NOTHING TO KICK ABOUT

Nothing
to Kick About

The Autobiography of a Modern Immigrant

by PETER GOGOLAK

with Joseph Carter

ILLUSTRATED

DODD, MEAD & COMPANY · NEW YORK

ISBN: 0-396-06820-0
Library of Congress Catalog Card Number: 73-3904

Printed in the United States of America
by The Cornwall Press, Inc., Cornwall, N. Y.

Contents

NOTHING TO KICK ABOUT

CHAPTER ONE

The "Must" Game

It was the Dallas game.

This was midway in the 1970 season, the first full year for the Giants with Alex Webster as head coach. Alex had taken over from Allie Sherman in 1969 after the Giants had lost the sixth straight of their six exhibition games. Under Alex the Giants had had a 1969 record of six wins and eight losses.

Absolutely nothing to brag about, and the 1970 season had started off even worse. We had distinguished ourselves by losing our first three games.

Then Alex had a "little talk" with the team.

Before a game, Alex is the nicest man you'd want to meet. At the pre-game pep talk in the locker room, right after the prayer, he emphasizes that football is just a game, the players should set examples of good sportsmanship for everyone watching, all we have to do is go out onto the field and play the sort of game he knows we're capable of.

Alex at half time, trailing 14-0, is quite another dish of tea. His language can take the blue out of your uniform.

So you can imagine what Alex's "little talk" was like on

the Tuesday—the day the coaches always analyze the pre-
vious Sunday's game—after we lost that third game to New
Orleans. (What made the defeat more binding was that New
Orleans was an expansion team.)

Alex talked for an elapsed time of about ten minutes.

Leaving out the four-letter words, it was about three.

He said he was going to give New York a winning team; he
wasn't going to coach a bunch of losers; there wasn't a man
on the team he wouldn't trade; he'd rather start off with a
whole new squad he could teach to win instead of a lot of
veteran bums who were willing to lose.

The next Sunday we won, and we won three more straight
—to practically everyone's surprise. Actually, even before
Alex's talk the team hadn't been all that bad, but the turn-
around certainly looked dramatic.

What all this added up to was that the Dallas game was the
biggest game that the Giants would play in four years.

Look at the record. We were four won and three lost, and
we were two games down to Dallas. If we won, we'd still be
one game down, but we'd have a shot at the playoffs. If we
lost, we were out of it. Dallas would have to lose four straight
for us to even have a prayer, and that Dallas team wasn't
about to lose four straight.

In other words, this was a "must" game. Unless we won—
a tie wouldn't help—we were just as good as out of the season.

What do you do for a "must" game?

At this time I was still a bridegroom. I'd married in May
and my bride Kathy and I were living in a pretty expensive
apartment ($420 a month) on the 23rd floor of a fancy brick-
and-glass high-rise apartment house on the northwest corner
of Second Avenue and 84th Street. It was called "Adams

Tower," why, I'll never know. For our $420-a-month we were getting a fair-sized living room, a smaller dining room adjoining a kitchenette, and a bedroom. The views to the north and the east were spectacular. We looked down on the East River and could see Hell Gate; we could see up Second Avenue for twenty or thirty blocks; and, on a very clear day, we could see Yankee Stadium.

This Sunday morning the alarm woke me at 7:30 A.M., as it does every day. I'm one of those people who slide out of bed almost the instant they wake up, so within a couple of minutes I was in the living room, gently jogging around and doing little knee bends and little jumps, just to get the kinks out. By this time Kathy was up and in the kitchen, in her bathrobe, getting breakfast ready.

I looked down onto Second Avenue and there wasn't a soul on the sidewalks. Only one car headed uptown. Sunday is a day of rest for everybody except football players.

Even that early in the morning, I began to get a feeling of how the day would go. You know how it is, some mornings you wake up and you know you can lick the world, and some mornings you're not so sure. This morning I knew I could lick the world.

It was a clear, glittering day. As I looked north I could see Yankee Stadium. I could feel the excitement and tension beginning to build inside me. I thought, in five hours I'll be up there on the field, and 65,000 people will be there to watch us play Dallas.

By 8:30 or so, Kathy had breakfast ready: For me, a big glass of fresh orange juice, three scrambled eggs, a twelve-ounce rare broiled steak, home-made muffins, and coffee. For her, no steak. An hour later we were dressed and off to Mass at St. Stephen's of Hungary Church on 82nd Street between First and York avenues. Entirely by coincidence, the former pastor, Father Benedict Dudley, is the chaplain for the Giants.

Father Dudley is quite a priest. In the first place, he has a square, solid jaw and he goes about 200 pounds in his cassock. His days with the Giants go back almost forever. He was a friend of old Tim Mara, the founding father of the Maras who owned the original franchise of the Giants, and a friend of his son, Jack Mara, who died a few years ago. Now Father Dudley is an intimate of Wellington Mara, the present owner of the team. A pleasant, amiable man with a vast fund of anecdotes, he is a tower of strength when needed. Father Dudley married Kathy and me.

When we have a tough game coming up, I always pray a little harder in church. This Sunday, I prayed extra hard.

A little after 10, Kathy and I were back at the apartment, and by 10:30, I was down in the apartment-house garage getting out the car. It's cold in November, and I have to be at the stadium at 11. The game doesn't start till one, so there's no point in Kathy coming with me. She generally comes up later with friends.

Driving up the East River Drive, I started really thinking about the game—first, about the opposing kicker. For Dallas it would be Mike Clark—Michael Clark, out of Texas A & M, formerly with the Eagles and the Steelers, and now with Dallas. Not one of the legendary kickers, but not bad. Suddenly I thought to myself: you know, all the other guys on the team are driving to the Stadium at this very minute from wherever they live, up in Westchester or over in Jersey, and at this very minute they're all doing exactly what I'm doing—

thinking about the game and who they'll be playing against. And a lineman or a back has to know his opposition a lot better than I knew Mike Clark.

On the way to the Stadium, I do one thing that most of the other players don't. I keep looking up to see if I can get a fix on how the wind is blowing.

God, how I hate the wind!

When I get to Yankee Stadium, if the flags are blowing, I think, Oh, Jesus! Yankee Stadium is one of the worst stadiums in the world to kick in when the wind is blowing. I don't know whether it's because of the open end, or where it's located, or what, but I do know that late in the season when the wind starts blowing in there at twenty or thirty miles an hour and swirling around in the upper decks of the stands, you get a football up there and you don't have the faintest idea where it's going. It's like kicking in a hurricane.

Sometimes I find myself thinking, well, if I miss one from 40 yards in a wind like that, no one can blame me; but instantly I know that I can't think like that, and I start to psych myself up. I think of the opposing kicker and I say to myself, let him miss one from 40 yards, I'll make it.

By this time, I had reached the Stadium and turned into the parking lot. Some of the other guys were already there, and another car was pulling in. Even this early there was a small crowd around the gate where the players come in, but we were all tense and nervous and there was no time for autographs. "Later, later," we said, and pushed inside.

On practice days the locker room is always kind of disorganized, guys milling around, jokes and wisecracks and "Where did you go last night?" and a record player on loud with some kind of rock music. Not on the day of a game—

especially this game. The locker room was almost silent. Like all the other players, I went to the little stool beside my locker and sat down and started to get ready. No talk. No jokes.

I may be the only player on the squad who doesn't go into the trainers' room to get ready for the game. I remember once going by the door and seeing them get Darrell Dess ready to play. Two trainers were working on him. Both his ankles had been taped, both knees—he'd had operations on both of them—both elbows, and when I saw him, the trainers were fitting on a shoulder harness. I remember thinking to myself:

"My God, how does he stand that kind of punishment? I absolutely couldn't take it."

How does a man live through being a guard on a pro football team? Yet Darrell told me once he liked it. He liked to hit.

One of the first things I did, as I always do, was to go over to the sock bin and pick out three pairs. There are about 300 pairs there, back from the laundry, most of them almost brand-new, but I like old socks that have been worn and are sort of broken down and comfortable. I always spend about five minutes looking for the three oldest pairs of socks I can find.

Then I went back to my locker and started to get dressed, same as always. One of the first things I always do is tape my own ankles. I know how to do it, I know how I like the tape to feel, and it's easier to do it myself than to take up the time of some poor trainer who has a lot of bigger problems on his hands.

When I was half dressed—again, as usual—I got a game

program and went into the john, sat down, and began to read. Before a game, the john is the busiest room in the State of New York. I've seen some guys go six times. Then I went back to the locker room and finished getting dressed.

The specialists—the kickers, the punters, the return men— have to be on the field to warm up fifteen minutes before everybody else, so by 12:15 I was trotting up the runway. It always gives me a warm feeling to come out onto the field for the first time, especially when, as that day, I had started out feeling tops. It wasn't freezing cold—about 45—the wind was only about five miles an hour, the sun was shining. The Stadium was only about one-tenth full, but, as usual, maybe a hundred fans were in the stands alongside the runway exit. And yelling:

"Pete, baby, go get 'em!"

"Score on 'em, you goddamned Hungarian!"

It made me feel good.

I like to start kicking from about the 25-yard line. Almost from the very first kick I can tell how I'm going to do on any particular day, and this day I still had the feeling that I had when I got up in the morning. I hit the ball exactly the way I wanted to. It gave the sound I want when I hit the ball exactly right, sharp and crisp, with what I call a "pop." After five or six kicks from the 25, I moved back to the 35, then the 40, the 45, and finally the 50. When I'm going good, I like to be kicking from the 50 when the other team, particu- larly the opposing coaches and kicker, come onto the field. Gives them something to worry about.

When Mike Clark started to kick, I followed my usual routine. I didn't watch him. Not openly. I peeked, to see how he was doing. It would be stupid to watch him—you know, as if I might learn something. But he knew I was looking, and I knew that he knew I was looking. Clark wasn't doing too badly, but I noticed he didn't make any tries from the 50. The thing about kicking from the 50-yard line, if you're doing it to psych the opposition, is that you have to make the kicks good.

By the time I'd made 20 kicks, in about fifteen minutes, the rest of the team had come onto the field to do calisthenics, and I went off to the sidelines to practice kickoffs. The fans love this. You're close to them and they can really see what you're doing. It's part of the game. Entertainment. Show business.

The Giants special-team coach, Jim Garrett, as always, came over with his three stop-watches to time me. The important thing in a pro game kickoff is not how far the ball goes, unless you get it out of the end zone, but how long it hangs up in the air. You can kick it eight yards deep in the end zone and some of these speed-ball kickoff return specialists they have nowadays will still take it and run it back out to the 35. The rule in pro ball is that if the kickoff is returned past the 20-yard line, it stunk. The only way to prevent that is to get the ball high enough into the air so that it hangs up there an absolute minimum of four seconds, long enough for your guys to get down under it.

The problem that every soccer-style kicker like me has to face is getting the ball high enough into the air consistently, so that it will hang. You can always get it high enough one time out of three, but that's not good enough. It has to be up there nine times out of ten.

Garrett, watching me, is a nice guy, but I have the feeling that I could kick the ball 100 yards up in the air, and Garrett's only comment would be: "Not quite high enough, Pete."

At any rate, this day, after I'd practiced maybe ten kick-offs, it was 12:45 and we all went back into the dressing room. Still no laughing, no joking. We all knew that this game was not for marbles.

You're sweating when you come in from the pre-game workout, even if the temperature is around 45, so everyone changes at least his T-shirt. I get a dull pain in my back from sitting on the bench most of the time in cool weather, so now I went into the trainers' room and had some analgesic heating ointment rubbed on me. Then I put on a light leather brace that I have for my back and went back to get dressed. My feet had gotten sweaty kicking, so I put on a new pair of socks. Sometimes, when I was kicking not-so-good before the game, I'd try on three or four new pairs, or maybe put on one pair over the other, anything to give me a new feel. This day I felt just right. Just one change.

The last thing I did after I was all suited up—I admit this is a quirk of mine—was to comb my hair. It sounds pretty silly, and it is. A thousand times guys have said to me: "This is one hell of a time for you to be worrying about how your hair looks," and I agree with them. It is. Nobody cares how your hair looks if you score the points, and you have a helmet on anyway. The funny part is that I'm not vain about my hair, what the hell, it's just hair, and I used to explain that long hair could spoil my concentration. I don't want hair flapping around my neck when I'm trying to make a 50-yard field goal. Besides, long hair is a pain after a game. After a game, all I want is a fast shower, get dried and dressed, and go home. I don't want to spend half an hour getting my hair dry enough to go outside. As far as I can see, hair styles just keep changing generation after generation until they end up back where they started. When I first started to play football in high school in America I wore my hair what seemed a little long (cut in what Americans call the European style), and people used to kid me because it was so long. Now they kid me because it's so short.

Maybe it *is* a vanity I'm not aware of; at any rate, the last thing I did was to comb my hair.

There were two other things to be done before we went out onto the field. First, Clifton McNeil, one of our top wide receivers, from Grambling College, got up on a stool at one end of the locker room to lead us in prayer. Clifton, when he wasn't running around the opposition, was a pretty good preacher. He never read the prayer, just made one up about sportsmanship, playing our best, not letting the team down—very good.

Then Alex Webster gave us his little talk. Webster is a nice guy, but he also is basically a tough guy. He would always pick up where Clifton left off about sportsmanship and so on, but he always ended up with: "Okay, let's go out and beat the piss out of these guys." That's Webster being nice. As I said, Webster at half time, down 14-0, is a totally different figure.

Toward the end of Webster's talk, my mind began to trail off. I began to think about the kickoff. I knew that I was going to kick off, because the real coin toss is done during the warm-ups. In pro ball, given two roughly equal teams and even breaks, it isn't supposed to make much difference whether you kick off or receive. But in Yankee Stadium, even leaving the wind out of consideration, for me there's a psychological advantage in kicking off. I like to kick toward the closed end. Somehow the perspective or the crowd behind the goal posts makes the distance seem shorter. If I have to kick toward the open end, the goal posts seem a mile away.

Anyway, Webster got through his pep talk and we were ready to go out onto the field.

There is no use trying to explain the feeling you get then to anyone who has never played, who hasn't been in the locker room, who hasn't been part of it.

It's an indescribable feeling of expectation.

We know we're going out, and 65,000 people know we're ready. Suddenly the little door opens and you can see that slice of the stadium directly ahead of you, jammed with people, color, movement, banners, and then the roar of 65,000 people.

I think: "This is it! Let's go, Petey, baby! Here we go! Let's go!"

I wouldn't be any place else in the world for any amount of money.

For a "must" game for us, this one started off beautifully. Really beautifully.

Within the first three minutes Greg Morton had thrown a pass to Bob Hayes for a touchdown, and we were down 7-0. Late in the first quarter, we got close enough for me to kick a 40-yard field goal, and the score was 7-3.

As a place kicker I don't criticize any team, much less my own, because when you're sitting on the sidelines you really don't know what's going on on the field. But all through the first half it looked to me as if the Giants just couldn't get going. Nobody can explain something like this about a team, not the coaches, not even the players themselves. Nobody knew better than the Giants that this was a "must" game, but they couldn't seem to get untracked.

Morton hit Hayes with another touchdown pass. Score, 14-3. It looked as if our "must" game was going right down the drain.

But the Giants fought back. On the series after the Dallas touchdown, we got close enough so that I was able to hit on a 42-yarder.

Then, with the game only three seconds from the end of the half and the ball on our 47-yard line, fourth and about four, I was getting ready to head for the locker room when suddenly I heard the yell: "Field goal team!"

Field goal team? They must be out of their minds. Kicking from 54 yards out? Well, it would be the last play of the half. As I trotted out on the field, I thought:

"Everything you've got, boy, everything you've got!"

What if I made it?

Dick Shiner, the back-up quarterback for Fran Tarkenton and my regular holder, was out there a little ahead of me, and we looked for the place where I wanted the ball spotted. And I mean spotted *right there,* not two inches away. You want a spot that's bare, if you can get it, and a little higher than the dirt around it. Dick marked the spot with his finger. We got into the huddle and Dick said:

"Okay, field goal. Play starts when the kicker is ready."

We broke and I went back to my position. God, 54 yards! All I could do was give it absolutely everything I had. And hope.

I made it.

I made it!

Fifty-four yards!

I kept my head down through the kick and I didn't look up till long after I'd followed through. Maybe a second. And there was the ball up in the air, looking as if it were floating toward the goal posts.

I don't want to make myself the hero of this game, but I went into the dressing room on Cloud 9, the roars of the crowd still ringing in my ears, the guys still pounding me on the back. That kick, besides being in the record books as one of the longest ever, is still a Giant all-time record.

Important as it was for my ego, it also had gotten the half-time score to 14-9. Instead of being down two touchdowns, we were now down only one, and coming at the end of the half, as it had, it had given the whole team a lift. You could feel it; you could see it. In the first half, the team had looked sluggish. It didn't look sluggish now.

At half time you really have only ten minutes in the locker room, so that kick celebration was possibly the shortest on record. The locker room at Yankee Stadium is one big long room. The minute we got in, the offense went to one end of the room with the offensive coaches. The defense went to the other end, with the defensive coaches. My locker is almost in the center of the row of lockers, so I did what I always do, I got myself a couple of orange quarters and went over and sat down on the stool in front of my locker and started to chew them. Me, the loner. When the offense and the defense are having crucial meetings, nobody needs Gogolak.

After a while I went over and got into one of the lines for the john—there are always lines at half time—then I went and got some new socks, found another old pair that suited me, retaped my ankles, put on the socks, tied and retied my shoes until they felt exactly the way they had in the first half.

There's no time wasted during the half, there are no speeches. The defensive coaches are too busy showing what went wrong in the first half, showing how the offensive players on the opposition were moving, pointing out mistakes, explaining exactly what had to be done. Same way with the offense, except that here the coaches analyze what the opposition defense is doing to stop the plays, discuss whether they ought to put in new offensive plays, discuss old offensive plays that did so well against whoever and talk about whether they should put them in here. There's no time for screaming.

Finally, with only a minute or so left, Webster talked to the whole team. You could tell from the way he talked that he was confident, too, that if the team could just pick up a little fire, a little snap, just a tiny bit of the extra charge that makes the difference, we could win. I think the whole team felt it. They'd won before, they knew that feeling of mo-mentum, so that suddenly the offensive line would be getting off a tenth of a second sooner, the defensive lineman would be charging a tenth of a second sooner.

We went back out on the field and proved it.

We knew then that we could beat Dallas.

On the first series of downs, the Giants simply outpowered Dallas, nothing fancy, just power, and went in to score.

Then Mike Clark, the Dallas kicker, hit two short field goals. The Giants came back with another touchdown, and the final score was 23-20, Giants.

We missed the playoffs that year by one game—the Rams beat us in the final game of the season in New York—but I think the Dallas game was the proudest game I've ever played in professional football. Three field goals for me, one the 54-

yarder, two points after touchdowns, we had won and I had put eleven points on the scoreboard.

After the game, in the locker room, it was almost as if we'd already won the division title. There weren't quite all the festivities you'd have then, but it was quite a riot, everybody yelling and singing and pounding everybody else on the back and yelling about plays:

"Did you see ole Tark——"

"When you made that tackle——"

"Man, you were lucky to get away with that, if that ref——"

Not a happier, louder bunch of guys in the Western Hemisphere. After all, remember it was Dallas we had beaten, we'd come from behind—behind against Dallas, mind you—and we had our "must" game.

After a while it quieted down and we began to get our showers, long, relaxing showers with plenty of interruptions, and finally we began to get dressed and go out, still getting slaps on the back and plenty of:

"Man, wait till Tuesday, this is *one* game I gotta see to believe!"

When you go out of the locker room at Yankee Stadium, there is a ramp going up and, just before the gates, a small room where the wives of the players or close members of the family can wait. When we've won, Kathy says, the talk in the room is so loud you can't hear yourself think; when we've lost, it's like the waiting room in a morgue. This day, well, I guess it was Babel.

There's one more thing before you can start home, the fans outside the gates. Again, it's a barometer of how the game went, like the family waiting room. If we lost, there are only a few diehards yelling: "You guys stunk!" and (to me, after I've missed one): "Go back to Hungary!" No autograph requests. On this day, there were two or three hundred people around us, slapping us, getting autographs, telling us how good we were.

Finally Kathy and I made it back to the parking lot and started back into Manhattan.

I turned on the radio, and—well, into each life some rain must fall.

Not a damned word about my kick. That was the Sunday that Tom Dempsey made his all-time record-breaking 63-yard kick for New Orleans, and old George Blanda kicked a 52-yarder in the closing seconds to pull out a win for Oakland over Kansas City. The radio was all Dempsey, Blanda, Dempsey, Blanda. I snapped it off.

"Why the hell couldn't those guys have waited till next week?" I asked Kathy.

Anyway, we got back to the apartment.

After every game we always have a little buffet for some friends, twenty people, maybe thirty, nothing elaborate, just delicatessen snacks like cold turkey and cold ham and roast beef, and some drinks. (My big standard drink is a spritzer, a couple of ounces of dry white wine in a tall glass, a couple of ice cubes, and fill it up with soda water.) We stand around, talking about the game, with the television always on in the bedroom so we can watch the West Coast games.

I began to feel better about the amount of attention my Giant kick had received on the radio.

At about 10 or 10:30, our party began to break up, and Kathy and I decided we'd like to go out and relax. Sometimes, after a game, especially after we've lost or I've had a bad day or the weather is lousy, we just decide to go to bed. Other times, we want to go out somewhere like P. J. Clarke's and have a drink or two. This night, we ran into Junior Coffey and his wife, and some other Giant players, and we sat around, talking about the game and having a few drinks. Along around midnight this small shindig broke up and Kathy and I were crossing 86th Street when we saw the next morning's *Times* on a newsstand.

There, on the front page, was a picture of me kicking my field goal.

"This," I said, "calls for a celebration!"

I bought ten copies of the *Times* and we all went back to our place.

Budapest: A Child in War

I ended up kicking field goals for the Giants because I was born in Budapest, Hungary.

In Hungary, as in most of Europe—east and west of the Iron Curtain—the national game is soccer. I remember very clearly, when I was only three years old my father giving me a forint for kicking a soccer ball ten times. A forint was about a dime. When my father said to kick it ten times, he didn't mean just kicking, he meant kicking it up off the earth, and then kicking it nine more times in the air before you let it hit the ground. Then, when I could do it ten times, my father raised it to fifteen times, then to twenty, and so on. He never raised the price, though. (Now I can do it five hundred times.)

There were two reasons why my father wanted me to learn how to play soccer. The first was that he was a frustrated soccer player himself, and a soccer nut. All Europeans are, of course. But the Hungarians are the worst of all. I can't understand why soccer isn't a much bigger sport in the United States than it is. It has so much more action than

19

American football or baseball. All through Europe and South America, it is *the* sport—baseball and football rolled into one.

To show you how rabid the Hungarians are about athletics, through three successive Olympic Games in the late 1950s and early 1960s, the Hungarians never finished lower than sixth in the team standings. This from a country of less than ten million people, competing against the United States and the Soviet Union. In Hungary, it's nothing to see a crowd of 100,000 at a soccer game or a track meet.

That explains my father's first reason for getting me to kick, he was a soccer-mad Hungarian.

The second was that Hungary was under Communist rule and the Communists are especially big on organized athletics. Partly because athletics keep the nation's manpower in working shape, and partly because they give the working people something to look forward to on weekends. Like the old Roman circuses I guess, they give the people a chance to vent all the frustrations that a totalitarian regime builds up. In Budapest, especially when a Hungarian team was competing against a Russian one, the stadium would be jammed with people, all of them cheering the Hungarians and booing the Russians. It was the only place you could boo the Russians and the police wouldn't crack your head.

I guess the Communists knew that themselves.

I remember I had an odd reaction at one track meet. I loathed the Russians as much as any other Hungarian. At this meet, the Hungarian champion, Kovacs, was competing against the great Russian 10,000 meter champion and favorite, Kuts.

All through the final laps the crowd was on its feet roaring: "KOOOVAAACS! KOOOVAAACS!" Kovacs did win, and the stadium broke into bedlam. Kovacs was mobbed. Just at that moment I happened to look at Kuts. He was off on the infield side of the track, all by himself, crying. And I thought to myself, "That poor guy." For those seconds he wasn't a Russian to me, he was a champion runner who had just been beaten in front of 100,000 people.

There have been times since on the football field when I've wanted to break down and cry myself.

Under a Communist rule, too, the athlete is the one person, outside the party members who play the political game well enough to keep from being sent into exile, who has a secure place in society. The working people, all the way up to doctors and scientists, either go along with the system and do what they're told, or they're out. The athlete has a lot more personal freedom, not to mention all the other perquisites he gets, like a good apartment, an automobile, and adulation.

In Hungary, the way up in competition is easier for even a moderately good athlete than it is here in America. Here, unless a kid is practically a superstar by the time he's in high school, he's likely to fall by the wayside. It's only by a miracle that he's able to go any further in athletics.

But in Hungary, and other Communist countries, there's a whole hierarchy of sports. There's a sharp distinction in America between professional sports and amateur sports. Not so in Hungary. There, the national soccer association sponsors the national team; then it also sponsors junior teams, and sub-junior teams, and so on down until finally you find it sponsoring teams at the grade school level, for youngsters of nine to eleven. It's as if, in America, the football Giants were sponsoring teams down at the grammar school level.

As a result, sports are much more competitive for youngsters in Communist countries than they are in America. Actually, everything is much more competitive for youngsters in Communist countries. Whether it's getting good grades in school or playing soccer, the boy has it drilled into him that if he doesn't succeed, he's going to end up as a bus conductor. In America, if a boy isn't too good at athletics, or in his studies, his parents sort of say: "Well, he's young, he's just growing up." In Hungary if a boy isn't too good at athletics—and I've seen this happen—his parents have him out running and kicking for two hours a day. If his studies aren't too good, his parents won't let him out of the house until he has improved.

And there is no argument about it. That is the old country approach as much as anything. While the child is at home, what the parents say goes. The child can rebel on his own time, and on his own money.

All of my childhood was lived against a background of warfare and terror. My parents met in the summer of 1940, when World War II had already started, but before Hungary was really involved in it. My father was a dentist, a doctor, and a Hungarian Air Force officer. That isn't as complicated as it sounds. My father was drafted into the Hungarian armed forces in 1932, when he was nineteen, and was assigned to the Air Force. In Hungary, then and now, the draft was much simpler than in the United States. When you were nineteen, if you were male and could walk, you were drafted. It was that simple. My father stayed in the Air Force long enough to be qualified as a pilot. After his stint in the Air Force, since he had always wanted to be in medicine, he went back to school. In Hungary, to become a dentist, or any sort of medical specialist, you have to get a medical degree first. So, after becoming a pilot, my father had become a doctor, then a dentist. He was still in the Air Force Reserve, of course. Every year he had to give a certain amount of time to his military duties, and as the war got closer, he was called up for longer and longer tours of duty.

In the summer of 1940 he was stationed at Kecskemet, which is almost in the center of Hungary, about seventy-five miles southeast of Budapest. My mother, who was studying to be a teacher, was there on vacation and by chance one afternoon they both happened to go to a big public beach to swim. A thunderstorm came up, with towering black clouds laced with lightning, and most of the people went into the huge reception hall where there were concession stalls and showers and lockers and things like that. It was in the hall-way of this building, waiting for the rain to let up, that my mother and father met. They were married the following year, and I was born on April 18, 1942, in Budapest.

All I know of those days, of course, is what my parents have told me, but they have told me the stories so often that sometimes I can't distinguish between what I remember, and what I've been told.

I've been told again and again, for example, that I took my first steps on May 3, 1943, because that's the day my father left to go to the Russian front with the Hungarian Air Force units that were supporting the Germans. He went first to Kiev, then Karkov, then Poltova, but on Christmas Eve he arrived back in Budapest and resumed his practice, that tour of duty done.

He was a man who believed in learning new skills. "You never know when they'll come in handy," was a favorite saying of his, and this was to prove true when we emigrated to America. If you are born and brought up in a country like Hungary, which has been at the mercy of ravaging armies for centuries—the Huns, the Magyars, the Turks (we had the Turks on our hands for going on two hundred years), the Austrians, the Germans and the Russians—you learn to start coppering your bets well in advance. So, while my father was running his practice every day from 3 P.M. to 8, he was spending every morning in the radiology department of the hospital, from 8 A.M. to 2 P.M., learning to be a radiologist. The terrible food that the Hungarians had been eating all through the war was beginning to catch up with them. Everyone's teeth were beginning to go bad. It was a very busy time for my father.

In the early summer of 1944, when the Russians were driving from the east and the Americans and the British from the west, Budapest began to see the first real military operations of the war. The British and Americans started bombing targets around Budapest. The raids increased until they seemed to come every day and every night. By September, the Russians were close enough so that they, too, began bombing and strafing. They were much less accurate than the Americans and British.

I remember the bombings and the air raid shelters we had to go to, only very dimly, but my mother remembers clearly that one of the hardest things she had to take, emotionally, during the raids, was carrying me to the bomb shelters with me crying all the way. I didn't want to go to the shelter, I just wanted to stay in my own warm bed and sleep.

Finally, things got so bad that my father sent my mother and me to Rabahidveg, which is less than twenty kilometers from the Austrian border. Part of the reason for this was safety, and part was that my mother was pregnant with my brother Charlie. He was born that December 29th. My father had come down for Christmas and he presided over Charlie's birth, complaining forever after that because of the war there was no electricity and kerosene was rationed. All the illumination he had was given by candles.

He told my mother that he was beginning to get the feeling that the Russian Air Force had him listed as a priority target area. First, when he had been in Karkov he had been strafed fifty times. Then, only a few days before he had come down to Kecskemet, our house in Budapest had been bombed and a big section of the roof and wall had been blown out. (My father had stayed in Budapest, working, because we were using up so much of our savings while he was in the Army that he simply had to earn more money.)

He was nearly killed when our house was bombed. He had been sound asleep, exhausted, when the sirens went off. It was raining, and he decided to chance it rather than go to the shelter three hundred yards away. But our old housekeeper forced him awake and said she had promised my mother to get him to the shelter whenever there was an air raid. She had practically dragged him to the shelter. Just as they got in, a bomb exploded, so close that it blew the door of the shelter closed behind them.

In the shelter, sort of joking with the housekeeper, he said:

"You were right to get us here. That might have hit the house."

It had.

When my father and the housekeeper got back, they saw that the major damage was to the roof. That *had* to be fixed.

It rained most of the time, and the whole house would be ruined if the roof were left off.

Almost everyone in Budapest had a similar problem. Roofing tiles were rationed. Even if you could get them, through all the red tape of the government offices, it would take weeks or even months. With the Russians getting nearer and nearer the city, the situation was getting worse. My father went to a roofer he knew and offered him double the price to fix the roof, and to throw in free dental work for his whole family. The roof was fixed in three days. (The dental work took three weeks, which shows you what roofers could command for their work then.)

By the time of Charlie's birth, all of Hungary was falling apart. The Russians had entered Budapest, so we could not go back there. The sky was almost always filled with airplanes; the roads were jammed with refugees, wheeling along their poor belongings. My father was ordered back into service, and we all moved to another small town called Csakanydoroszlo, where he was to be stationed and where we could stay with a cousin of his, who was a judge. We were there only from early in January until early in April, when we had to move to another small town called Csorotnok. By this time, my mother and Charlie and I were refugees ourselves; all we could take with us was what we could carry. We were housed in a school-building with hundreds of other refugees. Then at three o'clock in the morning all the pregnant women among the refugees, about eighty of them, were ordered to get into buses, to cross the Austrian border. The Russians were only twenty kilometers away, and it was thought that the pregnant women would be better off in Austria, in Gleisdorf, which was still held by the Germans, than they would be with the Russians. My father was to go with the women as their doctor. My mother was told that all the non-pregnant women and small children would go in the next bus load, as soon as the buses returned.

But the buses never returned—the Germans commandeered them. So there was my father in Austria, my mother and Charlie and I still in Hungary, and the Russians now only ten kilometers away. Then, someone came into the schoolhouse and shouted:

"The Russians are coming! Escape as you can!"

My mother took Charlie and me and, with some other women and children, we went and hid in a graveyard, in the grass and bushes among the gravestones.

Everyone wanted to get to Austria. The border was ten or twelve kilometers away, and the roads were jammed with people, walking, pushing carts, riding bicycles, driving horse-drawn wagons jammed to overflowing. Someone came and said there were two trucks for the women and children, so the Gogolaks went and were packed into the trucks like sardines. We started off. As we got nearer to the border we could see dead horses and dead soldiers lying alongside the road, victims of strafing attacks. We ourselves were attacked by a Russian strafer trying to kill refugees and clog the road. The plane came so close we could see the pilot's face. My mother pushed Charlie and me down and laid on top of us. We got to a factory where they had food—my mother holding onto both of us so we wouldn't get lost in the crowd—and that night we got across the border into Austria. The road was a shambles, but there was no other way across because the fields had all been mined. We were lucky to make it; by now the Russians had brought up their tanks and were firing into streams of refugees only two or three hundred meters behind us. I don't know how many people were killed, but we were told it was hundreds.

We crossed the border near a little town called Fehring. Here the roads had been blocked off by the Germans, so now we refugees were caught between the two armies. But the fields were not mined, and we escaped off into the hillsides. The Russians had come up so close to the border that the Germans had opened fire on them; the refugees behind us were pinned down by firing from both sides. There was no place for them to go; they all spent the night in ditches and in whatever holes they could find. In the morning someone stumbled across an old wine cellar and we all crowded in, two or three hundred people. Charlie began to cry, and my mother put him into an empty wine barrel. She went out that night to get him some milk, and gave a farmer her gold ring for just a litre of it. After a while, a couple of German soldiers came in and told us they were pulling back.

"You can come with us, if you want," they said.

The refugees decided to stay. If we went with the Germans, the best we could hope for was a refugee camp in Austria. No one knew how long the war would go on; no one knew what would happen. It seemed better to stay near Hungary. After all, we all came from Hungary. When the war did end, we wanted to be as close to our homes as we could. Almost all the refugees had husbands or sons in the Army, off fighting somewhere, and they knew that sooner or later everyone would try to get home.

Within a few hours the Russians did come, and ordered everyone out. They started to herd the refugees back toward Hungary. After we had gone about two hundred meters, they halted the column. They had a cartload of apples they had stolen, and they let the refugees help themselves. Then they went among the refugees, taking their watches, their rings and jewels, sometimes they even took their shoes. My mother had foreseen this, however. She had with her a handful of jewelry, worth perhaps a few hundred dollars, and this she had put inside Charlie's diaper, and so she saved it. The Russians escorted the refugees over the border, then they grew tired of it and let the refugees go on by themselves.

It was 300 kilometers to Budapest through a war-shattered countryside, all the way around Lake Balaton, the largest lake in Central Europe, and even though most of what I know of it I must have been told, I still see it in my mind as a nightmare. A couple of hundred people, penniless, begging for food, sleeping in fields, none of them used to walking like this. It took twelve days. I walked the whole way, except when some man would take pity on me and ride me on his shoulders for a kilometer or two, and my mother carried Charlie, except when someone would spell her. I remember, or I think I remember, crying:

"Mama, mama, leave me here, I want to die!"

Finally we got back to our house.

Or what had been our house.

God knows what the Russians had used it for, except on the ground floor. The ground floor had apparently been used as a bath center. The Russians had torn out our bathtub and brought it down from the upstairs bathroom. They had plugged up the drain and put it in the center of the living room floor. To get rid of the water, they had cut a hole in the parquet floor and tipped the water down into the cellar —there was about five feet of stinking water in the cellar.

They had built some sort of stove to heat the water, because a whole section of the floor had been charred away. The upstairs had been used for the toilet. All the Russian soldiers I ever saw were nothing but crude peasants—they didn't know what an indoor toilet was for. The upstairs floors were all ankle deep in excrement and the place stunk so you could barely go up there. My mother burst into tears. After all she had been through, to come back and find her home like this. All the furniture was gone except for a couple of dressers and buffets that were so heavy the Russians hadn't been able to move them.

After my mother stopped crying, she found a neighbor to take us in for a few days, which was a great imposition. All the stores in Budapest were closed and there was no food to be bought, no clothes—nothing. The only food was at public soup kitchens that had been set up in every section of the city.

There was nothing for us in Budapest, and we had no idea where my father was, so we made our way back to Kecskemet to stay with my mother's parents. It was better there, but not much. The Russians were there, too, and every time they needed a billet, they would simply turn my grandparents out of their house and take it over. We would all move in with a neighbor and every time we got back to our house we found that the Russians had cleaned out everything that had taken their fancy. This happened six or seven times, and by the time my grandparents finally got their house back for good, it had been stripped bare. But at least in the countryside you could get fresh vegetables to eat.

By the time the late fall arrived and the fruit harvest came in—this part of Hungary is great fruit-growing country—some order was being restored to the country. Some public services, the railroads, for example, were being put back into service. Every night a fruit train left Kecskemet for Budapest, and twice my mother hid in one of the fruit vans and made the trip. She wanted to see if my father had come back. The Russians checked these trains, and once they tried to check the car she was in. But she heard them coming and took off her belt, put it around the inside handle of the door, the doors opened out, and strapped it around an inside handhold. When the soldiers couldn't open the door they fired a couple of shots through it, but my mother was out of the way.

Both times, when my mother got to our house, she found that no one in the neighborhood had heard anything of my father.

It was only later, when my father finally got back to Budapest himself, that we found out what had happened to him. After he had delivered his busloads of pregnant women to Gleisdorf, he had moved on to Klagenfort. He was there when the war ended, and he became a prisoner of war of the British. The British were not hard warders. He was allowed to go anywhere he wanted to within a thirty-kilometer range of Klagenfort, which meant that he could go swimming in the Wurtersee. The countryside was beautiful, but the food——

"The Germans had left warehouses full of horsemeat," my father said, "and the British were using it to feed the prisoners and refugees. Horsemeat is perfectly edible, but you can get awfully tired of it."

Though the Russians had captured Vienna, and had set up their usual puppet government, it did not work as well in Austria as it was to work in Hungary—largely because the

Allies, in June, met with the Russians and enforced a joint Allied occupation of Austria and Vienna. The British, Americans, French, and Russians were assigned areas of occupation of the country and of Vienna, and the Russian troops roaming the countryside were obliged to return to their own sector. Once the Allied occupation had been established, in July, our father determined to escape. With a soldier who had been a member of his unit, he simply started walking. Through fields, of course, never on the highways.

The two made their way through country that had been held by the Russians, and my father said he had never seen such desolation—houses burned and ruined, not a soul around, not a domestic animal, no cows or horses, not a chicken or a duck. This in what had been prosperous farming country. He and the soldier walked until they got back to Fehring, again, and suddenly they came to a farmyard where, from the barn, they could hear mooing. They found the farmer who proudly showed them fourteen cows and horses.

"But how do you have them?" my father asked, stunned, "when all the other farms are ruined?"

"I've been stealing them, nights, from the Russians while they were moving back," the farmer said proudly.

My father and the soldier made their way to the town of Ivanc, where a patient of my father's, the Countess Sigrai, an American who had married a Hungarian count, had a villa. He told her of the incident of the farmer, over dinner, and she explained that the Hungarians, too, were profiting by the losses of the Austrian farmers. As the Russian soldiers fell back, they had begun to realize they couldn't keep this stolen livestock forever, so the Hungarians were buying it up to restock their own farms. She kept the two escapees overnight and in the morning took them, in a hay-filled wagon, to the railroad station. Inflation had already reached the point where it took my father a month's salary as a dental corps major to buy a ticket to Szombathely, twenty kilometers away.

At Szombathely, a loud speaker was announcing a welcome to all returning soldiers, inviting them to a room where they would be given food and tickets to wherever they wanted to go.

"The Motherland welcomes you!" the loudspeaker said.

The soldier said:

"Let's go!"

My father took him by the arm.

"In a police state, always do the opposite of what a loud-speaker tells you," he said, and started off in the opposite direction.

He led the soldier to a hotel where he knew an employee who had also served with him in the Army. This man took them into a small room and fed them bread and absolutely terrible cold cuts. While they were eating, there was a commotion outside. The man appeared, led them up a back stairs, and hid them under the beds in one of the rooms.

When the man returned later, he explained:

"Russian soldiers were here looking for escaped prisoners of war. It doesn't matter who you are. They get a list every morning with so many names on it, and they just pick up every man they find who might be a soldier till they have as many men as there are names. That's what would have happened to you in the railroad station. They would have loaded you into a train going to a prisoner of war camp to fill the quota."

This, my father found later, was perfectly true.

At one o'clock in the afternoon, my father and the soldier boarded the train for Budapest, 250 kilometers away. They arrived there at six o'clock the next morning—an average speed of about fifteen kilometers an hour.

And that morning at a neighbor's house he found my mother.

Just by coincidence, she had chosen the night before to make one of her trips up to Budapest on the fruit train.

Charlie and I were still at Kecskemet, so I can only imagine what their reunion must have been like after all those terrible months.

When they came down to visit us, it meant practically nothing to Charlie, of course. And, for myself, I'm afraid that after I threw my arms around my father, all I could find to say was:

"Good! Now we'll get something to eat!"

CHAPTER THREE

Flight from the Communists

Charlie and I stayed at Kecskemet for several months after my father came back from the war. Our parents were mostly in Budapest, trying to re-establish our home. Charlie and I didn't give them our undivided thoughts. Charlie was too young to know, but I sensed that the world was beginning to come together again. There weren't any enemy planes in the air, people didn't go around with the gray look of fear, the food gradually got better. I spent most of my time playing, helping out with whatever little chores a four-year-old can do, and getting in people's way. Charlie was less than a year old. Our grandparents took fine care of us, we were in a home where we were loved, and our parents came down to see us as often as they could—my mother, naturally, more often than my father.

It was almost a year before the house in Budapest was finally repaired and even today there are scars in the walls from the bomb explosions, though now the ivy has grown up over the walls so that you can't see them unless someone shows them to you. It took an entire year for the cellar to dry out from the water the Russians had poured into it. Fortunately, the roof had stayed whole and there weren't any big holes in the walls. But there was no glass in the windows, and glass was very hard to come by. What my mother did first was to block off all the windows with some sort of opaque material, leaving only one pane for the light to come in, and these panes were glassed. Gradually, as we were able to get more glass, the opaque material was taken off, and after months all the glass was replaced.

I realized later that we lived in a really lovely house in the Buda section of Budapest. Budapest, which dates back to pre-Roman times, was originally two small settlements on the banks of the Danube, at one of the few natural crossing places of the Danube River coming from the west to the plains of the southeast. Buda was the village built on the hills of the west bank of the Danube (the Danube flows almost due north-south here) and Pest was the village on the plains of the east bank. As the centuries passed and the two tiny settlements grew into today's modern city of 2 million people, Buda became more or less the residential part of the city, Pest the commercial and industrial part. That, of course, is a very simplified explanation of a very ancient and complicated and beautiful city—one of the most beautiful in the world, and renowned for the loveliness of its women.

The Buda section is quite hilly, as compared to Pest, and it has lovely winding streets with many fine homes. I am told that the city was even more lovely before the terrible seven-week siege in the winter of 1944-45, when nearly thirty-five thousand buildings were destroyed as the Russians and Germans fought, but I would have no way of knowing anything about that except for pictures.

Ours was a two-and-a-half story, eight-room house built on the side of a hill, with a lovely lawn, garden and tiny orchard of some twenty-five fruit trees. Directly across the street was a soccer field.

To get our house into the shape in which I remember it was largely my mother's work. My father helped her with the most revolting part of the work, cleaning up the unspeakable mess the Russians had left upstairs and bailing out the cellar, and he helped her with the heavy work. But most of it my mother had to do herself, for my father had to re-establish his dental practice if the family was to eat.

"Who else will feed you?" he used to ask.

Besides ruining the house, the Russians had taken every bit of his dental equipment.

The story of how he supported us then and how he began to re-establish himself is, I suppose, not really an extraordinary story for those days and that place.

Our whole economy for months revolved around the fact that when my father had been confirmed in the Catholic Church at the age of twelve, he had been given a solid gold watch.

It it almost impossible to describe the inflation in Budapest then in terms that mean anything today. My father says it was worse than the inflation in Germany after the First World War. The value of the forint fell so rapidly that a man would be paid his salary in the morning and find that by evening he didn't have enough money to buy potatoes for supper. My father was in Munich in the summer of 1920 when a glass of beer cost 50,000 marks; three weeks later it cost 420,000 marks. At the height of the inflation in Budapest, it cost 7.7 billion forints for a streetcar ticket.

What my father did was to sell his gold watch, bit by bit.

I remember one thing that he did. He came down to the country and bought a pig with some of the money he got for a tiny piece of gold. He brought it to Kecskemet, where it was slaughtered. The whole family turned out to butcher it and to cut it up into hams, shoulders, roasts—even to making sausages out of the intestines, and lard out of the fat. This whole operation was totally illegal, of course, and if we had been caught, we all would have gone to prison.

But, to repeat his quote: "Who will feed my family if I don't?"

He wrapped up all the cuts of pork and took them back with him in the train to Budapest. As the train was slowing down for a junction outside the city just at dawn, he threw all the pork cuts out on the ground and jumped out after them. He gathered up all the cuts and carried them into the city on foot. That day he went from house to house, selling the pig.

In addition to that, my father spent a good deal of time simply watching the gold market. It fluctuated almost hourly and if he saw it taking a downturn he would immediately start buying gold, knowing that it would only be a question of a day at most before the market would be up again, higher than ever.

My father was successful enough in these operations so that at the end of a month he had the money to buy a dentist chair, a drill, and sufficient instruments to start practice. By this time too, my mother had the house clean, and had scrounged enough furniture, so that patients could be admitted.

On August 1, 1946, the government stabilized the currency

by issuing new money and calling in all the old. Now nobody had much money at all, but at least prices got down to levels you could comprehend. Slowly the shops began to reopen, the trolleys and the trains were almost all running, there was electricity most of the time.

Slowly, however, the Russians were beginning to take over the country and to install the totalitarian government that is the only kind they understand.

A provisional government had been formed in December of 1944, after Admiral Horthy had been arrested by the Germans. It had been a coalition of Social Democrats, Smallholders, National Peasants, and Communists. The first elections after the war gave the Smallholders a big majority, and the Communists only 17 percent. The Communists, however, held the post of the Ministry of Internal Affairs—which means control of the secret police, of which Hungary had 160,000 at the time—and they began to take a bigger and bigger role in running the country. They effectively destroyed the Smallholders, the biggest party, but spineless when it came to leadership, by arresting all its spokesmen who opposed them; it did the same thing with the Social Democrats. (The favorite technique was to denounce a leader as a "fascist" or "collaborator," then have the secret police arrest him, after which he was heard of no more.) The Communists refused to let Hungary join the Marshall Plan; they successively nationalized the institutions of the country, starting with the banks, then the industries, then small landholders (any farmer with over twelve hectares was labeled a "kulak"), finally down even to the barber shops. When we left Budapest, there was not an independent barber in the city.

Housing was at an enormous premium, and it was there that my father first began to feel the real pressure of the Communists. Everyone was required to register his house, the number and size of the rooms, and the number of persons occupying them.

Now, our eight-room house may have sounded big for five persons (my father's mother was living with us), two of them small children. But, of the four upstairs bedrooms, one had been the maid's room and was quite small, and two of the other rooms were still uninhabitable. Downstairs there were four rooms, one was my father's dental office and one was his waiting room. (We also used it as the living room after all the patients were gone.) And there was only one kitchen, which would have gotten pretty jammed with a whole other family in the house.

The government was forever sending inspectors to the house—"a bunch of good-for-nothing bums," my father used to characterize them, "before the Communists took them on, they were pan-handlers"—and my father would bribe them by offering to fix their teeth. ("God help me if I run into an inspector with good teeth," he used to say. Fortunately, practically nobody in Hungary over the age of twenty had good teeth, and after they'd been to a government clinic once, they jumped at the idea of a private dentist.)

One day one of his regular patients warned my father that the government was really beginning to crack down on private housing. My father spent all his savings turning the upstairs into another apartment to get more people into the house. It went for nought. The government simply moved an engineer and his family of four into the upstairs apartment, for which my father got no rent—though of course he still had to make all the payments to keep it up. The Communists even nationalized the garden, and my father had to pay rent to be allowed to maintain it. When one of the fruit trees died, he had to go to the city authorities to get permission to cut it down—otherwise he would have been charged with "destroying the property of the people."

He told me that the worst part of the Communist regime was the uncertainty. The secret police were forever coming around, and you never knew why. Somebody could be arrested and if your name was found in his address book—a dentist's name is likely to be in a lot of address books—the police would spend an hour interrogating you, wanting to know everything you knew about this person. But they never told you why the man had been arrested in the first place.

When Charlie and I were old enough to go into the Young Pioneers—the Communist youth organization in Hungary, which gave you little red neckerchiefs to wear the way American Boy Scouts wear various colored neckerchiefs to denote their troops—we knew that sooner or later the secret police would come to our house in the middle of the night to get us out of bed and take us down to make us join. So, when we could, we used to sleep out in the backyard, beside the fence, in our sweat clothes, to be able to hop over the fence to get away. Every now and then I read in the newspapers about how someone here says that America is a police state. God, he ought to be *in* a police state for six months.

I never really appreciated this until long afterward, naturally.

I was just a kid growing up with a soccer ball.

Ever since I can remember, I had a soccer ball. I'd get one every Christmas.

Christmas is a much bigger holiday in Hungary than it is in America. It's much more religious, much less commercial. Christmas Eve is the traditional present-opening time in Hungary. Our dining room was locked all day every December 24th while our parents trimmed the tree—with real lighted candles—and the little Christ Child and his Christmas angels could come in and arrange the presents. At 7 P.M. mother rang a little bell and we all went in. First, prayers— then, presents. Then supper—haddock with paprika sauce. For two or three days we did nothing but eat marvelous Hungarian Christmas food—every kind of cake and cookie you can imagine, roast pork, duck, everything. Every midnight we listened to Radio Free Europe. Every Christmas I got a new soccer ball, which was a big present because regulation soccer balls in Hungary were pretty expensive then.

Besides all the kicking I did to earn forints from my father, I was forever over at the soccer field across the street, dribbling the ball up and down. On school days, I'd come home at three o'clock in the afternoon and my mother would fix me a piece of black bread with some lard and salt on it. Then I'd play with the kids in the neighborhood—I used to play with the tough kids because I always liked tough games —and with Charlie, when he got big enough.

I still remember how horrified my mother was one afternoon when she happened to look out the window and saw us kids playing in the garden with an old Army hand grenade that we'd found. It was live. We could all have been blown apart. That's one of the drawbacks of living where a war has been fought. There were still signs around, warning against unexploded bombs and shells that the sappers hadn't gotten around to cleaning up yet.

I was living the good life. I was surrounded by a loving family, I had a nice home. Even when I was young everybody in the neighborhood knew who I was—mosly because I was "Dr. Gogolak's son," but also because I was a pretty well set-up kid, husky, a good natural athlete. Most days, through the summer, my mother would take Charlie and me to one of the big municipal swimming pools dotted around Budapest and sometimes we'd go to Lake Balaton—the lake my mother and I had to walk around on our way back to Budapest after the Russian soldiers had let us go. Lake Balaton is seventy kilometers long and so shallow at the south end that an adult can walk out a kilometer before getting over his head. The water is warm most of the year, and it's Hungary's biggest resort. Everybody goes there. Sometimes, when he could, my father would come with us. My father used to take me to international track meets and soccer games at the People's Stadium in downtown Budapest.

I even found going to school a good deal of fun, even though my parents were the strict European types who thought that if you were getting straight A's, that was what was expected of you. If you got a B, you had a lot of explaining to do. My mother, having been trained as a teacher, would go over my homework with me every night—as she did practically the whole way through high school, and later with Charlie, and still later with my second brother, Johnnie, the only one of us children born in America.

Getting to school was the great fun. We used to go by trolley. The most exciting part was when you had just missed the trolley and had to run after it and catch the handrail and jump on—highly illegal. It used to drive the conductor out of his mind and get all the people cheering. If you made it.

Now and then, of course, there was a kid who didn't. We were a rambunctious lot on the trolleys. I guess it was a reaction against the strict discipline we had in school and at home, but it seems to me we were always fighting on streetcars, or in the streets.

There was nothing of the freedom I found later in American schools. Boys and girls were strictly segregated, and you bloody well did your homework. When it came time to recite, you went up to the front of the class, turned and faced it, and recited your lesson. We used to average about three recitations a day. We didn't have written examinations until the Gymnasium, which is roughly the equivalent of an American high school.

Of course, kids will always find a way to get around discipline, no matter how strict. I remember how we used to take advantage of one middle-aged woman teacher who was very near-sighted. Our classrooms were longer than they were wide. There were thirty kids to a class, and the seats were set in two long rows of two kids each. When this teacher called on a kid toward the back, if he didn't know the answer, the kid next to him would answer. That system always worked. For a while. The teacher may have been near-sighted, but she had extraordinarily acute hearing, and it didn't take her too long to pick up the differences in voices. I remember when one kid who knew he was going to have to recite but hadn't done his lesson anyway, got another kid to hide in the closet at the front of the room to prompt him. This was going along just great till the kid in the closet sneezed.

That was where the discipline came in. The teacher sent the kid down to the principal, the principal called the kid's parents, and the kid sat there until the parents came in.

Another way that discipline worked more strictly in Hungarian schools than in American was that the pupils didn't change classes—the teachers did. That way, you didn't have a couple of hundred kids milling around in the corridors at the end of every class. A kid found in the corridors when school was in session had to have a good solid explanation, or it was down to the principal's office. Parents get pretty tired of being called down to school. The school wouldn't let a kid out till his parents called for him.

I don't know whether this is a better way of teaching, all I know is that when I got into high school in America, they were teaching me mathematics I had learned two years earlier in Budapest. Teaching it the wrong way, too. I've never figured out why the columns slant the wrong way when you do long division in America.

I did well in school in Hungary, and I was elected president of my class in the sixth grade.

The only real problem I had was over the Communism issue. We had an hour's discussion every day about the great leaders of the Soviet Union. But at home, my parents used to talk frankly in front of Charlie and me about politics and government, and the whole family used to listen to Radio Free Europe every night, quite illegally. Most of what I learned from my parents was that the Communists, whether in Russia or Hungary, were dictators ruling their countries in the sort of arbitrary fashion that would have made a Romanov or a Hapsburg think twice.

I was about the only kid in the school who didn't join the Young Pioneers, despite the fact that my teachers kept telling me that I would have no future if I didn't and that when

I got to the Gymnasium I'd have a tough time. But my father wouldn't have let me, even if I had wanted to.

"The first rule in a dictatorship is, never join the party," he kept saying. "That way, when whoever is in power now loses his head, you don't lose yours."

He would never join the party himself, either, though he was forever being waited upon by delegations of three or four party members—most of them good friends of his—trying to show him the errors of his ways.

I'm eternally grateful that he was so hard-nosed about it. Maybe that's where I first learned not to go along with the crowd. If my father had joined the party and I had gone into the Young Pioneers, where would I be now? In Budapest, working in some government office.

I remember that my history teacher was one of those continually jumping on me about the Young Pioneers; I was the only kid in the class who didn't wear a red neckerchief. Once, and I'll remember this to my dying day, I had to give a recitation in world history. I knew it perfectly and delivered it perfectly, but she gave me a B. I went home in tears and my mother went charging down to the school. (I had given the recitation to my mother that morning before I'd gone to school, so she *knew* I knew it.)

"His material was correct but his presentation was faulty," the teacher said. The B stuck. Somehow, it didn't seem fair to give a twelve-year-old kid a B on the basis of whether he belongs to the party.

I'll never understand how my mother did all she did. Just running a house in those days was a major operation in itself, especially a dentist's house, with patients underfoot all day and, in this dentist's house, an unwanted family living upstairs. Though life had become fairly normal, my mother still had to get up at five o'clock in the morning to queue up for bread and milk, which frequently ran out. (Hungary used to be a rich agricultural nation, and still is, but the new masters had made a shambles of production in their efforts to collectivize farms, and they were taking all the produce they dared to sell for foreign exchange to try to make the country an industrial power.) On top of all that, my mother found time to take us boys swimming, to supervise our lessons, and to fight our battles at school.

Generally, as I said, life was good in those days. For relaxation, as I grew older, there was reading. I may be the only player in professional football who's read *all* of Jules Verne and *all* of James Fenimore Cooper's "Leatherstocking Tales" —*The Deerslayer, The Last of the Mohicans, The Pathfinder, The Pioneers,* and *The Prairie.* All in Hungarian, of course, all in paperback, and handed around from boy to boy. You have no idea how we read and re-read those books, and how we played cowboys and Indians—never having seen either.

When I became thirteen, I turned into a movie buff. There were no American movies in Budapest, but some of the Italian ones were pretty good. I remember getting into an adult one (you had to be sixteen) to see Gina Lollabrigida, and just when it got to the best part—meaning Gina was practically naked—someone recognized me and I was thrown out. I also picked up a little pin money by scalping movie tickets. There was only one performance a day, in the evening, and tickets were reserved. If you were waiting in line when the box office opened and bought six or eight tickets, you could net a nice profit by waiting a couple of hours till latecomers were getting desperate.

Most of all, I loved the newsreels. Some programs in Budapest were nothing *but* newsreels, a solid hour-and-half of them. I'd sit through them all, drinking in everything that had anything to do with the West, especially America. I'd go home and dream myself to sleep with visions of America.

But, of course, the biggest thing in my life when I got to be thirteen was soccer. I've already described how soccer teams were broken down by ages in Budapest, from the top professionals down to nine-year-old boys. I wanted to play soccer as much as I did anything else in my life, and since schools in Hungary do not have athletic teams the way they do in the United States, the only way I could play was to try out for the thirteen-to-fifteen-year age limit group on one of the pro teams.

One of the really top professional teams in Hungary was, and is, Ferencvaros, popularly shortened to Fradi. This team, before the war, was one of the great prestige teams of Europe. Even to be considered for a tryout, you had to be recommended. A friend of my father's recommended me, and the proudest day of my life was when I made the team, playing right inside. (The center was a curly-brown-haired, brown-eyed kid named Florian Albert who is now the Number One center in Hungary and is on the second All-European team.) I had a strong leg and a powerful shot, but I was short on speed—I was the playmaker, setting them up for other guys. As a matter of fact, I ended up as a defensive halfback on account of my lack of speed. I had a really good technique, but I doubt that I ever would have become a top player. At any rate, nobody in Hungary was happier than me the day I was taken onto the team.

We had practice twice a week down in the tough section of

Pest, which didn't bother me much—I was used to tough kids. I used to go down by streetcar, carrying my soccer shoes and wearing my jersey, and feeling mighty well pleased with myself.

We played soccer games every Sunday; Sunday was a full day of soccer for Budapest. I'd be up at six o'clock, go to Mass, and then start off with my father by streetcar to the stadium. I was getting my first taste of real organized competition, of professional sports. I carried my equipment and my green-and-white identification card (green-and-white were the team colors) so that I could identify myself to the officials. When we got to the stadium, I'd check in and find my locker and get changed. (One way this was different from the *real* professional team was that there were no showers, and the only pay I got was a sandwich my father would buy me in a cafeteria.)

But, from the pre-game ritual, I was learning discipline and, from the fact that I was generally playing against kids two years older, and bigger, than me, I learned competition.

The biggest thrill I had was one Sunday when we played before 50,000 people. That was about half the crowd that would come to see the professional team that played in the afternoon, but it impressed me that so many people would come early to watch us kids play. We won, and now I've even forgotten the name of the team we played against.

All this was soon to end, however, for the Hungarian Revolution of 1956 was on its way.

My father had first tried to get us out of Hungary in 1951. Cardinal Mindszenty had been sentenced to life imprisonment for refusing to go along with the Communists (the

Catholic Church alone still maintained its opposition to the Communists) and, in 1951, his successor, Archbishop Groesz, suffered the same fate. The year 1951 also saw the launching of one of those interminable Communist "five-year" plans, this one designed to turn Hungary into a supply state of munitions and agricultural products for Russia. Working hours were increased in all industries and when the workers rebelled, the unions were "disciplined." The shops began to look bare again, and we began to have food shortages once more. Food shortages in Hungary!

My father decided that we had had enough. He decided that instead of just describing to us boys what freedom meant, he would take his family and live it in the West.

Something that still surprises me even today in America, is how people take their freedom for granted. I have talked to hundreds and thousands of Americans, and only about one in a hundred understands that to millions of people living under dictatorships in Europe, America is still as much the land of dreams it was a century ago, when the oppressors were the monarchs instead of the Communists.

At any rate, Charlie and I had heard hundreds of stories and rumors about people who had managed to escape to the West—or who had been blown up or captured trying to escape. Ever since 1948, people had been fleeing Hungary; nobody knows how many, but by then it must have been up in the scores of thousands. Budapest is a very closely-knit city; sometimes it seems that practically everybody is related to everybody else, or at least *knows* everybody else. (That's how I got thrown out of the Gina Lollabrigida movie. I was recognized.) And *everybody* talks. There's no such thing as a secret in Budapest. Everything you do is repeated everywhere, generally as a joke. Hungarians are great for jokes.

One of them at that time was, you asked a Hungarian the population of Hungary.

"Ten million," he would say. "Eleven, if you count the ones who've been smart enough to get out."

A New England friend of mine once told me the story of a tight-fisted old Vermont farmer who bought a pig in the spring, fattened it all summer, and sold it in the fall. A friend asked him what he'd paid for the pig in the first place.

"Ten dollars."

"And what did you sell it for?"

"Ten dollars."

Pause.

"Not much profit in that."

Pause.

"Nope. But I had the company of the pig all summer."

That's a Hungarian joke.

The stories that Charlie and I heard at that time were a little grimmer. They all revolved about how to get across the 160-kilometer Austro-Hungarian border. All the roads were blocked, and between the road crossings there were watchtowers every two miles, staffed with Russian soldiers or with the Hungarian secret police. These watchtowers were elaborate military posts, manned by squads of armed men equipped with watchdogs. They went on regular patrols from tower to tower. They had set up huge searchlights and had supplies of flares to shoot up whenever the dogs started barking. In addition to that, the ground between the towers was studded with minefields.

One of the most familiar stories we heard was about the

man who got through the minefield by driving a cow ahead of him to explode the mines. Another was of some ingenious Hungarian who got a sackful of alley cats. When the patrol dogs started barking at him, he let the cats loose. How we laughed at the vision of the Hungarian escaping while the soldiers tried to get their dogs out of a fight with a dozen cats!

The first airplane hijacking I ever heard of was a Hungarian who forced a pilot to fly him to West Germany at gun point. Another Hungarian hid in the cab of a locomotive and forced the engineer at gun point to run a border crossing.

Not all the stories were funny.

A woman patient of my father's, escaping with her husband, stepped on a mine and her leg was blown off. Her husband tied a tourniquet around the stump and carried her over the border, drenched in blood. They both made it, and they both live today in the United States.

At any rate, my father told Charlie and me that we were going to spend New Year's Eve at Gyor, where he had relatives. (Between my father and my mother, we had relatives, or close friends, all over Hungary.) Gyor is a small city at the confluence of the Raab River and the Latja, which is an arm of the Danube. It is about fifty kilometers from the Austrian border.

New Year's Eve is another big fete in Hungary, a time of feasting on roast pork, a time when practically everyone gets drunk.

I don't think Charlie noticed anything odd, but I was nearly nine, and I wondered what we were doing taking three suitcases full of clothes just for New Year's Eve in Gyor.

When we got on the train, we split up. My mother took Charlie and one suitcase and my father took me and the other two suitcases. Traveling in Hungary then on a train headed toward the Austrian border was no laughing matter. Rakosi was Prime Minister, and he was a real tough old Stalinist. Plenty of the iron fist and damned little of the velvet glove, was his way of ruling. We knew that his secret police would come through the train, asking everybody where they were going, and why. The train was jammed—as always, back then —and there was very little talking and no joking.

We made the four-hour trip from Budapest without any trouble, but instead of going into Gyor, we got off one stop ahead, which struck me as even stranger.

There was a horse and carriage waiting for us outside the station, in which there already were four people—a mother and daughter, and a husband and wife. There were almost no greetings, no talk. By this time it was late at night—eleven o'clock, I should guess—very dark, and very cold. The horse and carriage started off, not towards Gyor, but towards the forest. We passed a few drunks, reeling down the sidewalks and singing, but nobody in the carriage said anything.

Finally it was too much for me.

"Where's the party we're going to?" I asked. "Where are the relatives? Where are we going? What's happening?"

"Shhh. Just keep quiet."

That was all the satisfaction I got.

Finally, deep in the cold black forest, the carriage stopped. Everybody got out, without a word. The carriage drove off and we all started walking down a path through the woods. Finally we came to an open space and, in the darkness, we could see the reflection of a few stars glinting on the swirling blackness of the river. We were on the east bank of the Latja.

"Now," said my mother, brightly but very quietly, "sit down. We're going to have a picnic."

I thought she had gone mad. A picnic at midnight in a forest in the pitch black?

But I sat down.

"We can't start just yet," my father said. "Someone is coming here to meet us."

So we waited. And we waited. And we waited.

Charlie was fast asleep, and I tried to, but I kept waking up. It was cold on the ground and no matter how I moved I couldn't find a comfortable place. At about 5:30 A.M. the dawn began to break and the birds started to cheep in the trees. By 6 o'clock it was full daylight, and my father stood up and began brushing himself off.

"We can't wait any longer," he said, "we might as well go back."

So we picked up our suitcases and walked all the way back to the railroad station. It must have taken us about three hours. We caught a train and went back home to Budapest. We never did get to the roast pork feast with the relatives.

Later we learned the whole story. We were to have been picked up by a man in a speedboat. He was a Hungarian who had escaped to Vienna. He was a real daredevil—he once landed a light plane on a street in Gyor to pick up a person who was trying to escape from the country, and flew him back to Vienna. He was devoting his life to helping refugees and fighting for freedom in Hungary. He returned to Hungary to fight in the '56 Revolution, and we never heard of him again. He had been due to pick us up at 5 A.M., but in the darkness he had missed the rendezvous. He knew the river like the back of his hand, but it's almost impossible with no light to pick out a landing place in the woods. He had come at 6:30, waited an hour, and then started back to Vienna.

On the way back he was stopped by a police launch, while he was still in Hungarian jurisdiction. If we six refugees had been aboard, we all would have gone to prison.

The oddest thing about the adventure was that neither Charlie nor I ever said a word about our New Year's Eve. Not to our friends, not to our classmates. And our parents hadn't told us not to. Somehow, instinctively, we knew that if you want to exist under Communism, you don't talk to anybody. Not to *anybody*.

Our second escape attempt, which was successful, came about almost by accident. Looking back, I'm convinced that for a happy life, and a successful one, the first thing you need is luck. So many times during the war we all might have been killed, except for one thing. Luck. We all might have been arrested in that speedboat on the Danube except for one thing. Luck.

If my father hadn't been introduced to a certain man in Budapest by mutual friends one day in 1956—just by luck— we might still be in Budapest. This man lived in a house only about ten kilometers from the Austrian border and he still lives there, so I'll omit his name.

Our first attempt to escape had depressed my father enormously. I know that he kept fretting to himself—he's told me so, many times—here am I, he thought, over forty-five years old, with a wife and two children and a diploma in medicine and dentistry for nineteen years, and I make the equivalent of $65 a month; my children are afraid to talk to other children in school, I spend all my time arguing about not being a party member and there are few people *I* dare to talk to, they want to turn us all into Communists. Is this any way to live your life?

But the failure of the first attempt had somehow convinced him that the gods were against him, that he was fated *not* to get out of Hungary.

Then came October, 1956.

The Hungarian Revolution just began. It wasn't organized. Nobody planned it. It just happened. The events that led up to it are so complicated—and anyway, this is not a book about Hungarian politics—that I am not going to discuss them.

The point is that everybody in Hungary was at the breaking point. The whole condition of life seemed insupportable, whether for workers, intellectuals, farmers or students. Everything seemed to be going wrong in the Hungarian Communist Party—and other satellite Communist parties as well. Stalin had died and Khrushchev had taken over; he had deposed the loathed Rakosi, but he had replaced him with Gero, who was hated just as much. (The people wanted the moderate Imre Nagy, who later briefly was Prime Minister.) The saying in Budapest then was: "In place of a bald assassin, we have a thin one." It was announced that the Russian occupation troops would be withdrawn and that new elections would be held—this was never done. Only a short while earlier there had been the uprising in Poland that had caused the Russians to break up the government and replace it with one headed by Gomulka. Hungarian intellectuals were excoriating the government; the university students were in full revolt, demanding, among other things, fewer courses in Marxism-Leninism.

October 6 was the day of the famous "silent parade" in

Budapest. (October 6 is a sacred date in Hungary; it is the anniversary of the executions of the leaders of the 1848-49 uprising.) Hundreds of thousands of people marched through the downtown streets, in utter silence. (Nagy was one of them.)

The violence finally broke out on the night of October 23. A vast crowd had gathered in front of the downtown head-quarters of the national broadcasting company. The statue of Stalin was toppled from its pedestal and smashed to bits; bricks were thrown and the first windows were shattered; the police fired tear gas first, then loaded rifles. All of downtown Budapest erupted into gunfire, screams, shouts of "They're assassinating Hungarians!" For hours that night, Budapest was the war returned.

It was then that my father decided to move. The man he had met earlier in Budapest had said that if my father ever wanted to try to escape again, to come to him. My father could have escaped by himself long before; it was his family that hampered him.

On Friday, November 30, we left Budapest for good. The first step was to get to the railroad station. My mother's brother had a college classmate who could get us an official car. (That is how things are always done in Budapest—some-body's brother knows somebody who knows somebody.) It was necessary to have an official car because the city was seeth-ing with riots and revolution, and we barely left in time. The Russians were not about to put up with any nonsense about a "free" Hungary. They sent in the tanks of two arm-ored divisions in the first week of November.

We carried no big suitcases this time. We all wore as many clothes as we dared and carried only a couple of small bags.

My mother took her jewels, wrapped around her stomach (for she now was seven months pregnant with Johnny), and her recipe book.

We were stopped by a Russian patrol on the way to the station, but the driver's papers were in order, and they let us through. On the train, it was the same as before, my mother took Charlie and I went with my father.

We got to the house we were looking for at about three o'clock in the afternoon. My father's friend told us that the regular guide who was to lead us to the border hadn't been heard from for three days; it was assumed that he had either escaped himself, or that he had been captured. No one knew, and no one dared ask. But there was a new man, said my father's friend, who knew the route and he would take us. The fee was the equivalent of $150 in Hungarian money for the four of us—$50 each for the adults, and $50 for Charlie and me together. Then my father took the rest of his money and split it up among us. It was just enough for each of us to buy a railroad ticket back to Budapest if anything went wrong.

We started out at 5:30 that afternoon, just as it was beginning to get dark. The guide told us that the Russian soldiers in the area were especially nervous; we must not talk and we must do everything he said, without question. (I didn't know till afterwards that my father was already so tired that he could barely see; he hadn't slept the two previous nights.)

The guide went out of the house first, to look for Russian soldiers. Then he motioned to us and we went out as he had instructed us. Charlie and I came out first, thirty meters behind the guide; then my mother and father, thirty meters behind us. We were supposed to act as if we didn't know each other and were just out for a walk. We had to leave everything behind. *Everything* except the clothes we wore. And my mother's recipe book and jewels.

Once we were outside the village, which I'm not naming for obvious reasons, the guide got us off the road and into the fields. We were safer there, but there also was a complication. The temperature had been about 60 during the day, unusually warm for that time of year, and the fields had turned muddy, with the heavy clinging mud of plowed farmland. Before we'd gone two hundred meters, our shoes felt as if they weighed ten kilos each, and we had ten kilometers to go. Toward midnight it began to freeze and the mud was not so bad.

The fields were dotted with haystacks about the height of a full-grown man, but the guide would not let us near them. When it got cold, he said, the soldiers and Hungarian border police used to get into them to keep warm. A couple of times we had to detour around villages, so I guess the distance we covered was closer to thirteen kilometers.

The person who had by far the toughest time was my mother. The pregnancy, the tensions she'd been under in Budapest, the pressure of leaving the homeland (Hungarians have a deep feeling of homeland), now the terrible mental strain of knowing that we might be gunned down at any moment, or captured and sent off to prison for God knows how long—all this plus the sheer physical stresses of having to walk pregnant, ten kilometers in the dark over plowed fields, up hill and down dale—made her bravery that night like something I can never forget. Her arms had begun to swell, she was losing the sight in her left eye. Every few hundred meters she would have to stop and rest. At first my father was only supporting her arm; at the end, my father and I were half-carrying, half-dragging her. "You go on," she kept begging. "Leave me here."

Now we began to see the flares going up. At first, when they were far enough away, in the stillness of the night we could hear the soft "pop!" as they were fired, then the faint hiss as they attained a height of three or four hundred meters, a faint trail of spark following behind. Then came a much louder sound as they exploded and suddenly there would be a huge glare of dazzling white light that illuminated every separate blade of grass. The light would last for eight or ten seconds, long enough for the guards in the watchtowers to scan the whole terrain.

They were much like the white sky rockets at an American Fourth of July celebration, but much bigger and a hundred times more brilliant. They were regular Army flares, originally designed to illuminate battlefields.

While they were still far enough away, and we could hear the pop or the hiss, we simply laid down on the ground—another trial for my mother.

But as we got closer, there wasn't enough time between the "pop!" and the explosion to get down, so we formed "haystacks," like those all over the fields. We huddled close together, our arms around each other, our faces down so they wouldn't catch the light.

We began to hear the most ominous sound of all, the sound of shooting. Every now and then, about every ten minutes, there would be the sound of a sudden burst of sub-machine gun fire. Then silence.

In the midst of this, Charlie got lost.

Can you imagine that? A ten-year-old kid, lost in the border zone in the middle of the night with flares going up and guns firing? And we didn't dare call to him. We just had to stand there with my mother whispering:

"Where is he, where is he?"

I know what we were all thinking—should we go back?

Finally, after what seemed like an hour but probably was only three or four minutes, Charlie showed up. If my father hadn't been so frightened for him, I think he would have murdered him.

"Where were you?" he hissed.

"I lost my jacket," Charlie whispered. "The money you gave me was in the pocket."

I could have murdered him.

We went on. I'm not sure that the guide himself wasn't lost —I still clearly remember crossing a railroad track three times. The tracks, like so many in that part of Europe, ran along an embankment elevated about two or three meters above the surrounding land.

One time, luck was with us again. We were at the bottom of the embankment, about to climb up, when the guide held us back. He had heard the sound of an a handcart coming along the tracks. It stopped just above us. Suddenly the glare of a searchlight swept out over the fields. If we'd been back only fifty meters, it would have had us dead. After it swept back and forth across the landscape two or three times the searchlight went out and the handcart went on.

Finally we came to the border fences. Here the guide really did know his business. He got us through the fences in about a minute flat, patted us all good-by, and was gone.

We dragged ourselves ahead for two or three hundred meters, and we were in Austria.

We had made it!

We had fled Hungary, and we were in the West!

CHAPTER
FOUR

Life in the Promised Land

After a few hundred meters more, we came to a road, and down the road two or three kilometers we could see the lights of a village. It was the little border town of Nickelsdorf.

That was the first thing that impressed me as we slowly started toward the lights. In Hungary, you wouldn't find a tiny village along the border with its lights burning all night long.

Actually, I think I was the only member of the family who *really* appreciated getting into Austria. Charlie was excited, of course, but I think that to him it was a big adventure more than anything else. He hadn't been exposed to as much of the Pioneer Youth thing as I had, and I don't think he understood really what we were getting out of, or what it meant to our parents. I didn't fully myself, until later, but even then I had some glimmering.

As for my parents, they were both so exhausted all they could think of was sleep.

The second thing that impressed me as we came into

the little village, was an automobile showroom with lights on and brand new cars standing on the floor. I asked about it the next day—or, rather, much later that same day—after we'd all had some sleep, and was told that it was a place that sold automobiles. Anyone who had the money could simply walk in and buy one. I couldn't believe it. Even an ordinary working man could buy one! In Hungary the state controls all automobiles, and while everyone dreams of owning a car, unless you're quite rich, or important, or have excellent connections, you never can get one. Even then you have to fill out endless forms and get all kinds of official permission, and then you have to wait years and years. Here, they told me that one private citizen owned the agency and he could sell as many cars as he wanted to other private citizens without any forms at all except a registration. And if you ordered a car one day, you could get it the next. I couldn't believe it!

At any rate, in Nickeldorf we found a border station where there was a guard on duty. He took one look at us and knew our whole story. He gave us food and something warm to drink—I think it was cocoa—and then led us out back to a huge barn that the Austrian government had converted into a refugee center. There were cots all along the sides, and a good many of them were already occupied. We hadn't seen a single soul since we had left the village in Hungary, but the people here had obviously been here only a couple of hours at most; they were sleeping the sleep of the dead and their clothes were as filthy as ours. We hadn't had time to get into our cots before the guard came back with two more refugees. The great exodus of 200,000 Hungarians from the Communists was in full swing.

We lay down on our cots and slept until late into the day.

When we woke, the first thing we did was to clean ourselves up as best we could, and then we had something to eat. The swelling had begun to go down in my mother's arms, her eye was beginning to come around, and she cried from happiness.

"It was the shock," my father told us. "She was in a state of shock."

None of us had realized how the Hungarian Revolution had stirred the rest of the world, but even in this tiny town in Austria all sorts of volunteers were doing everything they could for refugees—the most-needed item being transportation to Vienna, about sixty-five kilometers to the northwest. We were taken there, jammed into a tiny Volkswagen, by a twenty-year-old English student who had come over to help. We couldn't speak any English and he couldn't speak any Hungarian, but finally he managed to get us to the home of a Hungarian friend in Vienna. This friend had fled the country himself, and my parents had helped his family—whom he had had to leave behind—to join him. We stayed with him a few weeks, getting ourselves alive again—resting, getting our clothes and ourselves clean, eating and walking around the city, and then he took us to a real refugee reception center run by the Austrian government. We were there three days "being processed." When they heard we wanted to go to America, they sent my father to the American Embassy to fill out all sorts of forms, and finally we and a hundred other refugees bound for America were loaded into three big buses and were driven to a U.S. Army relief center at an Army camp just outside Munich, Germany.

The drive took us through the Bavarian Alps. They may

not be as famous as the Swiss Alps, but they impressed me as a fourteen-year-old boy. I felt that I was bursting with impressions—I couldn't see enough. I was outside of Budapest and Hungary for the first time. Vienna had seemed like a dream city. Vienna is actually a little smaller (in population) than Budapest, but it seemed to have so much more life; the shops were so brilliant, the sidewalks were crowded with people who were so much better dressed, who seemed so much happier than in Budapest; the restaurants were so much livelier with so many different kinds of food; people sat at the sidewalk cafes and argued; the streets were jammed with automobiles. And at night—night was unbelievable. Never, never, never, had I seen so many lights, so much brilliance.

And now we were taking our first step toward America.

One of the first persons I remember seeing when the buses drove into the camp at Munich was a Negro soldier. I had never seen a Negro before, but that was not what impressed me: I had never seen a man so big before. I imagine, looking back now, that he probably was about six feet tall, and he must have weighed 250 pounds.

"Daddy, daddy, look," I said, pointing, "what a rich country America must be if their Army can feed soldiers so much they grow that big!"

At the camp, we found more evidence of how Hungary had stirred the world. There we found that many of the nations of the West were doing everything they could to help the refugees—the United States, Australia, and Canada are the ones I remember most clearly.

The camp was jammed with refugees, but it was run as a model of efficiency, considering the babble of languages and that most of the refugees were absolutely lost. All they knew was that they had escaped to freedom, but what they had to do now, and how to do it, was a mystery. There were queues of people everywhere—at the information lines, at the processing lines, at the medical lines. (Everyone had to have shots, no matter what country he wanted to go to. One of the Army medical men giving shots in the American center was a Negro doctor, and everyone wanted his shots from him, so few of the refugees had ever seen a Negro before.) My father took my mother with him to every line they visited. In Europe, a pregnant woman will get you to the head of every line there is. Again, one of the things that sticks clearly in my mind was the food. We were fed in a U.S. Army mess, and I never would have believed that *anybody,* much less an ordinary soldier, could eat the way the American army did. I had never even seen an orange or a banana before, but here they were for breakfast—and as many as you wanted. And meat for breakfast? I couldn't believe it, but here it was—bacon, and sausages, and sometimes ham—and again as much as you wanted. Fresh milk? In Budapest, it had been a treat (the food shortage was on when we left, remember) but here it was the same old story—great pitchers of it, help yourself. I had never seen breakfast cereal before, either, and here it was.

I was amazed that some of the soldiers didn't finish all their food. They'd leave some on their plates and scrape it into a garbage bin. At home, I'd never seen *anybody* leave any food on his plate.

One of the things my parents had to go through was a long interrogation about their backgrounds. It was understandable. If the Communists had wanted to get an agent into a foreign country, the refugee program was a perfect cover—he could pass himself off as a poor victim of oppression who had fled his native land with only the clothes he stood in. No possessions, no money, and most important of all, no papers. Even after we were settled in America, the FBI checked up on us—one agent, years later, passed himself off as a book salesman.

There were also Red Cross women there, especially ready to help my mother as much as they could. The Red Cross was absolutely magnificent to us—they helped us all the way through until we finally left for our new homes in America.

Because my mother was pregnant, we had to stay in Munich until a special Army plane, with Red Cross nurses, was ready to take all the pregnant women in the camp bound for America at one time. There were about twenty. So it was not until January 2, 1957, that we boarded a U.S. Army hospital plane at Munich, all of the pregnant women strapped onto stretchers.

As the plane ground its way from the airport building to the runway, I was boiling with excitement. Never in my life had I ever been in a plane, much less one as big as this four-engined monster, and here I was on my way to America—the dreamed-of land. I don't think any fourteen-year-old boy in the history of the world ever had such a magnificent experience. All the sounds of the plane fascinated me—the roar of the engines (just watching them being started had been thrill enough), the mysterious whinings and grindings that meant absolutely nothing to me, but which I was sure were part of some arcane, complicated process that only God-like men could understand. The plane waited at the end of the runway for four or five minutes, the engines winding up into a blast that shook the whole earth, then slowly we started rolling. I was beside myself. Faster and faster we went. Suddenly I noticed we were up a little way from the ground, then higher and higher. I could see the airport buildings flashing below us, then the highways with the cars on them, then the houses, then whole farms and the bend of the beautiful Isar River, the plane turning and the whole wing dipping, then we were on our way.

For the first few hours, I was fascinated, simply looking down at the countryside (I *still* like propellor planes; at least you can see something and you feel as if you're in an airplane instead of high up in a movie house, the way the jets are) and trying to figure out where we were. There was the Rhine! Or was it? I remembered the maps in my geography book at school. It had been so much easier to learn geography from them than looking down at the real earth below.

Finally it began to get dark. The Red Cross women on the plane fed us, and after a time we landed at London to take on fuel. By the time we took off again it was dark, and I went to sleep. It was getting light as we approached Stephenville, in Newfoundland, and there was a driving snowstorm, a blizzard. I'd seen snow in Budapest, and I'd read about snowstorms, but nothing had prepared me for this. I couldn't see more than a few hundred feet out the window, the snow was driving by, the plane was bucking like a wild thing, the sounds of the engines screamed up and down, and I was absolutely frightened out of my wits. Finally we landed. Outside the wind was screaming almost as loud as the engine had been and the snow was blinding. All the pregnant women had been strapped to their stretchers again. Finally we made it into the airport building.

The storm was so bad that we had to stay overnight at the airport, where a very nice American guy played checkers with

me. It was mid-afternoon as we approached New York. The
pilot told us about the city over the loudspeaker—what the
buildings were, and the rivers, and so on. Speaking only
Hungarian, I didn't understand a word he said, but I didn't
need to. I could see, and that was enough! The plane circled
the city, then it headed for Newark. Again, I couldn't believe
it! So many roads, all interlacing each other, so many millions
of cars, so many buildings, and all of them so high!

We landed at Newark, and we were all put into dark green
Army buses and taken to Camp Kilmer in New Jersey. One
program that had been established in the United States, with
the blessing of President Eisenhower, was arranging for
American families to take refugees into their homes until
they could get established, and we were to come under that
program.

My mother, Charlie and I stayed at Camp Kilmer for about
ten days. It was an old Army camp that had been fitted out
for the refugees, much like the one at Munich, but nowhere
near as busy or crowded. I spent most of my time, from 8 A.M.
to 10 P.M., in the main lounge of the camp, watching television, which of course I had never seen before. I saw every
single cowboy film there was.

My father had left us after a couple of days to go to Plattsburg, in northern New York State, where he had a good
friend he had gone through medical school with—Dr. Charles
Petenyi, a pathologist. He had fled Hungary in 1947. The
first thing my father wanted, naturally, was a job. Dr. Petenyi
explained that father couldn't practice dentistry in New York
State without going through dental school again in the
United States to a school that New York would recognize—

after nineteen years of practice! My father had neither the time nor the money for that.

Because of his medical degree, however, he was qualified to practice medicine in a New York State hospital. There was an opening at the St. Lawrence State Hospital for the Insane in Ogdensburg, on the St. Lawrence River. Dr. Petenyi also mentioned that he knew some people at nearby Saranac Lake and that *they* had told him that the town had offered its hospitality, at the urging of (among others) James Loeb, the publisher of the local paper, to the refugees from Hungary. Saranac Lake was only about seventy-five miles east of Ogdensburg. That, I repeat, is the Hungarian way of doing things. There is always somebody who knows somebody who knows something.

So it was arranged that my mother and Charlie and I would go to stay at various homes in Saranac Lake while my father filled out all the forms for the job at Ogdensburg. In addition to establishing his medical *bona fides,* my father faced the same problem we all did—lack of English.

Our stay at Kilmer was over.

Our first step was to join our father in Plattsburg.

Leaving Kilmer, I realized that my mother and Charlie and I stood out as real refugees. We had some clothes and other personal belongings that had been given to us by the Red Cross, packed into tiny suitcases that had also been given to us. A very nice lady Red Cross volunteer drove us into New York City. I'll never forget that car—my first ride in a private American automobile. It was a 1955 Oldsmobile convertible with red upholstery and it had a button that if you pushed it, the antenna for the radio went up. On the way into New York the lady stopped at a Howard Johnson's and treated us all to coffee and ice cream. I wanted some sugar for my coffee, but I couldn't see any, and I was too embarrassed to ask for it. (Later I found that the sugar came in tiny little paper bags.)

In New York the lady took us to the Hotel Diplomat, and up to our room on the fifteenth floor. We were to stay there overnight and take the train to Saranac Lake the next morning; someone would come to get us and see us safely on board.

Naturally, I'd never been in a hotel before, much less one as big and important as this one obviously was. Charlie and I were all around the room, pushing buttons, turning on the taps, running the shower—generally being helpful to my mother.

We were up early the next morning, all packed and ready to go, long before the appointed hour. There was no sense telephoning downstairs for breakfast because it seemed unlikely that there would be anyone who could speak Hungarian. Finally, we decided to go downstairs and wait there.

Out in the corridor, a problem arose. We couldn't find the elevators. We went up and down the corridors, but we couldn't find them. There were signs but we couldn't read them. We saw other guests, but how could we talk to them? We had only twenty minutes to make our appointment with the Red Cross volunteer, so we went back into our room and and went down the outside fire escape. A full fifteen stories, my mother pregnant and Charlie and me carrying the suitcases. Looking down, the view was dizzying.

Finally we met our escort and were taken to Pennsylvania Station and put on the train for Plattsburg. It was a pleasant train ride for me, looking out at the countryside. The only sour note was that my mother bought Charlie and me an ice cream cone from the man who came through selling them and, knowing nothing about American money, gave him a dollar. He gave us no change.

We stayed with the Petenyis in Plattsburg only a few days, then went to Saranac Lake. I was to stay with the Loeb family; Charlie stayed at the home of Dr. Frederick Klemperer, and my mother with a wonderful widow named Mrs. Sally Billings. God bless them all!

All of the people at Saranac Lake couldn't have been nicer to us.

When we first arrived, there were stories about us in the newspapers, with our pictures. People stopped us on the street to welcome us, though we couldn't communicate with them except with smiles and handshakes. We were only beginning to learn the first phrases of English, but these good people were constantly coming to visit us. When Johnnie was born in February, thirty ladies got together and gave my mother a shower. Charlie and I agreed that that kid got more presents out of the shower than he and I had ever gotten put together. There was every toy you can imagine for a newborn infant, and all the things you give at a baby shower. I remember seeing my mother sitting in the middle of the living room floor crying, out of happiness, and not be able to tell the women how grateful she was. The local shopkeepers gave Charlie and me a complete outfit of everything we needed in the way of clothes. I'd never seen such hospitality.

The Loebs were magnificent. Mr. Loeb, I found out, was well known in Democratic politics in the United States, besides publishing the local paper. He had been chairman of the Union for Democratic Action, and President Kennedy appointed him Ambassador to Peru. The whole family was warm and close. Besides Mr. and Mrs. Loeb, there were two children a little older than me—Susie and Peter—and in addition to that, they had a French exchange student staying with them. The Loebs were a very musical family, too, and little as I know about music, I got the greatest pleasure out of the family musicales.

In Hungary, we kids had gotten the distinct impression that the average American family, after the day's work was done, piled into the family Cadillac and went to see a drive-in movie and eat chocolate bars with nuts in them. The Loebs didn't have a Cadillac, and I never even heard anybody mention a drive-in movie. I did get a chocolate bar with nuts in it, though.

I'm sure I made a thousand mistakes while I was staying with the Loebs, but only one comes to my mind. They had told me that any time I wanted something to eat, just help myself out of the refrigerator. I came home one day and there was no one in the house, so I opened the refrigerator. On the door shelf was an opened can with a spoon in it. The can had a picture of a leaping fish on it.

"Ah, ha," I said to myself. "Just what I want. A little salmon or whatever it is, and some bread."

I made myself a nice snack and was just finishing it when Mrs. Loeb came in. I had made a mistake. It wasn't salmon, it was cat food.

But good.

It was the middle of the school term when I got to the Loebs, and I was beginning to be—homesick, I guess is the closest word. It wasn't that I wanted to go back to Hungary, but everything was so strange and new. And our family had always been so close, even through the war. Even though my mother lived only twenty minutes away by car, and Charlie was just about the same distance, I somehow found myself missing them more than when my mother used to go up from the farm at Kecskemet to Budapest and be gone for three or four days at a time. Perhaps it was the fact that I couldn't speak English well enough. As I said, the Loebs couldn't have been warmer and more thoughtful, but I was too young to be able to feel that I was part of them.

God knows I worked hard enough at learning English. I had a Hungarian-English dictionary in my pocket all the time. Every time I saw a word I didn't know I looked it up— or as many as I reasonably could. If I'd looked them *all* up I wouldn't have had time to do anything else. The Loebs spent God knows how many hours trying to teach me English.

It was decided that I should go to school with Peter Loeb, who was a year older than me. The Loebs got permission from the school authorities for me just to tag along with Peter, sit in his classes and follow him around. Peter always acted as if it was a pleasure. How I would have acted with a kid a year younger than me following me wherever I went is a tribute to his sainthood. I wasn't expected to learn anything that first year except English, and the Loebs were perfectly right in sending me to school. There is no faster way to learn any language than to be thrown in with people who don't speak a word of yours. It may be painful, but it works.

Here was the first time that I really saw the difference between European and American schools. The kids here were so much more relaxed, more natural. They dressed so casually, and they changed classrooms, not the teachers. The corridors always seemed filled with kids. And dressed—they dressed any way they wanted to. In Europe, you *dressed* for school, you didn't just put on what was handy. And in Europe you *studied* for school—you were always a little tense and worried about how you were doing. It was forever being drummed into you that if you didn't get good marks in this grade, you wouldn't get into the next one, then you'd never get into the Gymnasium, then you'd end up with a job as a street sweeper. The Loeb kids studied and got good grades, but it was all so much more casual than at home. They'd study with a record player on. At home, I always went off by myself and studied until I had my lessons so that I could recite them to my mother. In the Saranac Lake school, the kids actually used to dance in the gym at lunch time. I can just see the expression on the faces of my old teachers in Budapest if they ever saw anything like that.

The only minor disappointement I had at the Loebs was that I wanted to play soccer. They not only didn't know how to play soccer, they didn't even have a soccer ball. They got out a baseball and some bats and gloves and tried to teach me how to play baseball. I appreciated the effort, but I didn't like baseball much. You don't get any exercise. There's no action. You just stand around most of the time.

My mother and Charlie and I stayed at Saranac Lake for two months. By this time my father was established in his job at the St. Lawrence Hospital. St. Lawrence was headed by Dr. Herman B. Snow, a famous psychiatrist, who was one of the innovators of the "open door" policy for patients, and who was very kind to the Gogolaks.

So, with a wrench, we said good-bye to the people we had met at Saranac Lake, the friends we had made—particularly the Loebs, in my case—and moved to Ogdensburg.

Ogdensburg is a lovely city with many magnificent views of the St. Lawrence River (I guess, from having been brought up on the Danube, I love rivers), and we lived in an apartment on the hospital grounds. I was enrolled as a freshman in the Ogdensburg Free Academy, the public high school, in April of 1957.

This was a different experience for me than going to school at Saranac Lake with Peter Loeb. My English was getting better every day—the Gogolaks spent every evening studying English—but it was by no means up to understanding a teacher's lecture on American history. It would have helped if I had known something about American history to start with, but Hungarian schools were much better on their version of Russian history than they were on American, so my going to the Free Academy was again simply an exercise in exposing me to the American way and the American language.

I was still at the stage of mentally translating, which is something you have to get over in order to speak a foreign language competently. In other words, if I wanted someone to pass the bread, for example, first I'd think of it in Hungarian, then I'd translate it into English.

I think fourteen is the worst age at which to try to learn a new language. You're not old enough to learn it as another skill, the way an adult can, yet you're too old to learn it naturally, the way a child does. Charlie was much better at English than I was. Even today, I speak Hungarian perfectly, but my English has an accent. Charlie, on the other hand, speaks perfect English, but he speaks Hungarian with an American accent. Our father always made us speak Hungarian at home, so we'd know at least two languages. He was fond of saying that a man who can only speak one language is like a man with only one leg.

Naturally, the kids being what they are, I was the butt of all sorts of jokes at Ogdensburg. I remember one kid patiently teaching me that the most polite thing I could say to one of the pretty young lady teachers was: "I'd like to screw you, dear." Something about his expression gave that little joke away, and I never did say it.

That summer my father bought me a soccer ball and Charlie and I spent a good part of our vacation playing soccer on the hospital grounds at St. Lawrence.

In the fall I was again enrolled, now as a freshman at Ogdensburg. My English was coming along fine, I thought. I could pretty well hold my own in a conversation, and I could read a book in English if it was easy enough. Though I must say that I think English is the most difficult language on the face of the earth. It amazes me that most Americans can only speak English. I should think that if you can learn English, you can learn anything.

Because by now I was older than most of my classmates, and because I had already studied most of what they were teaching me at Ogdensburg—with the exception of American history and English literature—I was determined to get through high school in three years. I guess it was my competitiveness coming out. If I already knew more than these kids, why should I be in the same class with them? My math was already at college freshman level.

That fall, therefore, I did practically nothing except study. I did notice that suddenly the girls seemed a lot zippier than the ones I had known in Hungary. They looked a lot more lively and interesting. They wore lipstick, and they swung their skirts with a gayer air, and—well, were just a lot more exciting than any girls I had known before. It was a pleasure to talk to them (I'd never bothered to talk to girls before). Also, it was wonderful to make body contact with them. The best way I found to do this was to ask them to teach me to dance. They didn't seem to mind very much.

In the spring I went out for the track team. Because I was pretty strong I had no trouble becoming the discus thrower and shot putter for the team, and I won enough events to get my name in the local newspapers.

Just before school was due to start in September of '58, Bob Snow, the son of the director of St. Lawrence Hospital, and Dick Maloney, another kid I had gotten to know pretty well, said:

"Why don't you try out for the football team? You're a pretty big guy."

By this time I was almost six feet tall and weighed 175 pounds.

I was of two minds about it. In the first place, I thought American football was pretty silly. I'd been to some of the games the previous fall, and they had seemed boring compared to soccer. It wasn't quite as boring as baseball, but the guys seemed to spend an awful lot of time standing around or huddling or lining up—doing anything except playing ball. I thought the uniforms were pretty crude, too, compared to soccer uniforms. How could you possibly move around with all those bulging shoulder pads and heavy helmets? On top of that, I didn't know *how* to play American football.

On the other hand, I noticed that the most popular guys in the school all seemed to be on the football team, and the girls seemed to fall all over each other to go out on dates with them. Leaving the girls aside, the big motivation of the Gogolak family was to *make it* in America. This was the land of opportunity. We'd read or heard all the stories about poor immigrants coming here and ending up rich and successful. We certainly qualified as poor immigrants. We'd come here with the clothing on our backs, a handful of jewels, enough Hungarian money to buy second-class tickets from the Austrian border to Budapest, and a book of recipes for Hungarian goulash. Now the thing was to become rich and successful.

I already had seen that the way to succeed at my present occupation—going to high school—was to get top grades and play sports.

So I went out for the football team.

I felt pretty silly when they issued our full equipment for the first time. Not only was it bulky and cumbersome to wear, it was also the first time I had ever seen—much less worn—a jock strap. And the shoes were high shoes, unlike soccer shoes, and the cleats were much higher. How can you move in these things, I asked myself, and promptly proved I was right. I was the last man onto the field and, coming down the runway with the whole team watching, I fell down.

Our coach, a great guy named Bill Plimpton, was also our social science teacher. (Why do American schools have such nutty names for courses? In Hungary, geography was geography and history was history, and at least you knew what you were studying.) Bill was a football nut, and he used to show film clips of all the football games in his classes. I made the team as a two-way end (offense and defense). The day before our first game, Bill suddenly woke up to the fact that he needed someone who could kick the football.

I was one of five or six guys who volunteered to try out. I'll never forget the look on my holder's face when he set the ball up, and I lined up at a 45-degree angle to the goal line. I could just see what he was thinking. What the hell is this? This guy is either going to kick me in the ass or he's going to put the ball up into the stands.

Stupidly, I hadn't practiced kicking an American football before. I caught the ball cleanly enough, and gave it a tremendous boot that sent it through the end zone. Unfortunately, it never got more than five feet off the ground. It would have been a great soccer kick, but it wasn't what Plimpton wanted. He picked some other guy for his kicker.

The team had a pretty fair season. By and large, the Ogdensburg Free Academy turns out good teams, and I played pretty well. But all through the season I was burned up at myself for that silly kick.

That fall, my father bought a television set, and we watched the college and pro games on it. I'll never forget the first pro field goal I ever saw. I was nuts about the New York Giants, even then. I thought of New York as the greatest, most exciting city in the whole world, and I thought that the guys who played for the Giants were the greatest heroes who ever walked the earth—Charley Conerly, Frank Gifford, Alex Webster, Mel Triplett, Pat Summerall. At that time I could give you the complete roster of every team in the league, size and weight, where the player had gone to college, how he had done last year. I may have missed a point or two in my social studies classes, but I never missed a point on how many passes Charley Conerly completed in 1957.

Anyway, the first pro field goal I ever saw, the Giants were playing the Cleveland Browns; the Browns had the ball on the Giants' 30-yard line, it was fourth and eight, and the announcer said: "An obvious field goal situation." It was obvious even to me.

Lou Groza trotted to his spot about ten yards behind the line of scrimmage. I said:

"Daddy, look at the funny way that man is going to try to kick the football!"

It *did* look funny to me, lining up directly behind the ball, and kicking it with your toe instead of off at a 45-degree angle and kicking it with your instep.

Groza kicked the ball straight through the goal posts for a 37-yard field goal—over the crossbar instead of under, like me—and I turned to my father and said:

"The paper says he gets $30,000 a year. *I* can kick a ball 37 yards."

At Ogdensburg Free Academy I found that they hadn't scored with a field goal in five years. Their kickoffs were averaging less than 35 yards. Still smoldering from my try-out kick, I said to myself, you've been kicking a ball since you were three years old. If you can't do any better than that first kick, you better just quit football.

So, next spring, I started to practice kicking by myself, or with Charlie. The field next to the hospital was used to pasture cows, so I think Charlie and I practiced with the smelliest football in St. Lawrence County.

My big problem was getting the ball high enough into the air, and getting it up fast enough so that opposing linemen wouldn't be able to block it. This was of the utmost importance later in pro ball, where some of those guys can reach up 18 feet. I didn't give much thought to trying to kick the American way. In the first place, I was too old to change. In the second, I think that soccer-style kicking has a lot of advantages. I think you can get more power into it, sweeping your leg rather than just kicking it straight forward. Also, you can steer the ball, make it hook or slice. (Sometimes you do that when you don't want to.)

But, kicking an American football, this style, has its disadvantages. A soccer ball is perfectly round. Basically, when you kick it all you have to worry about is making sure that it's going in the right direction, where you want it to. Since an American football is oval, and what you're kicking against is a parabola, you also have to worry about exactly where your foot is going to hit it. You have to hit it at the precise spot between where the nose of the ball is on the ground and its greatest circumference. You can louse up a soccer kick, too, but it's harder. If you don't hit an American football precisely right, you've blown it. Hit it a trifle too high, and the ball won't go up into the air. Hit it low and you'll get altitude, but no distance.

The biggest problem I had by far was the fact that I was doing something brand-new. To my knowledge, no kicker in American football had ever tried to kick soccer style.

I had no examples to follow. There was no one to teach me. There were no books on the subject. No one could say to me, when I flubbed a kick: "This is what you did wrong." No one could say: "You're hitting the ball too high"—or too low, or whatever it was.

I simply had to get a kicking tee, and go out into that cow pasture at the state hospital at Ogdensburg, and figure it out for myself. I had to figure out exactly where to hit the ball. Only experience taught me where to hit it and how to hit it; only experience taught me how to control—or compensate for—the hook or the slice of the ball.

I have figured out that I kicked a football, that spring and summer, rain or shine (you play football in the rain, you know), ten thousand times.

That fall I was the school's kicker, and glad of it. I was listed as an end, and I played end, as I had the year before, but when the team was practicing, I was allowed to go off by myself and practice kicking instead of going through all the tackling and blocking drills.

I don't know whether it's my soccer upbringing or not, but I'm not very much of a man for the continual body contact—hitting and hitting and hitting—that goes on without let-up in American football.

I don't mind hitting or getting hit, I can take care of myself. I just didn't like it scrimmage after scrimmage after scrimmage. I never could get myself worked up into that go-out-there-and-kill-the-son-of-a-bitch frame of mind that you have to work yourself into if you're going to be a good lineman.

The first time I kicked off for Ogdensburg that fall, unlike my first performance, the kickoff went out of the end zone, clearing the cross bar by five feet. Such a thing had never been seen before at Ogdensburg. I'm sure that when I lined up to kick off, every man, woman, child and dog in the stands, as well as the whole opposing team, had said: "What is that nut on the field going to do?"

I showed them.

That season, too, I made two field goals for Ogdensburg— more than they'd had in one season in all their history, and not a bad record considering that I had only three attempts, one from the 42-yard line.

My last two years at Ogdensburg were very good. My first and second years, I'd taken practically no part in the social life of the school. For one thing, the hospital is six or eight miles out of town, and my father had no car. And, of course, we used to spend every evening studying English. But now my father had bought a car, and I had gotten a license, and every now and then my father would let me drive in to town to go to a dance or school play or something—provided I got home at a reasonable hour. At first that was 10 o'clock, then it was moved up to 11.

Also, football wasn't the only thing I was doing. I played every sport I could get into, except baseball and soccer. For example—you may not believe this, and it's a small honor to brag about anyway—in 1958 I was the Northern League ping-pong champion in the sports carnival held at Massena, New York, a few miles down river from Ogdensburg. In track I was the sectional champion, and helped win the sectional championship for Ogdensburg, with a discus throw of 143 feet 5 inches, and in the high jump (5 feet 2 inches, I'm ashamed to say). I was on the intramural basketball team—high scorer in one game, with 17 points—and I was bowling for the Maple City Boys League. Mr. All-Round Athlete, that was me.

The newspapers were beginning to notice me. (I never dreamed that the day would come when I'd have headlines in the New York *Daily News* and *The New York Times*.) The Ogdensburg *Advance-News,* the Ogdensburg *Journal* and the *Adirondack News* (Jim Loeb's paper back in Saranac Lake) all had stories about me. I gave an exhibition of discus throwing and I was headlined "Mr. Discus." I was called (in headlines), "The Foot," "The Golden Toe," and "The Hungarian Goulash."

Also, I got first honors at the Ogdensburg Free Academy, which means an average of over 90; pretty high class for a poor immigrant boy whose native tongue was Hungarian and who did the four years in three.

During my last year at Ogdensburg, the question of college came up, and here my father laid down the law.

"An Ivy League college," he said. "I'm not going to have you going to someplace where, when somebody asks you what college you're in and you tell him, a blank look comes over his face and he says, 'Where's that?' "

I did get him to relent to the extent that I could apply to Syracuse, on the grounds that it generally had a topnotch football team, because by this time the feeling was beginning to grow in me that I could become a good enough kicker to end up in the pros.

So, absolutely cold and with no letters of introduction, I sat down and wrote to the director of athletics at Syracuse, Dartmouth and Cornell. I told them I was applying to their colleges for an academic scholarship—Ivy League colleges don't give athletic scholarships openly and my grades were good enough, and I was under no illusions that Syracuse would give me an athletic one—and how would they like to have a kicker who could drive an opening kickoff out of the end zone and who had made a 40-yard field goal in high school? I knew that the football coaches would laugh at this, so I offered to supply film clips.

I found out afterward what happened. Syracuse asked for the film clips and didn't believe them. "That has to be a phony," one coach said, looking at them. "No high school kid can kick a football out of the end zone. He had to have a 60-mile wind behind him."

Dartmouth—Bob Blackman was the football coach then and I don't know whether he ever saw the clips or not—put me on the waiting list.

Cornell asked me to come over to Ithaca and talk to them.

I went over, with my scrapbook full of newspaper clippings (kept by my mother, who *still* keeps them) in case they had missed any. Besides the admissions people—with my grades and my background, I wasn't too worried about being turned down for admission—I talked to Ben Mintz, who did publicity for the athletic office—and a wonderful guy who is still a friend of mine, Ted Thoren, the varsity baseball coach and the freshman football coach. His family background was Yugoslavia, and when he got to know me a little better he always called me: "Hey, Hunkie." My guide around the campus was a top varsity football player of White Russian descent—and they say America isn't a melting pot—named George Telesh, who later was voted captain of the football team and whom I played with.

So, to Cornell I went, to the College of Arts and Sciences on an academic scholarship.

CHAPTER

FIVE

The Good Years at Cornell

There's something wonderful about going to college. Fall in Ithaca is wonderful. The air is beginning to get crisp, just a hint of the turning season, the grass on the campus is a lush green. The young people; the air of excitement; registering for classes; finding out where you're going to live—to me, it couldn't have been more exciting.

Beyond all this, I was determined to make the freshman football team, though in my own mind there was a question because while I was husky and all that, the only real thing I could do was kick. I came up to Cornell as an end (that's where Ogdensburg had played me), but I absolutely couldn't run. What's the use of an end who can't gain five yards after he's caught the ball?

A man who was to become a friend, Gary Wood, came to Cornell as a freshman along with me. He was a quarterback. Naturally, the first thing a quarterback in college looks at is his ends. The highest compliment I ever got from Gary in freshman practice was:

"Well, at least, Gogolak, if I throw you the ball your hands are big enough so you don't drop it." Big deal.

I was already a loner by nature, but freshman football at Cornell reinforced it. We'd have practice, then I'd go off to practice kicking by myself. Everybody else on the freshman team would be down there sweating, and I'd be off with a kicking tee, all by myself, practicing kickoffs and field goals. Or kicking a soccer ball up into the air.

Sometimes I'd quit earlier than the rest of the team and somebody would say:

"Where's Gogolak?"

And somebody else would answer:

"Off at the movies."

It was funny and it wasn't. I would have liked to be one of the guys, but I didn't know how. I couldn't get into all the scrimmages. What would have been the point of that?

And I was a freshman. I really didn't know what the hell was going on around me. I went to a lot of movies by myself. On top of my loner role was the fact that I was Hungarian. There was my accent, my haircut, and my own belief that if you can't take care of yourself, who will?

I found out from Gary Wood that I stood out even in the meeting for freshman football practice. This was before the days of freak clothes on campus, but most guys going out showed up in sweat shirt, slacks and loafers. I showed up for the first drill in shined shoes, a suit, and white shirt with tie.

I stuck out!

But I made the freshman football team. This was because

almost every time the ball was put on the tee at the 40-yard line for a practice kickoff, I kicked it out of the end zone. Not into the end zone. Out of it. I was carried as an end, and I may have been the world's worst, but I could kick.

The proof of this came in the second game of the freshman season.

We were playing Yale. Somewhere in the game, we'd gotten to the Yale 41-yard line. It was fourth down and eight, and Ted Thoren sent me in for a field goal. Even the Cornell bench laughed. This would be kicking 48 yards. A 48-yard field goal from a college freshman kicker? I could see the whole Yale bench laughing, and there I was, trotting onto the field in my spanking clean uniform, and then I lined up at my 45-degree angle.

The whole stadium was laughing, though I didn't notice it. When I go out to kick I don't pay any atention to the crowd.

I lined up, I kicked, and the ball went right straight through the uprights.

Then I listened. Dead silence. Not a sound. Nobody could believe it. A 48-yard field goal? In a freshman Ivy League football game? From a guy who kicked sideways?

Then as I began to trot off the field, came the roars of applause. I began to understand what I had done.

The goal posts in college ball are ten yards behind the goal line, which meant that the ball was in the air for 58 yards, and still cleared the cross bar.

The Cornell publicity department did a good job for me. After our very first game against Cortland, a small college in New York State, in which I had kicked a 39-yard field goal, the Cornell *Daily Sun*—"Ithaca's Only Morning Newspaper"—had headlined "Cub Eleven Opens Season With 49-12 Win; Gogolak, Wood, Robinson, down Cortland." Now, there was a reason to headline Wood—he was later eighth-round draft choice by the New York Giants—and Robinson, who was a fine running back, but there was no reason to headline me, except that the Cornell publicity department had made such a big thing about having a soccer-style kicker on the team.

I loved the publicity, but it was helping me to become even more of a loner. If I had been an American, I don't think it would have been so bad. Or if, like Gary Wood, I had been a quarterback, a guy who played all the time. But, as a freshman, getting all this publicity both helped me and worried me. I was living in a dormitory at the time, as all freshman did, except the guys who came from right around Ithaca, and it didn't help. If you're a college freshman and your name is in the papers all the time, how can you strike up a friendship that doesn't sound artificial?

Even on the football team there was a little of it. I'd be a few seconds late for practice and there'd be that "so nice of you to show up routine."

Actually, I don't think that the loner reputation was all that much my fault. I had come up to Cornell as an end, and God knows I tried to play it. I was big enough and I was strong enough, but as Ted Thoren said to me:

"You don't have the finesse."

Ted was right. He made the point that by the time you're trying to play college football, you really have to have played at least three or four years. On a soccer team, I would have looked great, and the Cornell guys would have looked lousy.

But on an American football team, as an end, I looked lousy. I didn't have the moves. I didn't have the instincts.

The Yale game in my freshman year may have put the final stamp on the die. I kicked three field goals in that one (the 48-yarder was the first). We won, 16-14. I still remember the referee running in to me as I lined up to kick off, yelling "You're lining up wrong."

Later, I found out that Ted Thoren went to the varsity football coach, Lefty James (Tom Harp took over the next year) and told him that maybe Cornell should think of me as just a kicker. This was unprecedented in college ball at the time. As a matter of fact, it would have been unprecedented in pro ball. The pros were more field-goal conscious, which wasn't hard, since the top twenty college teams were averaging less than one field goal a season in those days, but even the pros didn't carry a guy on the roster who couldn't do anything except kick.

James, and later Harp, went along with Thoren's idea. James had at least six ends who were better than me, but he didn't have anybody else who could kick 48-yard field goals.

Once Thoren told James: "He's been hooking the ball. I think . . ."

"No, no, no!" James yelled. "Don't coach him!"

By this time, I was beginning to get newspaper headlines outside the Ithaca area. I'm not putting this in to blow my own horn—those headlines were to help me later when I was panting desperately to get a job in pro ball. I'm not sure they swung it, but they helped.

By the end of the freshman season, there had been stories about me in the Cleveland *Plain Dealer* and the New York

Herald Tribune, and in the fall of '61, I was in the "Pigskin Preview" in the *Saturday Evening Post* and in *Playboy.*

Reading feature stories about yourself in newspapers for the first time is a strange experience—at least it was for me. Just a straightforward account of what you did in a ball game is generally all right. Very few sports reporters have ever *really* played the sport they cover. By really playing, I mean getting up to the level where you're given a chance to try out for a pro team, and so they don't really know what's going on on the field and they make plenty of mistakes. (Some reporters try to make up for this by making a stab at finding out, the way Paul Gallico once sparred with Jack Dempsey, but that's just pretend.) But, generally, accounts of what happened in the game are right. "Gogolak kicked a 48-yard field goal, which made the score 10-7." Perfectly straightforward, perfectly correct.

The feature stories make you feel as if you're reading about somebody else. I still remember articles in the Cornell *Sun* —in fact, I still have the clippings of the articles: "Gogolak kicked six field goals in eleven attempts during the year. Old timers will remember . . ."

It gives you the eerie feeling that you're already a part of history.

In my sophomore year I began to feel as if I was more a part of Cornell. It's so big a place that I don't think you can ever get to *really* become a part of it unless you spend most of your life there. But as a freshman, I guess I had always felt lost. There were so many people, and so many things I didn't know. Except for football, all I did was live in the dormitory, go to class, study, go out with a couple of the guys for a movie or some beers, have a date or two with a girl, talk to my parents on the phone—that was it. Football did give me a sense of ego.

In the fall of '61, things began to change. I was taken into Delta Upsilon, the fraternity that most of the athletes went into. There, I started off with a bit of trouble. I didn't like what I'd heard of fraternity initiations in Europe—which are much tougher than American ones but which, somehow, in their peculiar undergraduate way, make more sense. Part of the Delta Upsilon initiation, I was told, was that you were supposed to bite the head off a live goldfish. I said the hell with it. What was that going to prove? I wanted to belong to the fraternity, but not that much. I said I wouldn't do it.

Delta Upsilon took me in anyway, and I must say I'm glad.

At Delta Upsilon I learned more about America in three years than I would have learned in thirty outside it.

It was the first time in my life I had ever actually lived with a bunch of Americans, real live Americans who, after the first couple of weeks, seemed to forget that I was a Hungarian—except for the ribbing I used to get occasionally about my accent—and a football player. (Football players were a dime a dozen in Delta Upsilon, and Gary Wood was more famous than I was.) They treated me like just another guy, so that I had the feeling they were acting naturally, not being "special" in front of me because I was a poor immigrant.

And there was a big cross-section of America in Delta Upsilon. Some guys (like me) were earning seventy-five cents an hour washing dishes to help put ourselves through college; some guys had gone to expensive prep schools and had Porsches out in the parking lot and never gave a second thought to money. Yes, I have to thank Delta Upsilon for teaching me how to get along with Americans of all sorts of backgrounds and creeds. I made a lot of friends there, and I still think of them as friends. I still keep in touch with a lot of them. There was Gary Wood, of course, and a wonderful older guy named Bert Antell, who lives in New York and is a great fraternity man—he goes back to Cornell every month—and Ben Lewis, who was an usher at my wedding.

I must say, however, that getting into the mainstream of American fraternity life didn't do much for my marks.

I still wanted to follow in my father's footsteps and become either a doctor or a dentist, and so I was majoring in zoology.

But, between endless gab-and-beer fests at Delta Upsilon and playing football, my grades began to slip. I never was anywhere near flunking, but I wasn't getting straight A's, either.

And, in my junior and senior years, football began to take precedence over everything. I had begun to think about the pros.

I didn't have the rapport with Tom Harp that I had with Ted Thoren, but I don't think that made any difference in my playing. A player doesn't have to like a coach, or vice versa. It's easier if it happens, but it's not important. Harp wanted Cornell to be a much better team than it could hope to be; Cornell didn't have the type of football machine that attracts the top high school players. I'm reminded of Dick Harlow's line about trying to coach Harvard when it was falling to a third-rate power even in the Ivy League in the late '30s: "My problem is, on any given squad, I've got maybe eight football players, the rest are a bunch of potato eaters." To Harlow, a potato eater was a guy who looked as if he should be able to play football but couldn't. At the training table, though, could he murder potatoes! That, to be frank, was Harp's problem. The difference was that Harlow's alumni never made a big deal about where Harvard finished in the Ivy League if only it beat Yale and, hopefully, Princeton. The Cornell alumni always wanted their team to go undefeated and be rated in the national standings.

While I was there, Harp had no such luck.

He had a great quarterback in Gary Wood—I've always felt that if Gary had been four inches taller and twenty pounds heavier, he would have been one of the legendary quarterbacks and I could kick, without any false modesty, and then there were maybe six or seven other guys who could really play football. Even in the Ivy League, you can't get by on a squad that thin.

Our record that year showed it. We were three and six, and the only pleasant part of the year for me, as far as football was concerned, was that the newspapermen began to pay serious attention to my kicking. "The coin toss at the start of a Cornell game is getting to be a waste of time," one wrote. "All Cornell ever wants is Pete Gogolak with the wind behind him in the fourth quarter." I hit one kickoff so hard it not only went out of the end zone, it hit the roof of the field house, which is another twenty yards away.

By now I had convinced myself that my future lay with pro ball. I assume it was a disappointment to my father (though he is not the sort of father to force a son to do something he's convinced he can't do), but I didn't have the sort of mind that would qualify me to be a doctor. In my third year at Cornell I switched from zoology to art. I may be the only player in pro ball who can tell the difference between a Durer and a Rembrandt.

I was under no illusion that all the publicity I was getting was going to win me a professional contract. I began to work on what I'd have to do for the pros.

The big thing there, I knew, is time. Timing, too, but also time.

The going figure is 1.4 seconds.

From the time the ball is snapped to the time you hit it, 1.4 seconds. Every kicker on the face of the earth would like to get it down to one second flat, but I don't think anybody ever will. On the other hand, if you get up to 1.5 seconds, you're in trouble. The line can hold off the chargers on the other side only so long; and the more tenths of a second you give the opposition, the more chance they have to get in on you.

In one game I played for Cornell, the opposing coach got two of his tallest players and the instant the ball was snapped, one of them jumped onto the shoulders of the other, then both stood up to try to block the kick. I think that the reason they missed—apart from the fact that I didn't even realize they were there, I was concentrating on the ball—was that they didn't understand (or their coach didn't) that a ball kicked the way I kick it doesn't come into the goal posts the way it does if it's hit by a conventional kicker. They were simply out of position.

Getting my field goal time down to 1.4 seconds required an enormous amount of work. No kicker can wait to make his three-step run till the ball is set; he has to start the instant the ball is snapped. If the ball isn't there waiting for his foot, the field goal is blown. That means the center has to snap the ball exactly where the holder wants it; then the holder has to spot it exactly where the kicker has marked; the kicker can only look down at where the ball is supposed to be. I'll admit that sometimes I've looked up too soon—I shouldn't have—and it always costs me three points. Basically, once I've started my run, there's no way to stop.

The holder has to have the ball just right—centered, almost vertical, the laces away from me. My holder at Cornell was Gary Wood, later to be my teammate on the New York Giants.

I punted for Cornell, too.

The logical thought for a coach is that if a guy can place kick he can punt, and so I punted.

In 1963 I was one of the three best college punters in the country. I averaged over 45 yards. But I knew that punting was no way to make a fortune in pro ball. Every team has to have a good punter, of course, but while the sports writers may talk about a game being decided in a "punting duel," punters don't put points on the score board. And that's where the owner of a pro team always looks when it comes to talking contract.

A lot of coaches feel that a missed field goal is as good as a punt. That's great for the coach, but not so good for the kicker. If the field goal is good, it means three points. If the field goal is missed, it's no skin off the coach's back. The opposition still has the ball on the 20-yard line. But on the kicker's record it reads: "Field goal, missed."

Punting is such a different way of kicking that, especially for kickers like me, it throws the whole timing off. The Giants used me as a punter for part of one season. I wasn't too bad, but my field goal kicking went to hell, which may or may not have been a result of the punting stint. Anyway, the Giants soon gave up on that.

By my senior year, my little brother Charlie had grown up to the point where he was the kicker for Princeton—also soccer-style. I think that one of the great non-confrontations of all time was when Charlie and I faced each other as kickers in the Cornell-Princeton game. The newspapers built it up—who wouldn't?—but the game was so one-sided that I could have kicked ten field goals and it wouldn't have made much difference. Princeton creamed us.

Apart from that disaster, Cornell had a couple of good games in '63—by which I mean games that we won, and that I helped win. The most important were the Columbia and the Yale games. We beat Columbia 18-17, and I had a 45-yard field goal. We beat Yale 13-10, and I had a field goal in the last forty-five seconds of the day. That year I set a new collegiate record for PATs (points after touchdowns) with forty-four straight, reached in the game in which we beat Penn. After that game, in Ogdensburg, my playing number at the Free Academy—number 44—was retired in honor of the number of PATs.

By now, my playing career at Cornell was over, and I was ready for the pros. Ready—I was anxious, eager and available. The question was whether the pros were ready for me.

I was under no illusions about making the pros. I had so many things against me that sometimes I despaired. It's hard to put them in order, but I guess the first one was that I played for Cornell. Ivy League. The pros didn't scout the Ivy League back then. Second, all I could do was kick. There wasn't a team in either the National or American Football League that carried a player, then, as a kicker. Third, there was my sidewinder style of delivery.

It all added up to the fact that while I hoped to be drafted, I wasn't at all sure that I would be.

What made it for me was that Ted Thoren and a man named Jack Guthrie, an all-out football fan who runs the All-American game, both knew Harvey Johnson, who is the director of player personnel for the Buffalo Bills.

They both told Johnson:

"Harvey, you've just got to come over and see this kid kick. He's unbelievable. He kicks them right straight out of the stadium."

If there was one type of player that Buffalo needed that year, it was a place kicker, so Harvey Johnson came down to see me.

The Cornell season was over at that time and I, not realizing what was going on, was a trifle annoyed when Thoren called me at the Delta Upsilon house to tell me that Johnson was in Ithaca and wanted to see me kick. My first reaction was to tell Johnson to go to hell. If he was thinking of drafting me, why hadn't he bothered to send one of his scouts to see me in action? But I decided that was silly. If he wanted to see me kick, I'd kick. I got some sweat clothes and my football shoes, and I went up to Schoellkopf Field.

Something that casual couldn't happen today. First, all football people now are so kick-conscious that it's not unusual to see a top-rated college kicker go on the first or second round in the draft. Second, the computer has filled in the gaps in the old hit-or-miss scouting system. The computer takes in the play of every kid playing varsity ball in practically every college in the country on every single snap from scrimmage, and by the end of the senior season it tells you the yardage gained by every running back, the number of completions, and the percentage of completions, of every quarterback, the number of tackles by every lineman and defensive backfield player. It can be done, but it's awfully hard to miss out on a pro prospect nowadays.

Johnson, Guthrie, and Thoren were all waiting for me when I got to the field. It was well into November then, the sun was shining kind of weakly through an overcast, the temperature was about 60, the field was a little soggy where it had frozen and then thawed. Thoren was the holder, Guthrie snapped the ball, and Johnson had a stop-watch out and a little notebook. I started kicking at the 35, then the 40, the 45, and the 50. Finally, after I hit one from 55 yards, I asked Johnson if he wanted me to go on.

He said:

"No, no, that's enough."

As we were walking back to his car, he told me that he was going to recommend to the Bills that they draft me. But he warned me that the Bills had other problems besides kickers. I liked Johnson then and I still do, but I sort of recognized that approach. I say "sort of" because if I had known then what I found out later, I'd be a lot richer man. Johnson was a very fine man, but he was management.

I found out later that Johnson was convinced that I would solve the kicking problem for the Bills. They may have had the "other problems" he talked about, but their big problem was a kicker. They were one of the top teams in their league at the time—one of the top teams in *any* league, I was later convinced—and they had players like Jackie Kemp at quarterback, Darryl LaMonica as back-up quarterback, and Cookie Gilchrist as a running back. Those guys could play on any team in either league. But the previous year they'd made only three field goals.

Johnson wasn't going to tell me that I was going to add punch to the Bills. What he told someone else later was:

"The Bills needed a kicker and I was looking for a kicker. I assume that Gogolak knew that, too—why else would I be driving over to Ithaca? I had a stop-watch on the kid and his time was good enough for the pros. When he asked me if I wanted him to kick any more, I was afraid to let him. Sure, he was kicking old pumpkins, but if he hit a 60-yard field goal with me watching, I could just see him asking for a $50,000 bonus and $30,000 salary."

"Old pumpkins" is what they call footballs that have been used in games. After a football has been used in a game, the leather loses some of its elasticity and stretches a little so that the ball is a little fatter than when it was new. Place kickers love fat footballs.

I don't think Johnson needed to worry about my price so much. I was too aware of all the minus signs I had against me—the Ivy League and so on—and my parents had brought me up to be a nice guy. I wasn't a tough, hard-nosed bargainer, and I wasn't famous, or lucky enough to have an agent to tell me what to do.

The really big deals like Joe Namath's $400,000 coup didn't come along until the next year, though there was big money involved even in 1963.

Two developments were bringing that big money into football.

One was the fight between the owners of the National League teams and the owners in the American League.

The National League owners were the old-timers, the Maras and the Halases. They'd put their teams together forty years earlier, when a pro football franchise wasn't worth much more than the paper it was printed on. They'd *built* those teams, and they'd *built* those franchises to the point where they were worth millions. They were ferocious about protecting what they'd spent all those years making. You can understand it. Or, at least, I could, being a Hungarian.

George Halas had put up every nickel he owned or could borrow to get the Chicago franchise in 1921, for $200. He was a player at the time, and coach, and after a game he used to be one of the guys who took off his helmet and went through the stands, asking the fans for money to pay off the expenses. This sort of experience sticks with you, and it's the sort of experience I can understand.

By the time I came along in pro ball, the old pioneers of the game had already beaten off one attempt to move in on their money—the All America Conference—by granting it franchises in such well-known football centers as Newark, New Jersey.

They also thought they'd get rid of the new AFL the same way. They didn't realize that the new AFL owners were a different breed of cat. These new AFL owners weren't really football men. They were money men. They saw that there was money in pro football, and they were attracted by the glamour of owning a team. They weren't about to be frightened out by the old NFL owners, and they had enough money so that they couldn't be forced into bankruptcy. (Which was the fate of many of the first All America teams.) They were the Clint Murchisons and the Lamar Hunts, the

Sonny Werblins and the Ralph Wilsons. (Wilson owned the Buffalo Bills.)

The new AFL owners not only weren't prepared to be beaten out, they were prepared to give pro football a whole new look. They weren't interested in the old NFL theory of building up a solid team over the years, they wanted instant stars.

This second development put the big money into football, and it was done through television. In 1964 the AFL sold the television broadcasting rights for all its games for the next five years to NBC for $34 million. That is big money.

I think that at least half of the stories about how the pro teams made sure of getting their top draft choices back in those days were absolutely true. For a *top* draft choice, a pro team would assign an assistant coach to chaperone the guy around to make sure that no other team got a chance to talk to him. The assistant coach would see to it that this guy got everything he wanted—meals in the best restaurants, all he wanted to drink, any show he wanted to see, a complaisant young lady to dally with every night—everything.

None of this for Gogolak. Harvey Johnson and the Bills were the only people who showed any interest in me at all as the draft date, December 1, came around. I'd gotten six or eight form letters from other pro teams that all started out: "If you would be interested in playing professional football . . ." and I'd answered them all, but nobody had answered me back.

When draft day came, I'm afraid I made something of a pain in the rear of myself to the Ithaca *Journal*. I didn't have access to any up-to-the-second news tickers on the Cornell campus, but I knew enough to know that the *Journal* had wire service news tickers in the sports department, and I had gotten to know one of the paper's sports writers, Kenny Van Sickle, well enough so I felt I could call him up. Poor Van Sickle! I don't think I called him more than six or eight times on the afternoon of December 1—he was working, mind you— asking if I had been drafted. The answer was always no. Finally, the next day, Buffalo did draft me. On their 13th round. At last I was able to breathe. I had been drafted. I was going to play pro ball. Or at least get a crack at it. The first thing I did was to call my parents and tell them.

That same day I got a telegram from the Philadelphia Eagles. I assume that they had sent it before I was actually drafted. It said that since I was now a free agent, how would I like to come down and try out for them? You know, if I had had any brains, I would immediately have started playing off the Eagles against the Bills. But not me. A twenty-one-year-old college senior, how could I know what to do? I didn't realize then that you got only what you were smart enough, and tough enough, to get. I let my pride get the better of me, too. I told the Eagles that if they didn't think enough of me to draft me, I'd be damned if I was going down for a try-out. I was going to stick with Buffalo. It made me feel better, but it didn't get me any more money. It hadn't done my ego any good that Gary Wood had been drafted by the New York Giants on the eighth round.

All I knew about Buffalo was that it had a pretty good football team. It went all the way to the Eastern Division playoffs in 1963, losing to Boston.

Back in those days the sports writers always qualified stories about the league: "A pretty good team, for the American Football League." Even I—I had seen my first live professional football game in America one Sunday in the fall of 1963 when I had gone over to Buffalo and watched the Bills wallop the New York Jets in the game in which Cookie (Carlton) Gilchrist set the all-pro rushing record of 242 yards in a single game and even I, on my way back to Ithaca, turned the radio on to listen to the New York Giants game. The Giants were my heroes.

After the Bills had drafted me, I never heard a word from them until late in February, when I got a call from Pat Mc-Gruder, a rich Buffalo contractor who was a vice-president of the team. He made an appointment with me to come to Ithaca and settle the terms of my contract. I was looking out the window for McGruder when he drove into the parking lot of the Delta Upsilon house in a big, fine new Cadillac. I went out and got into the front seat beside him. After some small talk, he reached into the back seat and got out his attache case. From it, he took a contract form and from an inside coat pocket he took a pen.

"Well, Pete," he said. "This is our offer. We want you in Buffalo, we need you and we like you. This is a one-year contract. A bonus of $1,500 for signing, and $9,500 for the season."

Two trains of thought went through my mind at the same time. One was that this was more money than I had ever heard of before in my life, in terms of my getting it. The other was that, compared to all the newspaper stories I had been reading about the $25,000 bonuses being paid to top draft choices, a $1,500 bonus didn't seem all that big, even for a thirteenth round draft choice.

At the same time a lot of emotions were bubbling up in me. I'd been brought up too properly—always be polite to your elders. I didn't want to start off with an argument with McGruder. And he seemed like a nice, pleasant man. I sort of felt that if I started to argue with him, he'd say, well, maybe we made a mistake, the whole deal is off.

I don't know how many months later it was before I realized that this was nothing more than a straight business deal to him. To him, I was just another football player who might be able to help his team, and he wanted to get me as cheaply as possible.

All I told him then was that I appreciated the offer very much, but that I was still considering going to dental school.

"Well, we'd like to sign you as soon as we can," he said.

He had the contract lying on his attache case, and he kept swinging the pen back and forth over it between his thumb and forefinger. I knew all I had to do was reach for the pen.

"Besides that," he said, "you know we're looking at some other kickers. And they can do more than just kick."

I still didn't want to sign. (I was so ignorant I didn't even know that I didn't have to be signed until the first league game, which wasn't until September.) It would have been great to get a check for $1,500 and a guaranteed salary of $9,500, but I didn't want to.

Finally I said no. My father had warned me not to sign too easily.

McGruder didn't seem bothered about that at all.

He just gave me a little laugh and said:

"Well, you think about it, Pete. I'll be in touch."

About three weeks later McGruder called me up and asked me if I could come over to Buffalo on the weekend. I had no car, of course, but my father said that he would drive me. McGruder lived in the kind of house a millionaire has—

magnificent—and at the moment he was alone. His wife was away and his son was off at Notre Dame. He took my father and me out for dinner at the finest restaurant in Buffalo.

I remember the dinner for two reasons. On the way to the restaurant, in McGruder's Cadillac, we had to do a short section on the New York State Thruway, and McGruder had to pay a toll. I was in the front seat beside McGruder, my father was in the back. McGruder gave the attendant a one-dollar bill out of a fat wallet and, as we were starting to drive off, he took a $50 bill out of the wallet and handed it to me.

My sole source of earned income at the time was seventy-five cents an hour washing dishes at Cornell, but I handed it back to him.

I said: "I don't want it."

He crumpled it up in his hand and stuffed it in my coat pocket.

"Keep it," he said. "I'm not trying to bribe you. You can use it. Keep it."

I kept it. I'd never seen a $50 bill before.

The other thing about the dinner that I remember was that McGruder said the speciality of the house was steak, and he recommended the filet mignon. I'd never had a filet mignon before and, my God, was it good!

After dinner, we went back to his house and went into the kitchen for some coffee.

While we were drinking it, he said:

"You know, Pete, the reason I invited you up is that I'd really like to get you signed."

My father and I had talked it over and we had decided that we'd ask for a $3,000 bonus and a salary of $13,000, and that was what I told McGruder. I also told him, which was perfectly true, that I had an appointment to go up to McGill University in Montreal to be interviewed as a candidate for their dental school. I'd applied at McGill because I knew that graduate students were allowed to play varsity football there. You see some pretty grown-up players on college squads in Canada.

McGruder seemed to think it over, though I'm sure he had it all planned out in advance. Finally he said:

"I'll tell you the truth. First, we don't know if you can even make the team. You're a college kicker and you're not used to kicking off the ground. You can use a tee in college, not in the pros. Second, as I told you, the only thing you *can* do is kick. It isn't as if you were also an end or a wide receiver or something. That means that even counting kickoffs you'll be in maybe ten or twelve plays a game. On the field, maybe five minutes for a whole game. That isn't much. What I can do is this. We'll put the bonus up to $2,000 and we'll raise the salary to $10,500."

I said I'd let him know; I'd like to sleep on it.

My father and I went upstairs. We agreed that, in the morning, if McGruder would come up to a $2,500 bonus and an $11,000 salary, I'd sign.

Maybe we should have held out for more. When I told that to McGruder the next morning, he burst into a big smile and held out his hand.

"Shake," he said.

He put the contract on the kitchen table, dragged out a pen and then handed the pen over to me. I signed. Then he got out his checkbook and wrote out a check for $2,500. Just like that. Like the $50 bill, I'd never seen a check for $2,500 before, nor a man who could write one.

On the way back home, my father and I stopped off in Syracuse, and I used McGruder's $50 bill—or a good part of it, anyway—to treat myself to a pair of really good shoes.

I wasn't entirely happy about the contract, because of the ones I had heard about. It was only later I realized how many mistakes I had made. For example, I didn't know I might have made a better deal by holding out for a second bonus if I made the team. That could have been $7,500 instead of $2,500. After all, how many rookies make a pro football team? I could have made a deal depending on the number of field goals I kicked, or the number of records I set, or making the All-Star game. Altogether, if I had known enough, I might have gotten my bonus money up to $10,000 or $15,000, because as it turned out I did have a great year. I kicked 19 out of 27 field goals, the Bills won their first championship, and I was second-highest scorer in the League, behind Gino Cappelletti. But Cappelletti, who played for the Boston Patriots, was a wide receiver as well as a kicker, so he had some touchdowns on his point score to help him.

My signing was only a moderately big deal in the newspapers. It was very big around Buffalo and Ithaca, of course, but it was totally overshadowed in the New York papers by the fact that the Giants had signed Gary Wood and that the Bills' first draft choice, Paul Warfield, had signed with the Cleveland Browns.

I had one minor tussle with the Bills during the summer. The college All-Star game was to be played in Buffalo on July 30 that year, on national television, and I hadn't been picked for it. The Bills called me up and asked me if I'd be willing to put on a demonstration of soccer-style kicking between the halves. That got my Hungarian back up. I told them that either I kicked for the All-Stars during the game or not at all. It ended with my not even going to the game.

From the end of June until July 21, when I was due at the Bills' training camp near Buffalo, I did nothing much except run and practice kicking at Ogdensburg.

The worst part of waiting for camp to start was the fact that I didn't have the faintest idea what to expect when I got there. I knew that the team I was trying out for was ten if not a hundred times better than any team I had ever played against; despite all my previous confidence that I could kick in the professional leagues, I now began to wonder if I really could make the Bills. My feelings weren't helped by a newsletter I got from the Bills listing the draft choices they had signed. There were three other kickers listed, all of whom could play some other position as well, including one player from Michigan State of whom the newsletter said: "He can kick 45 yards with his left foot and 55 yards with his right." It didn't explain what advantage there was to being able to kick with either foot, nor why he'd ever kick with his left foot if he had a 10-yard advantage with his right.

Came the day that I was supposed to report to the Bills; my father drove me up to Buffalo.

The Bills had hired a big motel for the training season in East Aurora, New York, about twenty miles outside of Buffalo. It had a big open field in the back that the Bills had graded for a football field. They had put up some goal posts, and built a locker room with showers and so on.

The first day of training was for the rookies only. None of the veterans showed up; but even so, I had never seen so many big guys in my life. At six feet and 200 pounds, I had never thought of myself as being small, and I certainly was as big as most of the guys I had played college football with and against. But among the twenty-five rookies who showed up in the Bills' camp, I felt like a midget. I was one of the two or three smallest guys in the bunch.

And almost from the beginning, I began to feel like one of the outsiders. Most of these guys, especially the top draft choices, had gone to similar colleges if not to the same college. The big football colleges. Ohio State. Michigan State. Penn State. If they didn't know each other, or hadn't played against each other, they at least had heard of each other. Who had ever heard of Pete Gogolak, a place kicker from a small Ivy League college? Nobody. So these guys were able to talk to each other right from the first, comparing notes about this Bowl Game or that All-Star Game. The only conversation I had was to explain where Cornell was, that I couldn't play any position on the field except kicker, and that the reason that I had this accent was that I had been born in Budapest.

Right from the first day, you could spot who the high draft choices were. They were the guys who drove up in the big flashy convertible cars, wearing the flashy sports clothes, with the flashy luggage. Me, I had put my $2,500 bonus in the bank. I wasn't going to spend a nickel till I was sure I had made the team. When I did make it, I took the $2,500 and bought a Ford Mustang. I often wondered what the guys did who were let go, after they'd spent all that money.

It would have been too rich for my blood. A total of forty-five players were trying out for the Bills, including draft choices and free agents, and only four made the team. Everyone knew that was about the odds from the beginning—less than one out of ten. So why spend all the bonus money?

On the first day, while there was a certain camaraderie

among the top draft choices, I could also see the wariness among them. There had been some of that at Cornell when I had started there, guys sizing each other up the first day. At Cornell, it had just been a matter of making a college fresh-man squad, and most of the guys felt that if they had been able to play pretty fair football in high school, they at least had a chance.

The feeling at Buffalo was totally different. Here, it was for real.

This was pro ball. This was for money. If you made the team, that was the first step toward fame and real *money*. It meant television, autographs, commercials, personal appear-ances—anything. It meant flashy cars and the flashy clothes. As you looked at the other guys you knew that any one of them, a half-step quicker, just that much tougher or better co-ordinated, could beat you out of all that and there you'd be, trying to catch on with some other team, trying out up in Canada or down in the minors or maybe off to high school coaching.

The first day was more or less organized chaos. We all took a physical, we were issued practice uniforms except for shoes (I naturally had brought along my own three pairs), we were assigned lockers and we were assigned roommates, two men to a room. Looking back, I can't even remember the names of any of my roommates back then, which isn't surprising. I had five different roommates in the first week. With forty-five men trying out for four openings, the coaches don't waste much time. Right from the start they had to see something in you, or out you went. Of course, if you were a high draft choice and you had gotten a big, fat bonus, or if you were a free agent with a pretty fair reputation, you would get a longer look, but unless you had one of those things going for you, you had to shine right from the start.

The next day the veterans began coming in, and the tension of sizing the other guy up began to build. You could almost feel it. Most of it was in the dining room, where the veterans were on one side and the rookies on the other, looking each other over like so many strange cats, the rookies estimating the men they had to beat out, the veterans thinking—I was to learn it later all too well when I was a veteran—"You suppose one of these kids is good enough to beat me out of a job?"

Most clearly, I remember three veterans. One was Jack Kemp, the first-string quarterback who's now a Congressman from New York. I remember him because he seemed to go out of his way to be nice to me. He was a great reader of books, not paperbacks like most football players, but books on history and politics, and he used to ask me everything he could think of about Hungary, and how it was living in a Communist country, and how the Communists ran things.

Another was Darryl LaMonica, Kemp's back-up quarterback who went on to become a great one himself at Oakland. He held a special interest for me because he was the place-kick holder.

The third was Cookie Gilchrist. Who is there who has ever met Cookie who could forget him? Twenty-nine years old then, six feet three and 250 pounds, he was built like a Greek god. Friendly, interesting, exciting—he was always doing something, mostly something that required spending money. He'd go into a gift shop at an airport and buy half a dozen fake antique swords, presents for God knows who. He opened a clothing store in Buffalo called Cookie's Closet. He helped form a syndicate that was going prospecting for something or other up in Canada, I never knew what it was, and once he jumped out of a helicopter to stake a claim. Now he's running a business out in Denver—he went to the Denver Broncos when he left the Bills in 1964, and made his home there—that supplies office cleaning services to business firms.

I'll never forget the first time I saw him. Here was I, a raw rookie, and here was he, with the all-time record for yards rushing in a single game. He drove up to the motel in the glittering sunshine in a pink Cadillac convertible, top down and along both sides of the car the big legend: "Lookie, Lookie, Lookie, Here Comes Cookie." Marvelous. How can your heart not go out to a man like that?

A Rookie with the Buffalo Bills

Moving from college to pro football has to be one of the biggest jumps an athlete can make. If you're a top college baseball player, for example, the pro league is a big step up, but it's basically the same game. Even if you don't make the team, they can send you down to the Triple A league for a little seasoning. None of that happens in pro football. You either make the team or you don't.

And pro football is ten times as sophisticated as college ball, so the guy whose job you're trying to get probably knows ten times as much as you do about how to play football, and he's waiting to make you look bad. Or let you make yourself look bad. There's no Triple A league to go down to. You're out. You're a free agent, on your own.

I had plenty of inner qualms. (The Bills tried out a total of five kickers that summer.) And a football training camp, at the start of a season, isn't designed to give you a sense of inner security unless you're an established star.

The Bills' locker room, in the makeshift quarters they'd rigged up at the motel, didn't even have separate lockers. All they had were little sections partitioned off with hangers for each player's clothes, with his name above them written with a magic marker on a piece of adhesive tape.

If you were cut from the team, you took your clothes off the hangers, and you had a choice about the piece of adhesive tape. You could either tear it off yourself or leave it for an assistant trainer.

The crack about a guy who was cut was: "He got a road map and a hamburger," meaning a final meal and directions to the highway for some other training camp.

With the Bills, cutting was done early in the morning, before practice.

Every pro team is always besieged with young guys in their teens who want to be ball boys or to help out any way they can, just to be around the players. The kids who get the jobs are generally the sons of some vice-president of the club, or of somebody with enough connections to get his kid in. Generally, on the Bills, one of these kids would knock at the door early in the morning, ask for a player and say:

"The coach would like to see you." Then he'd add the fatal sentence, "And he says to bring your play book."

You knew then.

Everyone calls the kid who comes for you "The Turk."

Lou Saban was the coach of the Bills then, and he always made the cuts himself. He was a very decent guy. If the player was a free agent, an experienced guy, Saban didn't have to say too much except, sorry. With rookies, he always was very kind. He'd give them a little set speech about how much potential he thought they had "but the problem I have is that I need a player with more experience, a player who can help us right away. You'll be real good in two or three years, but

The start of it all: The formal photograph of my parent's wedding. The bride's parents are seated at the left, the groom's on the right.

Oops. At age three you're not really a soccer player, but I'm trying.

Charlie and me outside our house in the winter of '46, after the war was over. God knows where we got the coats, or what I'm fishing for in my left-hand pocket.

The last posed photograph of the family in Budapest in '49, before we escaped to the West.

Early fame. Well, publicity, anyway. This 1957 photograph was taken for a newspaper in Saranac Lake, New York, when I was very big in basketball. Maybe not so big, either, I never scored as much as 20 points in a game.

A 50-yarder for Cornell against Lehigh. A good kick, even if my left foot is skidding and I'm way off balance. But look at the ball.

Photo by Philip P. Berelson

How to beat Yale, 13-10. It was only a 30-yarder, but it won. Note the Yale manager at the left of the 20-yard marker, kicking along with me.

LEFT: I wasn't too bad at punting at Cornell, either. You can look up the record.

Photo by Robert L. Smith

One of my favorite games and pictures—kicking for the Buffalo Bills against the New York Jets. It may look as though the Jets player can block the ball, but actually he's about ten feet from it.

Photo by Robert L. Smith

Making one for the Bills against the Chargers in the 1965 championship game.

LEFT: No rivalry here· This is November 1965 and I already regard myself as a big man in professional football—but I'm not above going to the Princeton-Harvard game at Cambridge to watch Charlie kick. Got a sidelines pass and here I am in front of the Princeton bench with Charlie.

Photo by Bill Mark

The next few photos illustrate my point about the intense concentration involved in kicking. In 1) holder Fran Tarkenton is awaiting the ball. Note the focus of our eyes. In 2) Dick Shiner already has the ball. Again, follow

Photo by Jack Pokress

Photo by Jack Pokress

the eyes. 3) Tom Blanchard holding, I'm still looking down. 4) Gary Wood holding, my momentum is bringing my head up.

I don't know how this kid got in here, but one of the nice things about training camp is all the free help you get. From the focus of *his* eyes, you can see he doesn't trust soccer-style kickers.

The first, and for years the only tackle I was ever credited with in pro ball. The ball carrier is MacArthur Lane, 6-feet-4 and 240, going full speed, which gives him an edge on me, plus I don't have any regular football pads on. But if you look closely, you'll see that Lane's right foot is about to come down on my kicking tee. He's going to fall over his own feet and I'll fall on top of him.

Photo by Dan Rubin

United Press International Photo

Teaching the coach. Alex Webster was a great running back for the Giants for years before he eventually became head coach, but soccer style kicking wasn't his dish. Anyway, the photographers posed us— me trying to teach him—before we played the Los Angeles Rams in 1970.

OPPOSITE TOP: Off season. This is no gag picture—in 1969 I actually did work in the kitchen of the "21 Club" in New York, trying to learn the restaurant business. Those things with me are crabs.

BOTTOM: Another of my favorite kind of pictures—me making three more points for the Giants against the Green Bay Packers on a sloppy field.

Photo by Dan Rubin

LEFT: Kicking off at Yankee Stadium, with Willie Williams making sure I do it right.

BELOW: Ah, sweet success. The bad guys in white, jumping up in the air, are Washington Redskins and they don't have a prayer of blocking this one.

Signing autographs at the stadium.

I need a player who can handle that position this season."

If the player *really* had the potential Saban was talking about, Saban would always say that he'd call around the league and see if any other team was in the market—and he would, too.

Guys took it different ways. Some knew it was coming and they took it philosophically. I've heard some guys go back to their rooms and just plain break down in tears. And then there are always the guys:

"Aw, that son-of-a-bitch never liked me in the first place just because I didn't kiss his ass as hard as he wanted."

The cuts made in the first five days were generally the free agents shopping around for a job. The coaches might go a little longer with a young rookie to see if he could adjust, but if a veteran wasn't making it, there was no sense keeping him around. Not only was he not helping the Bills, he might catch on somewhere else if he started looking soon enough.

Part of adding to my being a loner, besides my natural temperament, was that I never went through the real continuous worry about being cut that other rookies did. I worried about my kicking, of course, but I didn't have to worry on every single play about whether I was going to be a half a step late getting to where I was supposed to be, whether I was going to miss a block or a tackle. I never went through tackling drills. The Bills didn't want me tackling even on kickoffs, except out of desperation. My orders were to kick off, then back-pedal to be the final, final safety man. There are always enough players on pro teams who'll take a cheap shot at an opposing kicker to try to take him out of the game so that it just isn't worth risking a place kicker to have him going downfield.

I assume that other rookies, and even some of the veterans, sort of resented a guy who always had a clean uniform, who never was covered with mud and blood. I'd gone through that at Cornell and I knew there was nothing I could do about it.

You know, the cracks like: "So glad you could show up, Gogolak," and: "Gee, Peter, it's a pity you have to take that blanket off and go out in all this rain. You could get wet."

I just got used to it. What the hell, what I was being paid for was to get three points for these jokers when I went out on the field and plenty of times my three points made the difference between a win and a loss.

But in a way, I regret now that I was so sheltered. I never got close to any of my teammates the way a blocker and runner can form a close personal relationship because they go through so much together, and because they depend so much on each other. Sure, I depended almost a hundred percent on the center to snap the ball perfectly and the holder to have it at the right place and on the blockers to hold off charging opposition linemen long enough for me to get the ball up in the air, but that was only for maybe a maximum of six plays in a game. I wasn't really sharing the battle with them, play after play after play.

Training with the Bills was vastly different from training at Cornell. It made me realize that I was embarked on a whole new way of life. At Cornell, football was only a part of my life. An important part, naturally, but still only a part; we didn't start practice, under Ivy League rules, until late in the summer, and we only played nine games, so we were through by the end of November. With the Bills, it was nothing *but* football. We started in July and we were still playing in December. In the off-season I trained.

At the Bills the motel switchboard operator called every room every morning to make sure that every player got down to the dining room by 7:30 at the latest. Even if you didn't want anything to eat, you were fined $50 if you weren't in the dining room at 7:30. After breakfast you could sit around a little in the lobby or in your room, but you had to be on the field ready for practice at 9 a.m. Especially in the first days of training, almost everybody was ready for practice a little early, making brownie points with the coach.

Even there I had a little break, I don't use much tape and I like to tape myself. That saved time in the dressing room. Some of the players who used a lot of tape, players who had old knee injuries or something, would be with a trainer half an hour getting ready. There are also some guys who love trainers' room, they spend hours there every day, taking the whole works, heat treatments, a whirlpool bath, the business. I stayed out of the trainers' room as much as I could because I didn't care for the smell. The locker room was bad enough, the temperature could get as high as 95, and with everyone wearing about fifteen pounds of equipment, the smell of sweat would pervade the whole place. The trainers' room smelled of sweat plus all the linament.

Anyhow, you were out on the practice field by 9, wearing shoulder pads and a helmet and football shoes—I was still wearing the high ones I'd had at Cornell—even if it was so hot that the rest of your uniform consisted of shorts and a tee shirt. And a jock strap, of course. From the first day, the Bills insisted on the helmets and shoulder pads. To get used to them I suppose, but on a hot day in early practice that helmet can feel as if it weighs fifteen pounds all by itself.

We did twenty minutes of calisthenics, then the coaches

split the players up into groups—all the receivers here, the running backs there, and so on. I'd get a couple of footballs and a couple of kids to shag them and start kicking. There were always people to watch us, even from the start. Other guests at the motel, and neighborhood people with nothing else to do. I had my fair share of watchers because the Bills were beginning to build me up in their press releases. All the stories about being a refugee from Hungary and the only soccer-style kicker in pro ball and the only player who was being carried—or being tried out, at that time—just as a kicker, all had helped me to begin to get known.

When I saw I had an audience, I was just as much of a hambone as any of the other players. I'd put on a little exhibition for them.

At these early sessions the players always keep an eye out for the coaches. Especially Saban, but the other coaches as well. It was with them that you really had to make an impression. If I saw a coach coming over to watch me, I'd move the ball up from the 40-yard line to the 50.

The second day of training the owner, Ralph Wilson, came out to watch practice. It was the first time I'd ever seen him, and he looked like exactly what he was—a hard-driving, hard-nosed businessman. He didn't look as if he gave money away. Naturally all the coaches flocked around him. I was watching them through the bars of my helmet and presently I could see them all looking at me, so I shifted into high gear, really booting the ball. I guess Wilson was satisfied, because after he watched for a little while, he started looking some place else.

I'd kick through most of the first hour of practice, but you can only kick so long. The rest of the team, in the second hour of practice, would run through plays, and my biggest problem then was to try to pretend that I was doing something constructive. That's another problem that all kickers have. It's pretty damned boring not to have anything to do while the rest of the team is hard at work. Mostly, I'd play catch with one of the quarterbacks who wasn't in the action, warming him up for when he went in, or I'd shag balls that had gotten away—anything just to be busy.

After practice was over for the morning, there came the wind sprints—40 yards at full speed. I was in them, all right, and possibly the slowest man on the team. If it had been a good practice, there were only six wind sprints; a bad one and there were twelve. On a hot day early in the practice season, twelve wind sprints come down to just about torture. It may not sound so hard, but in most of a football uniform, after two hours of real work, it's murder. I've seen guys pass out at them.

After that, we all got showers and then dragged ourselves down to lunch. No matter how good a shape you try to keep yourself in, those first days of training just about kill you— you're just not used to playing football, that's all.

Breakfast was substantial and hot—juice, cereal if you wanted it, eggs any style, French toast, bacon, sausages, ham, milk, coffee. I'm a fairly substantial eater, and I could go through three eggs and five or six pieces of bacon with no trouble at all, but Jim Dunaway, a 300 pound farm boy from Mississippi who played tackle for us, would go through twice that—six eggs and so much bacon it was funny.

Lunch was mostly cold—all kinds of cold cuts, meat and poultry, and fruit and vegetables—sliced tomatoes, things like that. And milk. And gallons of iced tea and coffee. All this food was catered to the motel. I guess feeding eighty football players could have put the motel into bankruptcy.

After lunch, just flop into bed.

Everybody was always taking salt tablets those first days, and gulping down water by the pint, because you can get terrible muscle spasms anywhere, in your face, your arms, your legs. I've seen guys suddenly not able to walk. It's not the easiest life in the world.

At 3:30 everybody is back out on the practice field, mostly for team drill. Saban is a great guy for team drill. He's an average-sized guy himself, six feet and 190, black-haired and with a Slavic face. He's a Croatian. He's strictly no nonsense, not given to smiling, but he can really blow up. He's no Tom Landry, who never seems to show any emotion. Before the game Saban is a prize worrier, always pacing up and down. If a play goes wrong he throws his clip board up into the air and screams. But he's a great coach and a master defense man, and I'm glad he's back with Buffalo. He left after the 1965 season because Wilson wouldn't give him a long-term contract, but Buffalo has been going so badly the last few seasons without him that I'm sure Wilson gave him what he wanted this time. He specialized in line play on the defense, and the defense plays he used to draw before the games every Sunday were masterpieces.

Afternoon practice wasn't as long as morning practice, it only went until five. And there were always many more people there, two or three dozen football buffs, the ones who can't see enough football, and fathers with twelve-year-old boys playing in the Pop Warner League and giving daddy some vicarious fame, people with nothing else to do, and some of the girls who like football players. I suppose that any-

thing that has glamour attached to it attracts girls, but different things attract different kinds. Girls who find politicians
glamorous wouldn't be found dead at a prize fight, and vice
versa. And baseball attracts one kind, auto racing another
and football still another.

After practice, it was back to the showers and clean clothes.
Part of the reason for the shorter practice is that even in
Buffalo it can get bloody hot in the sun in the afternoon in
July. We'd sit around in the lobby in shorts and sandals and
sports shirts, and just look at ordinary people. They looked
as though their lives were a lot quieter than ours. Dinner was
at 6:15. We had steak three times a week, and at other times
roast beef or ham or fish—about anything you wanted in the
protein line—and baked potatoes, salads and desserts. After
dinner there were always meetings but normally they were
over by eight, and from eight to eleven was free time. We
always got Saturday afternoons off, too. But curfew was at
eleven, and with the Bills it was a $200 fine if you were
caught sneaking in late. (With the New York Giants, it was
$300.)

The first ten days I don't think anybody even thought
about getting out. Most of the guys stayed right around the
motel, not even bothering to go into Buffalo. There was a
television set in every room, and we'd watch that, or write
letters or read paperbacks or just go to bed. I always called
my parents every three or four days, just to talk. It wasn't
lonesomeness, it's just that we're so close. It may have been
hell getting out of Hungary, but when you have four people
who put their lives on the line for a chance to make a new
life for themselves, it forges bonds that don't exist for people

who've always been used to the good life, who never had to risk anything.

There were about twenty-five black guys on the Bills squad at the beginning, and I got along with them okay. As far as I could see, so did all the white guys on the team, even the ones from the deep South. To me, they were just football players, some of them good, some not so good, some really outstanding stars like Gilchrist. I read a good deal about how some people think black football players are still victims of some kind of discrimination, but I never saw it. Coming from Hungary, maybe I had a different point of view than a white American would have. To me, blacks were interesting because they were different. I've told how all the refugees from Hungary wanted their vaccination shots from the Negro Army doctor. And, coming from a different culture, I might miss things that might mean something to an American. If I hear a Serb talking to a Croat, I can tell whether he's being friendly, or needling him or really trying to put him down. It's not only the subleties of what's said, it's also how it's said, and all the nuances of the circumstances. In America, you can call a man a son-of-a-bitch in a way meaning to be friendly, and also in a way that means you're looking for trouble. (That's why I still have to be careful when I'm talking English. I don't know all the tiny differences.) When Ted Thoren used to call me a "stupid hunkie," for example, I could always tell whether he was just kidding or whether he was really damned mad.

So, with the Bills, there may have been things going on that just didn't register with me, but as far as I could see the blacks were treated just like the whites.

The blacks more or less stuck with each other, but that

hardly came as a surprise to me. After all, if there had been a couple of other Hungarian refugees on the team, I'd have been more inclined to pal around with them than with anybody else. Like people tend to find more in common with each other. The only thing different about the blacks that I noticed—outside of their color, of course—was that they seemed to have more fun than the whites. They were always ribbing each other about something or other that I understood only about half the time, they always had a stereo on or a record player, they laughed a lot more. Outside of that there wasn't much difference. They came in all sizes and temperaments. Some of them were nice guys I'd like to have known better, some of them were surly bastards I tried to stay away from. Just like the whites.

I began to feel a lot better about my chances of making the Bills after a couple of the other guys they had trying out for kicker—including the guy who could kick almost as well with either foot—were let go. I was kicking well, and the coaches and the veterans on the team began to treat me as if they sort of expected me to make the team. Just subtle things, like the tone of voice and the kind of comments they'd make in idle moments.

I began to go out nights sometimes at the end of the week. I never was much of a guy to be a good-time Charley, living it up all the time, boozing and so on, but I'm no plaster saint. I like a couple of drinks, and I like going out with a good-looking girl and enjoying her affections.

In Buffalo there's a place near the University of Buffalo that's kind of a college hangout, beer and stuff like that, and a juke box. It also got to be sort of a hangout for six or seven of the younger guys on the Bills. For one thing, we weren't making the kind of money to spend it the way Cookie Gil-christ did. We were only a little older than the college kids, and of course pretty soon everyone knew we were football players—sometimes one of the guys would show up bandaged even if he was as healthy as you are, just to give the girls a little extra thrill.

It's great for your ego when you're only twenty-one and you see the girls sizing you up while they're pretending they're looking somewhere else. It's great at any time, but you appreciate it more when you're twenty-one, and they all seem enchanting. Some baseball player once said, it's great to be young and to be a Yankee. Hell, there's nothing wrong with being young and being a pro football player for the only team in town. Especially if you're surviving cuts, as I was. I felt more and more that I would make the team, but no ball player, or damned few, is ever one hundred percent certain. Our cuts that year went from the very earliest one, that reduced the squad from eighty to sixty-four, then to fifty-five, then to forty-nine, then to forty, and at last to the final one made the Monday before the first regular season game to get down to the final playing team of—at that time in the American Football League—thirty-four men.

That last cut, and the one right after the first exhibition game are the ones that, for some reason, the players seem to fear the most.

The very first "game" that we played was at War Memorial Stadium in Buffalo. At that time it was probably one of the worst stadiums in the country. The game was listed as an exhibition, but it wasn't really. The Bills were going to play an inter-squad game, to give the fans in Buffalo a look at the team.

But it sticks in my mind, that first game I ever played as a pro, the first time I ever was handed actual cash for playing in front of a crowd.

A couple of days before the game, Saban had made his second-last cut of the season, so now the team was almost down to the strength that it would have to go through the exhibition season.

The locker room at War Memorial Stadium is so small that trying to dress an entire football squad there was out of the question. We all dressed in the locker room at the motel and went to the stadium by bus. It was a hot, muggy night late in August and it was a rough, tough game. Don't forget that all these players knew that there was one more cut to come and the coaches would make the decisions on the basis of performance in the exhibitions.

I'd played in college games, and I'd seen pro games, but never from the bench, and it almost stunned me—the precision, the toughness. Everyone has seen a pro player miss an assignment on television, but what hit me was how seldom it happened—series after series of plays would be run with never a missed assignment, and a man who missed one never missed it a second time. For a college player who'd seen some poor hapless end miss three in a row, it was quite an eye-opener. And the speed with which the pros reacted—a ball carrier might find an opening and make eight or ten yards, but the next time that play was called the defense had it figured and the runner was lucky to get past the line of scrimmage.

And the hitting—I thought I'd seen hard blocks and hard tackles in the Ivy League. There may have been one or two in a game as hard as these guys hit *every* play.

I remember, all through the game, thinking to myself again and again:

"This is for real! This is the pros!"

I think I felt it the strongest after the game was over. Here were all these guys covered with sweat, stinking of sweat, bruised, blood on their jerseys and hand-pads, and all I could think was, this is for real, the kid stuff is over—the professional athlete, back to the days of the Caesars.

We all piled into the bus and started back to East Aurora. There isn't the same feeling after an intra-squad game that there is after a game against another team. Then, if your team won, even the guys who might have made a mistake or two don't feel too bad because, after all, we've won and they'll show them in the next game. But after an intra-squad game, the guys who made the mistakes are miserable—who knows, another game performance like that and they'll be off the squad.

The lights inside the bus were dim and it was rocketing along the road between Buffalo and East Aurora, I guess the bus driver was in a hurry to get home, and—I'll never forget this—one of the assistant coaches started down the aisle. I knew we were supposed to get $50 for every exhibition game, but I didn't have the faintest idea how we were going to get paid. What this assistant coach was doing, he had a sheaf of brand new $50 bills in his hand, and he was handing one to each of the players. No receipts or anything, you just took the $50.

Where do you put a $50 bill in a football uniform? The same place you carry cigarettes, inside your stocking.

The other game of the exhibition season that I really remember was against the Jets in Tampa. I still wasn't positive that the Bills were going to keep me, because there had been a lot of newspaper stories back in Buffalo stating that if the Bills wanted to win the championship that year, they couldn't afford the luxury of having a player who couldn't do anything except kick.

At any rate, the Jets game was being televised back to Buffalo, and I distinguished myself right at the start. We scored a touchdown first, and I went trotting out onto the field to kick the point after—and missed.

I was so stunned I couldn't believe it. I didn't feel anything. I went back and sat down on the end of the bench and just felt numb. Nobody said a word to me. I could barely hear the fans jeering.

The problem with kicking field goals in the pros is that the goal posts are on the goal line instead of ten yards back, the way they are in college, and when you kick, you're kicking from only nine yards out. Those goal posts look as though they're right over your head. But I knew all that, and I'd been practicing for more than two solid months. What had happened, I figured afterward, was that I hadn't gotten my foot under the ball enough. It went up, hit the crossbar, and dropped back to the field. Figuring it out didn't get that point back.

A friend of mine was watching the game on television in a bar in Buffalo, and he told me afterward how the whole bar moaned when I missed the attempt and the guy next to him yelled: "Send him back to Hungary!"

I redeemed myself later in the game, though. The Jets scored on us and their kicker missed the point after, so the score was 6-6. Then, late in the first half, I kicked a 32-yard field goal, and we went into the locker room with a 9-6 lead. In the third quarter the Jets scored again to make it 9-13, but in the fourth quarter we scored—I made this PAT—and the score was 16-13. It was deep into the last quarter, and I was sitting on the bench thinking about flying back to Buffalo, my mind a million miles away from the game. We had the ball on our own 40-yard line, a play was run, and I was looking up at the clock to see how much longer I'd have to be sitting there, when suddenly I heard the yell:

"Field goal team!"

I had almost exactly the same feeling I had later at the Giants-Dallas game.

I couldn't believe it. I looked out on the field and the ball was on the 50-yard line. The thought flashed through my mind that the record for a field goal in a regular pro game was 56 yards. I'd be kicking from 57 yards.

I ran out onto the field thinking, what the hell, we have a three point lead, I'll hit it as hard as I can, even if I miss we have the ball game. The ball was snapped, I sort of half-closed my eyes, took my steps and hit that ball as hard as I've ever hit a ball in my life. I looked up and I could see the ball way up in the air, sort of floating toward the goal posts. It seemed to go so slowly it was like watching the sun set. I could see all the guys on the Jets, standing up and turned around so they could watch—and it went through! It cleared the crossbar by four feet!

Everybody on the team jammed around me, slapping me on the shoulders and the ass, yelling all sorts of congratulations, and above it I could hear the roar of the crowd. As I trotted over toward the bench everybody was up, cheering.

It was the most magnificent feeling I'd ever had in my life.

My friend in the bar in Buffalo told me the place broke

into bedlam and the guy on the stool beside him fell off onto the floor.

It may have been that kick that assured my staying on the Bills. There were two other plus factors. The first was that that year the pro teams had begun to realize that a player who could kick field goals, especially from 50 yards out, could be an asset to the team even if he couldn't double as a wide receiver. After all, I had scored seven points in the Jet game, more than anyone else. And that year several pro teams—I think three—had "kick only" players. The second plus was that the AFL owners were much looser than the NFL owners. They were willing to take chances. They realized that they were bucking the establishment. Not only the NFL owners and the set-up of pro ball at that time, but also the whole general atmosphere. The general public still thought of the AFL as a second-rate league—largely, I think, due to the newspapers and television. It wasn't due to any malice or conspiracy. It was due in part to what is called a cultural lag, the length of time it takes you to see what's happening right in front of your face. At this time there was no super bowl where the best AFL team could show what it could do against the best in the NFL, though I would have put Buffalo up against any NFL team that year. When Cookie Gilchrist, for example, broke the all-time scoring record, he got about half the publicity that a Jimmy Brown would have gotten, though I think Gilchrist was up in Jimmy Brown's league. Gilchrist was just playing in the AFL.

The day after we played the Jets in Tampa, I went all through the sports pages of the New York City newspapers, and I couldn't find anything except a box score of the game. Nothing about a pro-record field goal, even though it was an exhibition game. And the Jets were a New York City team. But this was the season before Werblin put the Jets on the map with all the masterful publicity he was able to get out of the Joe Namath signing—and Namath's own playing and personality, of course.

After the Jets game we still had three more exhibitions before the regular season started: Kansas City at Wichita, and Boston and Houston at Buffalo.

The magic of being with the pros was still with me, and by now I knew that I had made the team.

There was one final bit of hazing that the rookies who were still around were supposed to go through. I'd gone through the dining room hazing with as poor grace as possible. The business of getting up and having to sing, or telling why you thought you were a great football player, or what your college claims to fame were—all that stuff is designed to make you feel as much like an idiot as you possibly can. At least, that's how I felt.

The final bit of hazing was getting a haircut. Three or four of the veterans would get hold of a rookie in the locker room and, using a pair of those clippers that the trainers used to shave you when they were taping you up, would give you a haircut that was supposed to make you look like a jackass. And did. You know, Cherokee haircuts, circular haircuts, top knots, total clips, a big strip out of the middle—anything.

There was a lot of horsing around, and one of the veterans would pretend to be a hair dresser and use a high voice to explain how he was going to make this haircut an artistic triumph. It got my back up. Maybe I'm more hair conscious than I should be, but I felt exactly the way I did with the goldfish head-biting in the Delta Upsilon initiation back at Cornell.

I said, the hell with it.

If these guys were going to cut my hair, they were going to have to fight me to do it.

"Not me," I yelled when the first of the veterans came at me. "Get away from me, you stupid bastards!" And I shoved him away as hard as I could.

Pretty soon three or four of them were after me, and the fooling began to go out of it. I know damned well I wasn't fooling. I was fighting them off as hard as I could—Cookie Gilchrist was one of them, which shows you how stupid I was—and we were making quite a ruckus. They would have taken me, I know that, except that Lou Saban heard all the noise and came in to see what the hell was going on.

"All right, all right!" he yelled at the top of his voice. "God damn it, knock it off! What the Christ are you stupid jerks doing? Just starting the season and one of you god-damned fools ends up with a broken wrist fighting in a locker room!"

He was boiling mad and the whole thing ended right there.

So I was the only rookie who didn't have his hair clipped. As I said, now I sometimes wonder if I shouldn't have given in. Sometimes I think you should pocket your pride. The other rookies must have been sore at me for being the only guy who got away with no hazing, and the veterans must have thought to themselves, that wise guy rookie. Again, it set me apart from the rest of the guys. Everyone else goes through it, what sets you apart from them?

But that's all water under the bridge now.

A Star at Buffalo—under Option

The whole life that goes with playing pro ball seemed exactly my dish of tea—flying in jets all over the country, seeing the country and different cities, staying at top hotels and motels, eating the best food, knowing that people were looking at you and saying: "See that guy—that's Pete Gogolak, the place kick guy for the Buffalo Bills."

When we broke training camp, I took an apartment in Buffalo with a friend of mine, Larry Hrebiniek, a Ukrainian who had been a roommate of mine at Cornell and who had been captain of the baseball team. He was taking a management training program with the Ford Motor Company in Buffalo, and when he heard that I was coming to Buffalo, he said he was looking for an apartment, and why not get one with two bedrooms and split the cost? So we did. Two bedrooms, a living room and a kitchen, furnished, in a good section of Buffalo near the university, for $160 a month.

(My second year, I roomed with a rookie linebacker for the Bills named Maury Schottenheimer. Ford had transferred Larry away someplace. Larry had been a pretty serious guy.

137

I guess Ford doesn't go looking for the roistering type for its management trainees, and a nine-to-five routine doesn't lend itself to partying. Maury was totally different. He had made the team and he was absolutely lapping it up, being a big man in Buffalo. Wine, women and song—nothing but the best.)

The Bills had a really big team in 1964. We started off by winning nine in a row, and I was having a great year. As I said, I was to end up the second leading scorer in the American League, with 105 points, and 19 field goals in 27 attempts. Also, as I said, Cappelletti beat me out. I was actually leading Gino by three points going into the final game, and I have a faint feeling that Gino's quarterback wanted him to have the record, because he threw him two touchdown passes during the game, and Gino had the record out of reach. Gino is a fine guy, though—he's now running a restaurant in Boston— and I sent him a telegram of congratulations.

Of the regular games that year, the one that sticks out in my mind again, is one we played against the Jets, this one in New York. The newspapers may not have thought much about the American League, but we drew a crowd of 62,000, while the New York Giants were playing Dallas at the same time in Yankee Stadium. The Giants drew a crowd about the same size, but you would have thought that it would begin to sink in that the American Football League was no second-rate operation. One thing that I noted when I read about the Giants game—they lost, 31-21—was that the team had no place kicker. Pat Summerall had retired and Don Chandler had gone to Green Bay. The kicking chores were being handled by Bob Timberlake, a third-string quarterback from Michigan.

One line about Timberlake was that "he's put some excitement back into the conversion attempt after a touchdown —you never know whether he's going to make it or not." I think he was 4 field goals for 21 attempts.

So the Giants needed a kicker.

The real thrill for me about the Jet game was that this would be the first time I had ever played in New York, the terrific city that I had first seen as a penniless immigrant kid. And now the New York crowds were coming out (at least partly) to see how well this crazy Hungarian could kick.

Of all the cities I played in, this was the one where I really wanted to show them.

The Bills flew down from Buffalo on Saturday, stayed in a big motel in Queens overnight, and the pre-game drill got me into a state where I was almost high. All I could keep thinking was: "This is New York! This is New York!"

When we came out onto the field, on a perfect playing day, the roar of the crowd almost deafened me. All the other fields I'd played on before seemed small-time compared to Shea Stadium. I was practically beside myself.

We started off fairly even—the score was 7-7 at the half. The Jets scored first with Dick Wood as their quarterback. Jackie Kemp couldn't seem to get untracked, so Saban took him out in the second quarter and put in Darryl LaMonica. LaMonica promptly hit Glenn Bass with an 80-yard touchdown pass and that tied it up.

The third quarter was even, too—neither team could score. We had one of the top defenses in the American League, but the Jet defense seemed all fired up for this game. Our offense couldn't even get within field goal range. I was beginning to get the feeling that I wasn't going to show anybody anything in my New York City debut.

Finally, about halfway through the fourth quarter, we got the ball to the Jets' 40-yard line, and it was fourth and about six. For a couple of seconds I could almost feel Saban hesitating. The team had tried three or four times to run or pass in a fourth and yardage situation, and the Jets had held them each time. But the 40-yard line. That meant a 47-yard field goal, which is a gamble itself. Finally Saban made up his mind.

"Field goal team!" he yelled, and we went out.

What you need on the field goal team, besides a center, a holder and me are some big, strong, fresh lineman who can hold off the opposition. Darryl LaMonica was going to hold for me. A lot of coaches don't like to have the playing quarterback hold, on the theory that his mind will still be brooding on what he did wrong on the last series of plays, or planning what he's going to do when he gets the ball back, but LaMonica was the regular holder, and a good one, so he was staying in. I trotted over to find where I wanted the ball spotted. I looked for a flat place with the grass worn away so it was a little bare. Sometimes you used to be able to get a little dirt in your hands and build up a little tiny tee for the ball while you were pretending to pat the ground to make sure it was flat and even, but the officials got too damned smart. Now they come over and look at the spot and if it's been built up a little they kick it flat. I picked my spot for LaMonica and he held his toe against it so he'd remember. The reason I pick the exact spot instead of the holder is that because of my style of kicking—swinging my foot in an arc just the way you'd swing the head of a golf club—I want to be able to spot the exact place where I will plant my left foot when I make the kick. The setting of the left foot is maybe the more important. I don't want that left foot sliding out from me.

By this time LaMonica was kneeling down, holding the huddle, which was very brief.

"Okay," he said. "It's a field goal. We start when the kicker is ready."

We broke and I swung around to where I was going to start my run, three steps. I got myself set and bobbed my head at LaMonica. Here's where it starts. Your ideal center is the guy who looks back between his legs once and spots exactly where the holder has got his finger on the ground. Then the center looks up to see how the opposing line is set. After all, the instant he snaps the ball, he becomes one of the most important blockers on the line. He's got to straighten up, loaded for bear against anybody who's trying to get through. So when I nodded to LaMonica he raised his hands for the ball, and it was snapped. The instant the ball is snapped, I start my run. It's the holder's responsibility to have it where I want it by the time my foot hits it. I don't have time to look for the ball. I have to keep my head down, my eye on the spot where the ball will be.

This time the ball was there, perfectly, and I hit it like the one in the exhibition. It went through. I felt glorious. This time those 62,000 people were going mad, for me. Even though their team was the Jets and we came from a small city upstate, they had read the stories about this Hungarian immigrant who could really boot them, and now they'd seen it for themselves. The whole bench was on its feet, yelling and pounding me as I came in, and even Saban gave me a couple of slaps.

There'd be no point in showing any false modesty over a kick like that. Those are the ones that make up for the 36-yard ones you miss in the final minute of play when a field goal would pull the game out. Then, you don't even want to come off the field. You just want to find some hole you can crawl into and wait till everybody has gone home.

Well, that kick broke the tie, and about five minutes later I kicked another one, this time from 32 yards. The score was 13-7. There were cheers for that one, but nothing like for the 47-yard one, which was my longest one up to that time in regular season play. Then, in the last two minutes of play, Cookie Gilchrist broke loose on a 67-yard run for a touchdown, and the final score was 20-7.

All my instincts about playing in New York were proved right by that game—*Newsweek* magazine carried an article on the Gogolak brothers. (Charlie was having a fantastic year at Princeton, three field goals in the Dartmouth game.) *Life* magazine had had an article on me at the end of the '63 season in Cornell, but that one was run mostly as a sort of curiosity piece—not that I ever objected to being in *Life*—based on the fact that I was a Hungarian, and a soccer-style kicker. The *Newsweek* one I'm sure was based almost entirely on the fact that I had played in New York. I could have made the same kick against Boston, and I might have gotten two lines.

I was walking on air for most of the week, but all that ended when we played Oakland out at Oakland. After Shea Stadium, the Oakland stadium then was a pretty sorry place, a high school stadium. For all I know, as a high school stadium it may be the greatest thing that was ever built, but not for pro games. It was not built to control crowds. We lost 16-13, on the last play of the game. We'd been leading 13-10, and then, in the very last second, Tom Flores threw a 35-yard scoring pass to Art Powell in the end zone. Of all the action pictures I keep stored in my mind, I still remember watching Powell jumping up and down in the end zone, holding the ball over his head while the crowd streamed out over the low stone wall of the stadium and mobbed him. I know how he felt and it didn't make me feel any better.

On Thanksgiving we went out to play San Diego at San Diego for the last game of the regular season, though San Diego had already locked up the Western Division championship and we had the Eastern title. (We were 11-1 and the second team, Boston, was 9-2-1, so even if we lost and Boston won, we would still have the title.) For a time, it looked as if we *were* going to lose to San Diego, which wouldn't have done our morale any good. Besides the letdown that would have come from losing our last two regular games in a row— that gnawing "are-we-running-out-of-gas?" feeling—San Diego was the defending American League champion and we would have to play them again at Buffalo for the league title. If we had lost this game, we would have been at a big psychological disadvantage in Buffalo, home field or no home field.

At the end of the first quarter, we were down 10-zip, but in the second quarter we scored 14 points, so we were ahead 14-10. Then, in the third quarter, San Diego scored another touchdown, making it 17-14, and early in the fourth quarter, they got still another, making the score 24-14. It certainly looked as if we had blown it. Sid Gilman's team was just running over us. Gilman, the San Diego coach, has always believed in powerhouse teams, and this powerhouse was ruining us.

But then, somehow, we suddenly seemed to come to life. Down by 10 points with only about six minutes to go, our defense started holding them, and our offense began to move. I got a field goal, and only about two minutes later, with Kemp hitting and Gilchrist running, we got a touchdown, so the score was tied.

Then, with only three seconds left to play, I got a 33-yard field goal to put us ahead 27-24. I felt just as Art Powell had in that San Diego game. I acted just like a kid. I did two forward flips down the field. It must have looked pretty silly from the stands, a full grown football player in full uniform doing flips, but I didn't care. I was just exalted. I think it was mainly relief. Ten or fifteen minutes earlier I'd been so damned sure that we were going to lose and I could just see us playing San Diego in Buffalo. My first field goal had made me feel a little better, then the tying touchdown had brought me back to the feeling that the end of the world hadn't come, yet. Then, that final field goal—I was on top of the world again. It wasn't as sensational as the one against the Jets, but I was named the AFL player of the week because of it.

It was the same old story. It doesn't do you any good to be sensational someplace where it doesn't matter. You have to be sensational at the right time in the right place.

The game for the championship at Buffalo was something of an anticlimax. Maybe the psychological edge had passed to us after the game in San Diego. Maybe San Diego did come in feeling "if we can't beat these guys with a 10-point edge and six minutes to go, maybe we just plain can't beat them." Anyhow, San Diego scored only one touchdown in the whole game. Meanwhile, good old Cookie ran for 144 yards, caught two Jackie Kemp passes for 22 yards more, and Kemp himself threw for 168 yards, 10 completions out of 20 attempts. I went two for two in field goals. So we beat San Diego 20-7 and we were the American League champions.

The game was played in really nasty cold weather, and it made me see how, if any of the stories about pro football players taking drugs are true, they might try it under circumstances like this. (There had been one of those perennial stories about drugs and athletes in some magazine the week before the game.) Personally I've never run into a pro player I ever thought was taking drugs. Maybe there are some; I just don't know them. I'm not counting pain killers like the cortisone shots that the trainer or the doctor gives you as taking drugs. Most of the players I knew and know are too conscious of their bodies to "take drugs." My own personal opinion is that anybody who fools around with drugs or stuff like LSD is out of his mind and should see his nearest friendly psychiatrist at once. For a pro football player to do it, he'd have to be a raving lunatic. Even cold sober and in your right mind you can get racked up playing pro ball—I don't mean broken ankles, I mean a broken back or a broken neck—and I should think that trying to play while you were fooling around with hard drugs would be the same thing as trying to commit suicide. I guess all real drugs affect the mind. What would happen in a game if you took one that made you think you were seven feet tall and then got hit by an offensive tackle who was six foot five and 285 pounds? It's the hard way to learn that you're really only six foot two.

But after that winter day in Buffalo, I could see—especially if your team was losing and you were a thirty-three-year-old defensive player with eleven or twelve years of getting knocked around behind you—where you might figure all you needed was one little pep pill to get you through the game. I don't know. Personally, I'm afraid to take aspirin.

Well, after that game, I figured on relaxing and enjoying myself for a little while. There were some parties around Buffalo and I did just that, relaxed and enjoyed myself. The winning share of the championship for the players was $3,200. After Uncle Sam and the State of New York got through taking their cut, it was $2,300—for me, at least, as a bachelor. What did I do with it? I bought one hundred shares of Holiday Inn stock.

At Cornell I had worked a couple of summers at Holiday Inns and I had become fascinated with the hotel business. I had reached the conclusion, as I said, that I just didn't have the kind of mind that's suited to becoming a doctor or dentist. I liked everything I had seen about the hotel business. It meant learning how to run a restaurant and I've always loved good food. It meant meeting people and getting along with them, and I like doing that. I think I'm good at it. After the championship game, I went back to Cornell to take some of its famous courses in hotel and restaurant management.

In my travels around the country it had always seemed to me that the Holiday Inns were well located and well run. Therefore, most of my bonus money went into their stock. I still have some of the stock left, and I wish I had it all. I sold part of it too soon.

I bought some presents for the family and some clothes for myself with the rest of the bonus, and that was that.

What had me a little teed off, again, was that the American League was so much of a second cousin. The winner's share in the National League was over $7,000 that year, and all the top players were being asked for testimonials for this breakfast food and that soft drink, and they were all out on the banquet circuit getting a few hundred bucks for an appearance. I contrasted all this with what happened to us on the Bills. What happened to us? Nothing. Not a damned thing. Not even Cookie Gilchrist or Jackie Kemp got an endorsement or a speaking engagement. And the Bills could have beaten any team in the country that year.

Sometime in the spring of 1965 the Bills called me up—Saban, it was—and said:

"Pete, we'd like to sign you up before May 1. You had a good year, and we're prepared to raise you $1,500, to $12,500."

I hadn't really expected to be offered a stunning raise. But this was so small that I don't think I even had the strength to laugh. I just gasped.

"$12,500?" I asked. "Lou, you must be joking."

I guess Saban knew that the figure was ridiculous, because instead of arguing about it, he said:

"Well, what were you thinking about?"

I was ready for this one. I had figured out that Cookie Gilchrist was probably getting around $25,000 or $30,000. (Ball players will never tell you what they're making, except in retrospect, and then they always lie. I'll say what I was really getting with the Bills, but I'll only give you a guessing figure for the Giants. No ball player in his right mind would ever ask another ball player what he's making, and no ball player in his right mind would ever tell you. Would you tell someone else what you're making? But I think I had figured out that this was roughly Cookie's salary bracket.) Now, I knew that Cookie was a big star, a top running back. People came to see him play. But I wasn't exactly anonymous, and I had given the Bills more points than Cookie during the season, partly thanks to him, and I was the second-highest scorer in the league. So I was ready.

"$20,000," I said, and I could hear Saban gasp. I think he'd been ready for $15,000 or $18,000, but not this.

"Pete," he said, "you're crazy. You're just a kid, a second-year player. Sure, you were a big help to the team last season, but suppose you have a lousy season next year? You can't expect to make all the money in one season."

Same old story. I told him he'd better get a lot better figure than $12,500 before we could talk. We chatted a while and hung up.

The calls from Buffalo began to become more frequent as the weeks went by and May 1 approached, the date the option clause in my contract became effective. A standard football contract means that the player agrees to play for one year for whatever team he signs with, for whatever terms he signs for. The option clause requires a player to play the following season for the same team that holds his contract. He cannot sign with a different team. After that, as of May 1 of the following year, he becomes a "free agent." (All football contracts run from May 1 to May 1.) Not signing a new contract after playing your first year is called playing out your option.

I was beginning to think more and more that I might just play out my option. I knew that I would rather be playing and living in New York than in Buffalo. I also knew that the Giants were desperate for a kicker, and even if they weren't interested in me personally, other teams might like to look at the AFL's second-highest point scorer.

I still felt that Buffalo had taken some advantage of me when I first signed up, mostly because I was young and dumb. And I didn't think they were making up for it with a $1,500 raise. Their final offer, as contract time got close, was $13,500, but by then I was beginning to get my Hungarian up.

I knew there was a lot of risk involved in playing out an option. I *had* to have a good season, and so did the team. If the team went into a tailspin, and I had a lousy season—or either—I'd be out of football. Ralph Wilson would be mad at me—he was anyway, I found out later—and no matter what my record, he would think of me as a malcontent. There had been a couple of other players who had run out their options, and nobody ever heard of them again. I would be the first "name" player to exercise his option. My neck would be out a mile.

There was a good deal going on in football at the time that I didn't know much about. First, the talk about a merger between the two leagues began to sound serious, precipitated by the fantastic bonuses that the American League owners were paying college stars.

It was here that the differences between the old-line owners and the new showed up most clearly. To the old-line owner, the player was "his" player. He got him straight out of college, paid him while he was being "brought along," and expected him to be "a member of the team" forever after, or until he was traded, whichever came first. The notion of a player using his option clause would have left the old-line owner aghast.

To the old-line owner, football was a kind of holy crusade.

To the new owners, football was basically a business. Big business. The new owners recognized a lot sooner than the old timers that television would bring money into football in huge folding wads—millions at the signing of a contract instead of ticket sale by ticket sale. And the new owners were willing to lay out a bundle to get another bundle back.

I began to get some glimmering of this basic business conflict when I decided to play out my option. I really hadn't the faintest idea of what I was stepping into.

I had no idea that the papers and magazines would describe me as "the player who forced the pro football merger." I may have been a precipitating factor, or the precipitating factor, but there were a lot of other forces at work.

At any rate, I didn't sign my contract before May 1, and I hadn't signed by the time I reported to training camp. The only thing I had gotten out of having helped the team win the championship—apart from the bonus—was that now I could wear a championship ring.

By this time I wasn't the only guy on the Bills who had the notion of playing out his option. There were five or six others who had come to camp unsigned, but as the weeks went by, Saban kept calling the unsigned into his office, pointing out all the risks we were taking, and one by one the others all signed. I think Lou was being fair with us—most of the things he said were perfectly true. But he was a management man; he had the power of hiring and firing, and I knew that however fair he wanted to be, he was still talking for Ralph Wilson.

I didn't notice any difference in the attitude of the other players to me that year. Nobody ever said anything, because your contract terms with your team are something that other players regard as none of their business. Some of them may silently have been offering me their best wishes, and some of them may have been hoping I'd fall flat on my face, but no one ever said anything.

The newspapers were different, however, especially in Buffalo and some of the American League cities we played in. I don't know whether the sports writers, consciously or unconsciously, were on the side of the owners or whether they just plain didn't have the foggiest idea of what was going on. I still don't know all the wheeling and dealing that went on in the merger of the leagues and how the National League owners were able to get such whacking sums just for letting American League teams into their cities. But I shudder to think of the plotting that went on.

At the end of the '64 season I was pretty much the fair-haired boy with the newspapers in northern New York. I had helped win the championship, I had been "Player of the Week," I was the second highest scorer in the league, I had been the most accurate kicker in the American League. (Sixty-five percent completions, when they used to think that fifty percent was pretty good.)

But now I began to see more and more stories and columns pointing out that, after all, I was only one player, that there were plenty of other good kickers and still more coming out of colleges; I was only a second-year player, what if I had a lousy year; the team would go bankrupt if it had to pay out the kind of money I was asking to every player who had a good year.

Some time in August, Wilson was quoted as saying that my salary demands were "totally unrealistic" and that if he gave in to them I would be the highest priced place kicker in all football except for Lou Groza of the National Football League's champions, the Cleveland Browns. This promptly gave rise to rumors that I was asking $30,000. I decided it was a great time to keep my mouth shut.

In the end, my gamble paid off. In the first game of the season we beat the Boston Patriots, then one of the powers in the AFL, by a score of 24-7. I made one field goal, but I missed one, and the papers started writing "It's a 10 percent cut for you next year, Gogolak." (Ten percent was what the Bills could have cut me if I had a bad year and they made me an offer at all.)

The next game was against the New York Jets, and in this one I was off to the best year I've ever had in pro football, so far.

Joe Namath was quarterbacking the Jets by then and Joe played a hell of a game.

He completed 19 passes out of 40 attempts, for 258 yards and two touchdowns. The only problem, as far as Joe was concerned, was that Jackie Kemp had an even better day. He connected for 25 out of 42 for 304 yards.

The Bills also got a pretty solid contribution from me— the equivalent of two touchdowns. I hit four field goals out of five attempts for 12 points, and kicked two PATs. Total, 14 points. The final score was Bills 33, Jets 21.

By now we were off and winging. In the first week of October I was already the league's leading scorer, with 33 points. We beat Oakland 17-12 but the next week we took our first loss of the season, to our big rival, Sid Gilman's powerhouse, the San Diego Chargers. They beat us big, as the saying goes, 34-3, and the fact that I had the only score of the game for us was no consolation at all.

Then we got untracked again. We beat Kansas City, 23-7, to which I contributed 11 points, three field goals and two

PATs. Then we beat the Boston Patriots again in a game that was almost a carbon copy of the Kansas City game. The score again was 23-7 and a Boston paper wrote: "It's the same old story. Gogolak was the hero of the game again with the same old three field goals and two PATs."

On November 25 we played the Chargers again. This time we tied them, on a field goal that I kicked in the last nine seconds, and the tie was enough to clinch us at least a tie for the Eastern championship.

The biggest game I had all year was the next game we played, against the Houston Oilers. I set a club record of five field goals, from 12, 12, 47, 34 and 19 yards out, and kicked two PATs as we beat the Oilers, 29-18. I missed two field goals, both over 50 yards, but handing in a total of 17 points made me feel pretty good. Houston had a pretty fair country quarterback and field goal kicker themselves that day, George Blanda.

On December 5 we beat Kansas City again, this time by 34-25, and I set a new record for both pro Leagues for most successful place kicks in a single regular season—twenty-eight. (Gene Mingo of Denver had set the old record of 27 back in 1963.) We had the eastern championship all wrapped up. Again, I was second highest scorer in the League, 115 points, twenty-eight field goals out of forty-six attempts.

We went out to San Diego on December 26 to play the Chargers in the old Balboa Stadium for the league championship, and we were so charged up that San Diego never had a chance. Never scored a point. We won, 23-0, and my contribution, as the Boston paper would have said, the same old thing—three field goals and two PATs.

What a way to end!

The only regret I have about that whole season was that the merger of the two leagues hadn't taken place the previous June instead of waiting for the next June. If the merger had already taken place, we would have played the Green Bay Packers. In the Super Bowl the next year, Green Bay played Kansas City and won, but if the Buffalo Bills team I played on couldn't have beaten both of those teams, I'll eat a football.

After we won the championship game, Wilson called me in and said:

"Pete, we want you on our team next year. I'm sorry about all the hassle we went through this year, but we'll make it all up to you."

Well, he sounded sincere enough. All I know is he hadn't said a word to me all season. Somewhere along the line Saban had said that he wanted to talk to me again, and later there was a rumor that by then—I think it was in October—the Bills were willing to meet my $20,000 figure. But by that time it was too late. By now I figured that I had a bargaining position.

So, when Wilson talked to me, I told him it could wait till next May 1. I took my championship money and my championship ring and went back to Ithaca to my classes in hotel management.

I Jump Leagues—the New York Giants

At this point a new figure came into my life, Fred Corcoran, a wonderful, full-living Irishman who has been on the sports scene practically all his life, who has a wonderful fund of anecdotes about all sorts of people, and whom you probably know best as a promoter of important golf tournaments like the Westchester Open. At this time Fred was representing some professional athletes, though now he says he's soured on it.

"Now it's all lawyers," he says, "and they want you to be in their office no later than 2:30 P.M. so they can be sure to catch the 4:30 out of Grand Central for Scarsdale. I tell them I used to be able to get more done in thirty minutes at Toots Shor's bar with an owner than in thirty hours in an office with his lawyer, but no, now they're afraid to get out of sight of their briefcases."

Anyway, Fred had first met my brother Charlie the way he always meets people, through a friend of a friend, some Princeton alumnus who was a great fan of Charlie's. That was during Charlie's final year at Princeton. As it turned out

Charlie was to be the Number One draft choice of the Washington Redskins.

"And," Corcoran's friend told him, "he doesn't have the faintest goddamned idea what he's getting into when those sharks start talking contract to him, so why don't you take him over?"

Corcoran conducted his business with Charlie the way he generally does—he took him to Shor's for dinner and then to a hockey game.

So, Fred was handling Charlie, and that's how I met Fred. We were introduced at the Lambs Club. The Bills were playing the Jets the next day, and, of course, he knew that I was playing out my option. I told him I knew that I could get into trouble if any approach was made to any NFL team, but I also told him that the Giants had been my heroes ever since I had come over from Hungary, that I loved New York, and that the Giants looked as if they needed a kicker.

All he said in reply was that I was exactly right about the Giants and that if I wanted him to look after my interests, he'd be glad to do it when the time came.

"And that will be after May 1," he said. "With all this merger talk, there's more wheeling and dealing and long-distance phone calls and what's-the-latest-rumor going on in football than I've ever heard before in my life. All you have to do is make one fancy little mistake and you'll be so deep in trouble that you'll never get out of it."

That was the only contact I had with Corcoran before May 1, except for a lunch that Charlie and I had with Corcoran at John Bruno's Pen and Pencil to introduce us to his lawyer, Mike Mooney. I guess Mooney is an exception to the way Corcoran feels about lawyers.

I took Corcoran's advice. I wanted to play by the rules of organized football, and I was going to play by them. I felt I was doing the right thing, and I was going to go ahead and keep on doing it—sort of the way I felt about not joining the Young Pioneers back in Hungary. How I would have felt if Ralph Wilson had come even halfway to meeting my salary figure in the spring of 1965, I don't know. I wanted to play in the NFL, I wanted to make the kind of money the NFL paid—don't forget I had done all this kind of thinking long before there was any real talk of the merger between the leagues; as far as I knew, they were going to be separate forever, like the National and American Leagues in baseball—but if Wilson had offered me $16,000 or $18,000 in '65, I might still be at Buffalo.

Back in Ithaca, going to my hotel management courses, I slowly began to feel like a man living in the eye of a hurricane. From the newspapers, the news magazines and the sports magazines I began to realize that tremendous things were going on in football about which I really knew nothing. It was like knowing that I was living in a period of false calm, that out there somewhere the winds of the hurricane were screaming at a hundred miles an hour, that sometime soon they would hit.

To bring it home to me, as the merger talks between the two leagues got more specific, I used to read more and more about myself as the key player in the middle of it all (though I wasn't doing anything except going to class), and more and more reporters would call me up for an interview.

I began to get edgier and edgier.

The Bills called me a couple of times during the early spring, but by now I felt that I had made my decision and I was going to stick by it. I told them to wait until after May 1.

On May 3 Corcoran called me at Ithaca and said that Wellington Mara, the owner of the Giants, wanted to meet me.

Suddenly I felt all the tension go out of me. I felt as if the hurricane winds had blown away. I was going to meet Mara, and there could be only one thing he wanted to talk to me about: I was going to play for the Giants.

Corcoran emphasized that neither he or Mara wanted it known that Mara was talking to me—there had already been stories in the newspapers that Mara and I had been meeting secretly to try to work out a deal. They sounded logical, but they were wrong.

The next day I took a plane from Ithaca to New York, fooling the whole world by traveling under the name of Smith, and I got to Corcoran's offices in the Time-Life Building on Sixth Avenue late in the afternoon. Mike Mooney was there and we all went downstairs and got into a chauffeur-driven Cadillac. Fred told me we were going out to the Winged Foot Country Club in Westchester, to which both he and Mara belonged, and that Mara would meet us there. He'd thought of Toots Shor's, Fred said, but he'd decided against it "because every blabbermouth in the world lives there."

The talks between the leagues had gotten to the point where they had agreed to merge, but not until June, and so far neither league had signed a free agent from the other. But if Mara signed me, all hell would break loose.

We got to the club about 7:30 and went into the grill room where, strangely, Mara was the only guest in the whole place. We went over to Mara's table and Fred loudly introduced me as George Smith, for the benefit of any waiter who might overhear. We all sat down and had a very pleasant dinner.

All through the dinner, Mara emphasized that he didn't want any publicity except what would be issued by the Giants' front office. It could take the blast of the storm that was sure to hit when it was announced that I had signed.

(I heard later that Vince Lombardi called Mara from Green Bay and told him he was the biggest fool on the face of the earth for going outside the league to look for a place kicker.)

I left most of the talking to Mara and Corcoran. Mara said, sure the Giants were interested in me, but first he wanted to talk to his coach, Allie Sherman, to make sure that it was all right with him. Sherman was in Europe and wouldn't be back for a couple of weeks.

Then they got around to money.

"We can't give him a bonus," Mara said. "That would be bribing him to jump leagues."

"Then you can make it up to him in salary," Corcoran said, and went into a long spiel about how valuable I was, how many points I had put on the scoreboard for Buffalo, how I was being exploited, and so on.

Mara smiled.

"How much?" he asked.

"How about three times what he's getting at Buffalo?"

Mara said: "Weeelll . . ."

We didn't settle a deal right then and there, but I finally got just about the three times that Fred had asked for.

I stayed overnight with Corcoran, whose home adjoins Winged Foot, and I went back to Ithaca the next day.

The Giants announced my signing on May 19, and everything that Corcoran and Mara had told me was going to happen, happened. I was wrong about the winds of the hur-

ricane blowing away. They surrounded me, engulfed me. For
two solid weeks the sports headlines in the newspapers were
about nothing except "the grid war," and how I had precipitated it. You would have thought that Willie Mays had suddenly signed with the Boston Red Sox.

"War" was the favorite word. It was emphasized that I was
the first top-ranked player in football history to jump leagues.
(There had been an end for the Bears in 1961 who had
jumped to the Oilers, a guy named Willard Dewreall, but
he had not been a star.)

Then, according to which side the particular sports writer
happened to be on, I was either a self-centered, egotistical
ingrate who had jumped leagues solely for my own financial
gain without regard for what I was doing to the whole game
of American football, or, I was an independent Hungarian
immigrant who had learned that in America a man is supposed to make his own way in the world, and I was a hero for
not bowing to the entrenched power of football owners. I
stuck by my guns. I still believed I was right. I was going to
hold to it even if it meant that I'd never play professional
football again.

Wellington Mara was the principal target, after me. No
one appreciated Mara's guts more than me. In the eyes of the
other NFL owners, he had broken a cardinal rule of their ex-
clusive club. He had traded with the enemy. The story went
that George Halas telephoned him and used language that
melted the receiver; that Lombardi, after his call, didn't speak
to him for six months. But Mara had known what would
happen when he signed me. He had made the deal with his
eyes open, and he stuck by his guns, too.

After a few days those stories began to disappear in the

flood of rumors, charges, and countercharges by the owners themselves.

The AFL owners cheerfully poured gasoline on the flames; they announced that they were interested in *all* the top NFL players and would pay the highest rates; it was openly announced that they were making offers to such Giant stars as the powerful young running back, Tucker Frederickson.

The Giants charged that Houston and San Diego were "tampering" with Giant players; Oilers' president Bud Adams said that the Giants were "tampering" with his players.

Oh, it was a merry brouhaha while it lasted. Meanwhile, I was getting such publicity as I had never gotten before, all over the country, and the Giant public relations people did everything they could to help it along. God knows how many releases they put out in those last weeks of May and early June. I was interviewed by newspapermen, by radio people, by television commentators.

All good things must come to an end sometime, however, and early in June the NFL owners "capitulated," as one newspaper put it, and signed the agreement that had been in negotiations for months.

I don't know what the writer meant by "capitulated." The agreement provided for retention of the present teams, and for a common schedule. In addition to which, the AFL agreed to pay the NFL $18 million over a period of twenty years, plus interest. The New York Giants got $5 million "indemnity" for allowing the Jets to play in their territory, and the San Francisco Forty-Niners got $5 million from the Oakland Raiders for the same reason.

For that kind of money, I'd "capitulate" myself.

I first met Allie Sherman, the Giants' head coach, at a cocktail party the Cornell Club of New York gave for me sometime in June, and he seemed like a very nice, pleasant, quiet guy, friendly but not a back-slapper. Not like Lou Saban at all or even Tom Harp. But I liked Allie from the very start, and no coach could have been nicer to me all the time I played for him.

In July I went to the Giants' training camp at Fairfield, Connecticut.

At first, everything was peaches and cream. The main reason, as far as I was concerned, was that this team had been my goal—the New York Giants. Finally I was going to play for the team that I had idolized, in the city that I had dreamed about.

And, somehow, there was a "big city" atmosphere about the whole training camp, everything seemed more sophisticated. In Buffalo you'd have maybe two or three reporters out at a practice, but here it was nothing to see eight or ten. They came from newspapers familiar around the country— the *Daily News*, the *Times*, the *Post*—and their own names were familiar from the columns and stories they wrote.

The other veterans seemed glad to have me, as did the coaches, and I think the rookies looked at me with a little awe. I like to think so, anyway; it's nice to know you're one of the "name" veterans, just the way I felt once about Gilchrist and Kemp and LaMonica.

But, after a week or so, I began to have my first feelings of doubt. Remember, the Giant teams that I had idolized had been the ones of the early 1960s—'61, '62, and '63—when they won three consecutive eastern division titles. They had lost all three of the play-offs, twice to Green Bay and once to

Chicago. They might have won two of those if the quarterback had called the plays I was giving him from in front of the television set in the Delta Upsilon house in Ithaca.

A lot of my idols were still with the team—Dick Katcavage, Rosy Brown, Dick Lynch, Homer Jones, Aaron Thomas, Spider Lockhart, Del Shofner, the indestructible Joe Morrison, and Greg Larson, one of the top centers ever to play ball. When Larson was snapping for a place kick, he could look back once between his legs, memorize exactly where the holder wanted the ball to come, then look up to see how the defense was playing him, then look back between his legs for the holder's signal, snap the ball and be up blocking with the best of them, all in a split second. Greg was the leader of the offensive line, and he should have been. After his second knee operation they said he'd never come back. I've seen him in the weight-lifting machine working his knee back, his teeth clenched in pain and the sweat rolling off his face, but sitting there in that contraption, swinging the weights up and down, up and down. Dr. Anthony Pisani, the Giants' orthopedic surgeon, said it was the greatest example of sheer unbelievable effort he'd ever seen. Larson is one of those guys who's always a half hour early for practice and stays half an hour late, a guy who has to warm up an extra ten minutes to get his knees working. And many a time when I needed a center to practice place kicks, Larson was there. In Buffalo, trying to get a regular center to practice place kicks was impossible—it was beneath him. Let some other guy do it, it was only practicing for three points. Larson knew better. He knew the timing problem.

There was Gary Wood, my old pal and fraternity brother and holder from Cornell. We had a fine old reunion. He was back-up quarterback to Earl Morrall, and he was to be my holder.

But where were the other old-timers? Dick Modzelewski, Rosey Grier, Erich Barnes, Sam Huff, Y. A. Tittle? Gone. Gone, and I was sorry.

I began to hear stories that some of the players who had gone had had fights with Sherman—that Sam Huff had gotten into a shouting match with him for not replacing Y. A. Tittle with Glynn Griffing at quarterback during the championship game with the Chicago Bears. (Tittle was intercepted five times in that game, and Huff thought Griffing was moving the team better.)

One of the first things I also had to do at this time was to get settled in New York. I wanted to live in Manhattan. Nowhere else would do. Gary Wood would have been a natural roommate, but Gary had gotten married and bought a house out on Long Island. Gary had no use for the fleshpots of Manhattan. On the other hand, I didn't want to room with some guy who was a wheeler-dealer, a swinger. I'm not against fun and games, but I didn't want to room with some guy where I'd come home on a Thursday after an evening out and find the place jumping with strange blondes.

What solved my problem was meeting Aaron Thomas. Somehow, Aaron and I struck it off from the start. Aaron was a hell of an end for the Giants for eight years, from 1962 through 1970. He was a very nice, quiet, reserved guy whom you didn't get to know easily. (When he left the Giants he was a stockbroker for a year; now he coaches football out in California.) Though he and I got along fine, and I knew he had a wife and family out in Oregon (he'd gone to Oregon State for college), it wasn't till I mentioned to him one day that I hadn't been able to find a roommate that he mentioned that he was available. He was living a bachelor's life. He was four years older than I was, and he was a settled, quiet guy. We agreed to room together and we found ourselves a great two-bedroom furnished apartment at 136 East 56th Street, on the corner of Lexington Avenue and right near the 59th Street subway station so that we could take the subway up to the Stadium for practice. It was also quite a while before I found out that the reason Aaron was "baching it" was because his young son was critically ill with ileitis on the West Coast. The boy recovered, but Aaron never talked about it.

When the Giants had begun to toboggan downhill after the 1963 season—their '64 record had been two wins, twelve losses, for a seventh place finish—the talk began to go around about the terrible trades the Giants were making, giving away future draft choices (which meant they wouldn't be geting good young players to build with), in the hopes of getting veterans who could perform right then and there, today.

When you get a small halfback named Dick James and a defensive lineman named Andy Stynchula in a trade for Sam Huff, you're not making much of an impression on anybody.

In addition to that, you're upsetting a lot of balances. I don't mean the balance of personal relationships, I mean the balances of playing together. If you've played defensive backfield with Sam Huff for four or five years, no matter who replaces him when he's traded, it's going to take months of playing together to get used to the new man's system, to his timing.

Of course, all players get older and you have to bring younger ones up, but the trouble the Giants were facing was that they had gotten rid of so many veterans in such a short period of time that all the balances of the team seemed to be upset at once. For what my second-guessing is worth.

Of course the Giants had bounced back to a seven-seven record in '65 for a second place finish in a tie with Dallas, and the people who'd been jumping all over Sherman the year before began to say:

"Maybe he knows what he's doing after all. He's a smart football man, you can't take that away from him."

What I really saw as the Giants' problem after we'd been in camp less than a month was that the team had absolutely no defense. None at all. It had a couple of competent men in the line, and a couple of fairly good men in the backfield, but that doesn't add up to a defense. That's just hoping your opponents will make a lot of mistakes. Like a lot of other football people, my philosophy is that a team is as good as its defensive line.

I said to myself: "Jesus, this team just doesn't have the horses. The Bills could beat this team by two touchdowns."

I foresaw a long, hard, busy and unrewarding season ahead for Peter Gogolak, like when Tom Harp used to figure that a missed 50-yard field goal was as good as a punt anyway.

I was kicking pretty well in practice, hitting them pretty regularly from out around the 48-yard line, and some optimist in the *Pro Football Almanac Forecast* wrote: "Despite holes in the line to plug, the Giants have tremendous young backs on the offense and defense—plus 100 points from the AFL."

I could have given him a piece of news. You don't rack up any hundred points as a place kicker unless your offense can get the ball inside the 35-yard line for you more often than not. Anyone who tells you a kicker can make more than fifty percent of his placements from the 40-yard line or beyond is either having you on or doesn't know what he's talking about.

Disaster didn't strike immediately. In an exhibition game we beat the Steelers, 16-14, to which I contributed a field goal and a PAT.

On October 16 that year, we upset the Washington Redskins in a game that had been billed as a contest between two brothers—Charlie and me. Charlie, of course, was playing for the Redskins by this time. The Giants won, 13-10, but neither Charlie nor I really distinguished ourselves. He made one and missed one, and I made two and missed two.

The relationship between Charlie and me as far as field goal kicking is concerned is this: we sincerely applaud each other, are sincerely glad when the other booms a real beauty, provided it's not against the team we're playing for. On any given Sunday, if he kicks a 48-yard one, and I kick a 47-yard one, he has my sincere congratulations. And vice versa. Provided it's not against the Giants.

I'd prefer to forget the entire '66 season. The game against the Redskins was the only one we won all season and we ended up in last place with a record of one win, one tie, and twelve losses, to give the Giants their worst record of all time.

The only thing that I'll mention about the season is a blocked kick that got into the newspapers because my old soccer instincts came out. We were playing Dallas in the Stadium—we lost, but it didn't make any difference because Dallas had already clinched first, and we had clinched last—and toward the end of the first half, I went in to try a 12-yard field goal. Perfectly routine. A kicker who can't make that can't play for Ogdensberg Free Academy. The ball was snapped, the holder set it perfectly—and the line let Mike Gaechter of the Cowboys through. He was through so fast the ball hit him in the chest and bounced up in the air. Without thinking, I caught it with my left foot and drilled it between the goal posts.

After a discussion, the officials decided it didn't count, and the ball was brought back to the 20. Well, it was that kind of season. A non-field goal to my credit.

Actually, I didn't have that bad a year, if you consider the percentages—13 out of 21 and I scored 77 points.

The only good things were my reunion with Gary Wood and the fact that after the season I began to get some of the perquisites that I had missed out on before. Thanks to the Giants speakers' bureau, I began to get some speaking engagements, and to make personal appearances, all of which, besides paying a little money, I figured would stand me in good stead when my playing days were over.

Then, in January of 1967, I was inducted into the Army.

I mean inducted on the spot.

I had registered for the draft when I had become eligible, and on August 24, 1966, I had been called down for my physical, I had been classified 4-F because I have a condition called "spina bifida occulta," which means congenital separation of vertebrae, which in turn means that while I can play football, the Army wanted nothing to do with me.

Toward the end of January 1967 I was told to report to Fort Dix, New Jersey, for reexamination, and I went there on January 25. The doctors examined me again, told me I was perfectly fit, and I was inducted there and then.

This time I was in the middle of a publicity storm that I had had absolutely nothing to do with.

I might have guessed, of course, for all anyone had to do was to read the newspapers. A Michigan Congressman named Lucien Nedzi had gotten headlines coast to coast by charging that professional athletes were getting special consideration from the Armed Services either by outright deferment or by enlistment preferences. There were endless newspaper feature stories on the subject, with long lists of all the top pro athletes and their classifications—whether they were deferred, exempt, in the Reserve or National Guard, and so on. Nedzi was a member of the House Armed Service Committee, and the Committee held hearings on the topic.

Besides their classifications, the medical state of all the famous athletes was gone into in long and excessive detail by the newspapers.

Did or did not Joe Namath have a bad knee?

Was there, or was there not, something wrong with Mickey Mantle's legs?

And so on and so on.

The minute I was inducted, I found myself in the middle of all this. Did I have a bad back or did I not? How could I have a bad back and play pro ball? Was I getting a fair shake or not? One football executive said my induction was symbolic of the Army's desire to "look good" in the newspapers. "Army Crusade Against Pro Athletes?" asked the New York *Daily News*.

My own attitude was simple: I would have preferred playing ball, but if the Army said "come," I was coming. In Hungary I wouldn't have been asked, I'd have been told, and I'd have been serving four years instead of two. I felt this was the least I could do for America. This country had been good to me and two years in its Army was no great sacrifice.

The Army gave me a week or so to put my affairs in order, and then back to Dix I went.

I was still taking basic training about five weeks later when I made a misstep on the top of a flight of six stairs, and I slid down the damned steps right on my backside. I'd already sprained my back when I was on snow-shoveling duty, and I'd been to the dispensary a couple of times for something to take the ache away—it wasn't really a pain—but now I'd really hurt the damned thing. Now it *was* a pain. I had trouble walking, and I was losing weight. I ended up losing nearly thirty pounds, and the Army decided to fly me to Walter Reed Hospital in Washington for special treatment.

And treatment I got. I never realized there were so many tests doctors could give you, so many exercises and manipulations.

Slowly, I began to get better. The pain began to ease, I began to gain weight back, I began to be able to walk. Finally, I was well enough so that I could jog. Walter Reed sent me back to Fort Dix to finish my basic training.

Because of my hotel and restaurant courses at Cornell, I was put in the operations unit that does all the housekeeping arrangements at Dix, and I used my spare time trying to get back into shape to play football. I had found out two things about the Army: That I would be able to get a number of weekend passes so I could play some games with the Giants, and that whatever leave I didn't take in the Army could be piled up at the end of my tour so I could shorten my term of service by that much.

So, a month after the regular football season of 1967 had

started, I was able to play for the Giants again. By this time I had finished my basic training and had been transferred to Fort Belvoir, where I was a clerk. All I knew about the Giants I got through the newspapers and a few letters. Football players aren't great letter writers. I knew that Sherman had chosen Chuck Mercein, the old Yalie, to do the place kicking for him, but Chuck was waived through the league and then put on the taxi squad before the season started. When that happened, the kicking was turned over to a guy named Les Murdock, a free agent out of Florida State who had been released by the Green Bay Packers a short while earlier.

The season started out as though it was going to be a fitting sequel to '66, though the Giants won their first game, beating the Cards in St. Louis, 37-20. Fran Tarkenton was the Giants' quarterback, and he threw three touchdown passes. The papers were full of stories about Fran's scrambling tactics, even the Fort Belvoir post newspaper—again proving that you have to play in New York to get nation-wide publicity.

The next week, the Cowboys beat the Giants at Dallas, 38-24.

On October 1 the Giants played the Redskins at Washington in what I gather was a wild and wooly game. The final score was Redskins 38, Giants 34. The Redskins won on what must have been the weirdest play of all seasons. A Redskin receiver ran the wrong pattern, turned around, and fell down. The ball was already in the air, headed nowhere near him, but it hit a defense man's helmet, bounced in the air, and fell in his lap.

My brother Charlie didn't play in the game. He had been

the highest scorer on the Redskins the previous year, but he had pulled a hamstring muscle. Later he was put on the disabled list.

I noted carefully, however, that my replacement, Les Murdock, had kicked only two field goals, neither of them very long.

Belvoir is an old regular Army post quite close to Washington with all the amenities, including a football field. I was in the post newspaper quite a few times, so I always had guys who were only too anxious to shag balls for me, or hold, and to talk football long afterward. I was getting in almost as much practice as if I had been with the Giants, though under different circumstances. The food wasn't Giant training table food, but it reminded me of the Army camp near Munich. There was plenty of it, and it was solid.

Meanwhile, on October 8, the Giants beat the Saints 27-21, at New York, and Allie Sherman jerked Murdock as his kicker, right in the middle of the game. Murdock had missed a 19-yarder and had another one blocked. I don't know exactly what happened, but he had my sympathy. I've missed 19-yarders for one reason or another, though the only time I've had any blocked is when the protection broke down.

I had talked to some of the Giants people—Mr. Mara himself every now and then—and told them I felt ready to come back. I told them I was still underweight—I was only about 195—but if they wanted me, I had all these weekend passes stored up, and I could get some leave in addition, in order to work out with the Giants. Practicing with amateurs, no matter how willing, helps keep you in shape but you can't get your timing down without practicing with the actual guys who are going to center and hold for you.

On Saturday, October 14, the Giants put out a double-barreled announcement: That Mercein was being reactivated, and that I was going to start practicing with the team on Monday. In the game on the 15th, the Giants beat the Steelers, 27-24. Chuck missed a 22-yarder.

The following Sunday, with me in there to help, the Packers beat us 48-21. We played pretty good ball till about half-way through the third quarter—we led at the half, as a matter of fact, 14-10—but then the roof fell in. The Packers just about ran us off the field. The only scoring I got was three PATs, but I did all the kickoffs. One went to the two-yard line, not an effort I would brag about, but Jim Garrett told me it was the longest Giant kickoff all season.

We won the next game, against the Cleveland Browns, but it marked the beginning of the time, I think, when people began to wonder what the hell was happening to the Giants in the second half? I don't think there was any way we could have beaten the Packers, no matter how well we had played. The Packers were just too good that year. But at one point we were leading the Browns 35-17, and we just barely lasted it out, 38-34.

That was an important game for me, personally, because I was kicking against my old hero, Lou Groza. God, I thought to myself, when I used to watch Groza on television, did I ever think I'd be on the same football field with him, kicking against him? Groza and I each made all the PATs, four for him and five for me, and he kicked two field goals while I kicked only one. But Lou's longest was 37 yards and mine was 47—in addition to that, mine came late in the game when we had only a one-point lead, and it meant that the Browns couldn't settle for a field goal in the closing minutes.

They had to have a touchdown to win, and they didn't get one.

Still, people talked about the size of the lead we had blown, and they talked about it more after our next game against the Vikings at Bloomington. There we had a 24-7 lead at one point, and we blew it. The Vikings won, 27-24.

The following game, at Chicago, the Bears all but wiped up the field with us. Maybe they *did* wipe up the field with us. The score was 34-7, and one of the New York writers who covered all the Giant games said it was the poorest game we'd played all season. He was right.

Of our last five games, we won three. We beat the Steelers at New York, 28-20, a game in which we lost Tucker Frederickson for the rest of the season after he tore up his knee, and Jim Moran, one of our defensive tackles, broke his leg. We beat the Eagles at the Stadium, 44-7, a game where I racked up 14 points, three field goals and five PATs. Then we lost both of the next games to the Browns by 24-14 and to the Lions by 30-7. We won the last game of the season against St. Louis, 37-14. That gave us third place in the Century Division of the National Football Conference.

That finish gave each of us $900, which wasn't as much as I'd gotten either of my years with the Bills, and it certainly didn't give me any visions of living big for the rest of the year, even if I hadn't still been in the Army with a year to go. I had 46 points for the season, nowhere near my team-leading 77 points in the scoring department that I had had the year before. Of course, I had missed five games, which accounted for a good part of it, and I hadn't gotten enough practice with the team, which may have accounted for an additional small part.

In December the Army told me I was going to Germany in January. I wasn't exactly sorry to leave Belvoir, partly because I'd agreed to kick for one football game for the Belvoir football team. The blocking wasn't even up to what I had gotten at Cornell, and the opposing players seemed to have only one idea—rack up Gogolak, the pro. One time three of them hit me at once, hard as I've ever been hit in my life. I thought to myself: "For God's sake, you get paid over $30,000 a year to kick a football. Suppose one of these $90-a-month buck privates breaks your knee? *Then* what the hell are you going to do?" It was the first and last time I played football for Fort Belvoir.

On the other hand, I wasn't overjoyed about going to Germany. I had sort of half-hoped that I'd be stationed somewhere within airline striking distance of New York, so that in the '68 season I could do what I'd done in '67—keep in shape and go up weekends to play. This meant that I'd lose the '68 season, and a football player has only so many seasons in him. So, for a while, I was feeling pretty damned sorry for myself until I suddenly thought:

"Gogolak, they're shipping plenty of guys out of here to go to Vietnam. How would you like to try that on for size?"

I ended up by telephoning Pat O'Hara to tell him what was happening. Pat O'Hara is another of those wonderful Irishmen. A lawyer, a great friend of Mara's and Fred Corcoran's (he lives near Corcoran in a house that abuts Winged Foot Country Club), a great friend of the players, a football nut, a bubbly, baldish extrovert. You go out for dinner with him at 6:30 P.M. and at 2 A.M. you're in P. J. Clarke's, still talking football. He does some legal work for the Giants, and he was the guy who called me up most often from the Giants in my first months in the Army.

When he heard what I had to say, he said:

"Well, there goes a hundred points for the Giants next year."

I tried to laugh.

"Yeah," I said, "or they try out some new kid who starts making them from sixty yards away and I come back and find out that I'm out of a job."

That was a worry, too—it's always a worry to any player who's past his third year.

Pat—his real name is William J.—tried to reassure me, but I still wasn't all that happy.

By this time I was a technician fourth grade and assistant assistant manager of the Officer's Club at Belvoir, and my orders read to report to European Army headquarters in Heidelberg.

The Air Force plane that flew us over landed at Munich, which is the biggest and busiest U. S. base in Germany. Most of the flight was at night and it was inevitable that I spend a lot of time thinking about my only other trans-Atlantic flight, the one from East to West. Here I was again in an American military plane, headed exactly where I'd come from in the first place. When we landed at Munich, I wangled it so that I could get a ride out to the Army camp where the Gogolaks had first been processed, where I'd seen my first big, black American soldier, and marveled at what it must have taken to feed him. And here I was, an American soldier in an American uniform, back at the same camp. All of a sudden I felt proud of the uniform I was wearing even if it did only have the stripes of a T-4.

At Heidelberg the Army detailed me to one of the resort hotels they ran in Germany for troops on leave. There were three in Berchtesgarden and four in Garmisch-Partenkirchen, where Army people paid $1 a day for room and meals. My God, what an Army! A room and meals in Garmisch in the off-season would cost an ordinary, careful traveler $20.

The Army-operated hotel I was sent to was in Garmisch and was called the Four Arrows. The manager was a German named Rudi Hoffman. All the hotels were run by professional, non-Army people, most of them Germans. It seemed as if the hotel was right at the foot of the Zugspitze, the highest mountain in Germany, over three thousand meters high. I used to look out the window of my room every morning and the mountain seemed so close you felt you were looking straight up the great rock cliffs to the snow on top. I arrived there in the deepest part of the winter. The snow was piled high on both sides of the streets; the only part of the earth you could see were the jagged cliffs of the mountains that were too steep to hold snow. Otherwise, since Garmisch-Partenkirchen is set down in a little valley in the midst of the Bavarian Alps, everywhere you looked were the dazzling mountains glittering with snow.

In the hotel, besides a first-class restaurant and all the lounges, was a night club with orchestra and dancing and some first-rate entertainment. Not at all bad. The only time I left Garmisch on any kind of a furlough was when I went to London for four days with a guy named Jim McKrindle. He was a Scotsman who was a professional hotel manager in charge of one of the other hotels. He and I kind of struck it off, and I had never been in London. When he said he was going there for a long weekend, and offered to take me along,

I jumped at the chance. He showed me all around, and one thing I did do was to go to a Saville Row tailor and have a dark blue suit made. I had always wanted a Saville Row suit made, and they did it in three days. I still wear it.

Except for that, I stuck pretty close to the hotel business. I met a lovely blonde Bavarian named Ricci, whose father owned a Mercedes-Benz dealership in Munich, and she and I became quite romantic. I had bought a second-hand Volkswagen for $300, so getting to Munich to see her, when I had a couple of days off, wasn't much of a problem.

After a month or so in Garmisch, I began to worry about the kind of shape I was letting myself get into. My German wasn't any too good—it was picking up a little because almost all the employees of the hotel were Germans, but it wasn't anything I'd brag about—but I did find out that Garmisch had a town soccer team called the Garmisch Füssball Klub, made up of local people like electricians, shopkeepers, workers of all kinds, that played in the Bavarian League. I got an introduction to the coach, and got a try-out. It was hardly big-league soccer—I think the biggest crowd they ever drew at a game was one thousand people. But, damn it, I made the team! Right halfback, and I had to beat out the guy who had held the job the year before.

At first, going out for the team, I felt as though I were reliving my days at Ogdensburg. A strange country, where I could barely speak the language. (I could speak about as much German as I'd been able to speak English.) As for actually playing, at Ogdensburg my problem had been that I'd never even held, much less kicked, an American football. My problem in Garmisch was that I hadn't played soccer for fourteen years. But, as I said, I made the team and traveled all around with them in their creaky little bus, playing places like Tegernzee and Mittenwald, drinking beer by the liter and eating blütwurst.

I decided that I wouldn't really bother to tell the Giants that I was playing soccer in the Alps any more than I told them I played football at Belvoir. It seemed wiser not to.

For conditioning, you couldn't beat the Garmisch F.K. Besides playing on about twelve inches of packed snow, we did our running on the landing slope of the ski jump that had been used for the Winter Olympic games back in 1936. If you want to strengthen your leg muscles, try running up and down a ski slope a few times every day.

The Germans were pretty snobbish, arrogant, and standoffish at first, but eventually I got so that I was on pretty good family terms with the members of the team, and with the fans, and then with most of the townspeople. I think I was the only American soldier who ever got to be really part of the town life. (Of course, we never wore uniforms in Garmisch.) Even with other Germans, the Garmisch people were pretty cliquish—it's the same in all resorts, the natives against the visitors—but I ended up with quite a few friends. I made the same contribution to their soccer team that I'd always made to a soccer team—one hell of a good shot when I kicked the ball, but the slowest man on the squad.

I only had two contacts with the Giants the whole time I was in Germany. First, along about March, John Dziegiel, one of the co-trainers, sent me two brand new (deflated) League footballs, air mail special delivery. I got them blown up and started practicing kicking on a field behind the hotel. The Germans passing by used to stop and watch me. The style I was using to kick was nothing new to them, but they couldn't figure *what* I was kicking, and why I kept getting it up in the air so high when I obviously could have gotten more distance with a lower trajectory.

The second contact was Pat O'Hara, who came over to see me. What other pro team would pay to send a guy 3000 miles off-season to see how a player was doing? I got reservations for Pat and his wife at the Markplatz hotel, showed them around town (which didn't take long, considering the size of Garmisch), and took them to the Spielbank, the local gambling casino. Casino gambling is legal in Germany and is run by the state, and I lost 80 marks.

I remember once the three of us were sitting on the terrace of O'Hara's suite with a bottle of Liebfraumilch. O'Hara was wearing the lederhosen he had made the mistake of buying (*nobody* looks good in lederhosen except possibly the original cow) and one of those green Tyrolean hats with a little red feather in the band.

"Ah, if Wellington Mara could only see us now," O'Hara said.

"See *you*," I told him, "you're the conversation piece."

Late in 1968 the Army figured that since I had not taken leave for almost two years, it owed me three months time. And so, well in time for the 1969 season, I returned to the United States, and the Giants.

Ups and Downs with the Giants

The 1969 season started with the firing of Allie Sherman as head coach, and his replacement by Alex Webster. It must have been an enormously difficult decision for Wellington Mara. After all, Allie had been his own personal choice, and a man thinks a long time before he finally decides that his hand-picked selection, a coach he has praised and stood by year after year, simply has to go.

More than that, the Giants are Mara's whole life. He isn't one of the owners who has a lot of other interests and to whom a pro football team is an ego-builder and a business investment. Mara inherited the Giants from his father; he's going to run the team his whole life, and he's going to leave it to his kids. He has ten children, eight boys and two girls, and he always brings a couple of them to every game. (Mrs. Mara is practically *always* at every game.) In addition, while Mara is devoted to his children, he believes in teaching them the facts of life early. The boys, in sequence, work at the training camp every summer, and they get no special treatment because they're the owner's kids. They help pick up the

181

locker room after the players have left, piling up dirty socks and smelly jock straps just like the attendants. Mara believes that there'll always be seamy work in life, and his kids should learn about it first hand. I agree with him.

But, because he feels so deeply about the team, the team always comes first with Mara. The team simply has to be the best he can make it. And so, Allie Sherman was fired.

Never on God's earth would I want to be a head coach in pro ball. You have a run of good seasons, as Sherman did, and everything is peaches and cream. Then you start losing, as every coach has to, and the world falls apart.

The first thing that happens is that the fans get on you. All right, they pay $9 for a ticket, they want a winning team, they're entitled to boo when you blow a game. But when it goes on and on, as it did with Allie—I don't see how he took it as long as he did. Allie is a great man in my book. Perhaps he was too *nice* to be a football coach. Off the field, in manner and speech and dress, he acted and looked more like a polished business executive than a head football coach. Allie took more punishment from the Giant fans than I ever could. I've had my share of booing, but I've never had twenty or thirty thousand people singing "Good-bye, Allie" at me and waving white handkerchiefs.

Another thing about Allie's harassment is that a lot of stadiums, especially the older ones like Yankee Stadium, don't have efficient crowd controls for professional football. Football draws a different type of fan from baseball. I've seen the Yankees play at the Stadium, and a line of ushers and stadium cops is generally enough to keep most of the fans off the field. Football crowds would no more be stopped by a line of ushers than by a loudspeaker asking them to please behave themselves. I don't know whether it's because we only play seven games at home all season and the fans try to get all their emotions out in those seven games, or whether it's because we play in colder weather than baseball so that some of the fans use it as an excuse to get tanked up on pint bottles of whisky, or whether it's because we play a lot more physical game than baseball. Whatever the reason, once you finish a game, a player's next problem is to get back to the locker room in one piece. Anything hanging loose from you—like a chin strap—is legal game as a souvenir, and some fans try to tear the helmet right off your head. Orderly, a lot of football fans are not. The worst ones are the teen-agers who want to see if they can hit you.

I remember after the final loss of the '66 season, Sherman actually had to sprint for the safety of the runway, chased by a howling mob.

As I say, how Sherman took it as long as he did I don't know, but finally at the close of the exhibition games that began the '69 season, every one of which we lost, Sherman lost his job.

Mara had been at the last game, which was played in Montreal on a cold, gray, miserable night, against the Pittsburgh Steelers. We lost, 17-13, and after the game we had a players meeting. Even the coaches weren't allowed in. Unfortunately, it amounted to nothing. All it was was forty professional football players, some of them pretty damned good, all of them angry at themselves and at the whole world, blowing off steam. The general tenor of the meeting was: "What the hell is going on here? *How* can we lose this way? *How* can we lose every single exhibition game?" The reason the meeting came to nothing was that nobody knew the answer. In the plane on the way back, Mara sat by himself in the front, away from the team and the coaches, talking to no one, looking out the window at nothing except the lights on the ground. He drove straight home when the plane landed, and the next morning he telephoned Sherman and told him the bad news.

How did the team feel? Well, we already felt so bad that we couldn't feel much worse. And most players feel that who the coach is is a management perogative. It doesn't make any difference whether players like the coach or not, except to themselves. Sure, it's easier on your digestion if you play for a guy you get along with rather than a real bastard, but it revolves around respect. The players have to be able to respect the coach as a man who knows what he's doing, what he wants.

Both Sherman and Webster got respect, different as they were. I've never seen or heard of a coach anywhere in any sport who put in the time that Sherman did. You'd come back from a night in town, making the 11 o'clock curfew by the skin of your teeth, and from Sherman's room you could hear the faint whir of the projection machine as he re-ran, for the umpteenth time, the film clips of some play that either had worked or hadn't. As everyone has said, he could diagram a whole series of plays on a blackboard, figuring out every possible contingency and planning for them, till you didn't see how the series could fail. And, when he had the horses, it didn't.

Sherman wasn't standoffish. He liked a couple of drinks at relaxing time—"pops" he called them—as well as the next man. He could lose his cool and scream as well as the next coach during a game. When we won the final game of the '66 season against St. Louis, he came into the locker room and kissed every one of us. Football really has to be man's whole life, to be in his soul, before he can, of his own free will, kiss forty football players who've just finished a game. Or any other time, as a matter of fact.

And if Sherman's system had worked, by that I mean that if he'd had the luck and the players, Allie would be enshrined up there right now with coaches like Vince Lombardi. Allie had one system, Lombardi had another.

My brother Charlie told me a Lombardi anecdote that ends up as kind of a gag, but to me the point of it is how Lombardi thought of a football team. (Jerry Kramer's famous crack illustrates my point about how it doesn't make any difference whether the players like the coach or not. "He's fair," Jerry said. "He treats us all alike. Like dogs.") Charlie was kicker for the Redskins the first year that Lombardi took over, and their first game was against Baltimore.

"We had to take the bus from Washington to Baltimore for the game," Charlie said, "and the story was that the Redskins knew they were so bad and the Colts were so good that the coaches had to get whips to drive the players onto the bus for the game."

It wasn't that bad, of course, but the game was—Baltimore won 52-14, with Colt rookies playing most of the final quarter. Lombardi practically had one long series of heart attacks on the field.

After the game, the players were getting dressed when Lombardi walked into the locker room.

"Whatever you were playing out there," he said, "it was disgusting. I've never seen anything as disgusting. Get back into your uniforms and back onto the field, and we'll start right now with the fundamentals."

So he got the whole team dressed and back on the field of the deserted stadium, standing in a circle around him, and then—Charlie said—he picked up a football and held it up over his head.

"To start with," he said, "this is a football."

I believe all that. That's true. Then I think the story becomes a gag. Some lineman is supposed to have said:

"Excuse me, coach, could you slow down a little? You're going too fast."

I think that basically Kramer was probably right—allowing for the exaggeration that makes the gag—about Lombardi. I never played for him, of course, but from what I've heard from Charlie, and what I've read, he was a perfectionist who demanded total performance from his players. If you could do, and did do, what Lombardi wanted, you were one of his fair-haired boys. If you couldn't, he didn't want you on his squad in the first place, and if you didn't, you were on your way out.

For a long time, Lombardi, in the public mind, to the reporters and people who didn't know anything about football except what they saw on television, was the hero-coach. He was the winner. Whatever he did must be right.

In the same way, if Sherman had suddenly returned to his winning ways he would have been the hero-coach, and there would have been endless magazine and newspaper stories about how his dedication, his systemization, was the way to produce a winner.

People who think this way leave two factors out of consideration. One is the one that I've always thought—and still think—so important.

Luck.

The second is that, while Lombardi was at Green Bay he always had that solid nucleus of the really top players who aren't the stars but who are the ones you have to have to make the stars possible. The tackles. The guards. The linebackers—not the middle linebackers who have been getting the headlines ever since Sam Huff, but all the linebackers.

After the old guard on the Giants began to disappear, Sherman—by and large—didn't have that nucleus. Or, he did have a nucleus, but not big enough. He had one of the really top centers of all time, Greg Larson. But what would happen if Larson broke an ankle?

In my first years on the Giants, defensive linemen used to come and go like ping-pong balls.

Even the draft choices the Giants picked didn't work out more often than they did.

In '64 the first pick was Joe Don Looney out of Oklahoma, one of the finest natural athletes I've ever seen, a big 240-pound fullback who had set all kinds of records in college, an All-American every place you looked. How could you miss with Joe Don Looney?

The way you could miss was that Looney wasn't with it. Maybe he was such a high-powered star in college that he figured he could do anything he wanted to, I mean *anything* he wanted to, and get away with it. He didn't understand that pro ball is a business, and pro teams don't give a good Goddamn what kind of headlines you got in college—they want performance. And they get it, or else.

More than that, Looney's mind didn't work the way other people's did. Nothing seemed to register.

The first thing that hit me about Looney was that he checked into our dormitory in training camp at Fairfield at

11:30 one evening in the very first week of training. When even the veterans are out to impress the coaches.

Sherman was in the lobby, and he looked at his watch. Check-in time, remember, was 11 P.M., and the fine was $300.

"Joe Don," Sherman said, "check-in time is eleven. This is going to cost you $300."

"But, coach," Joe Don said, "I was out on a great date, and I had a half-an-hour coming to me."

"What does that mean, you had a half-an-hour coming?"

"Well, last night I checked in at 10:30. So I had half-an-hour coming."

Now, that may sound like a wisecrack, but the problem with Looney was that it wasn't. That's the way his mind worked. He was serious about it. In early one night, out late the next.

Sherman didn't see it that way. The fine stood.

Another stunt Joe Don pulled, I thought Sherman was going to put an axe to him. Twice a week, from 3 to 4 P.M., we had what was called "press time." We were all supposed to stay in the dormitory so that the reporters could come in and talk to us. It made sense. It gave the reporters a chance to ask all the questions they wanted, and it meant that when we were practicing the reporters wouldn't try to buttonhole us and take our minds off what we were doing.

Unfortunately, one 3 to 4 P.M., Joe Don decided he wanted a nap. A guy from the *Times* went up to Looney's room and rapped on the door.

"Go 'way! I'm trying to sleep!" Looney said.

The reporter knocked again.

"Come on, Joe Don," he said. "It's press time. I'm from the *Times*."

"Go 'way!!" Joe Don roared.

The reporter rapped a third time and Joe Don charged out of bed. Now, besides being big and strong to start with, Joe Don was also a body-building nut, always squeezing rubber balls in his hands and pressing weights—he could press 300 pounds. He was always looking at himself in the mirror. He pulled the door open so hard it came off its hinges—literally.

"Goddamn it!" he shouted, "I told you to leave me alone!"

He picked up the guy from the *Times* and threw him downstairs.

Sherman almost had apoplexy.

What finally cooked Joe Don's goose with the Giants was that he didn't like to practice. He'd practice enough to know the plays, then he figured that from that time on, practice was strictly for the peasants. He knew the plays, he could perform when they needed him.

Sherman talked to him.

Y. A. Tittle talked to him.

Coaches and trainers talked to him.

And they went up to *his* room to talk to him, they didn't call him down, the way they would have with another player —even a veteran.

It was no use. Joe Don wouldn't practice, and the Giants cut him at the end of the training season.

He was such a hell of a football player, though, that he caught on with the Colts. Lasted the season, was cut. Went to the Lions. One season. Cut. The Redskins. One season. Cut.

It's a pity.

Another guy was Jeff Smith, a linebacker out of the University of Southern California, a colored guy. A great big guy, who came up in '66, a great year for college stars—the year of the big bonuses. He had all the ability in the world, but it was impossible to coach him.

As I said, pro ball is ten times as sophisticated as college ball, and what was star play for USC didn't get passing grades with the Giants.

But Jeff left the Giants in style.

At the end of the season he bought a Cadillac and drove it into the garage under the building at 10 Columbus Circle, where the Giant offices are, and took the elevator to the 28th floor. He got hold of Ed Croke, the head of promotion for the Giants.

"Mr. Croke," he said, "I bought me a Cadillac and I've got it in the garage downstairs. How do I get to California?"

Croke knew Jeff.

"Well, Jeff," he answered, taking him by the arm, "take the elevator back downstairs to the garage. Get your car and pay the attendant. When you drive out of the garage, turn left. At the first traffic light, turn right. That road will take you to a big bridge. Cross the bridge and keep going until you get to California."

The Giants never saw Jeff again.

Another rookie who didn't pan out was Don Davis, who also came up in '66, and for whom the Giants paid an arm and a leg. They gave him a whacking bonus and a long-term contract—$150,000 was the reported figure—that they were still paying off till a couple of years ago. If Davis used his head about his money, he shouldn't be hurting. He was also a black man, and huge, right out of Los Angeles State, six foot six and, when the Giants signed him, 290 pounds. He was a defensive tackle.

He checked into training camp at 325, thirty-five pounds of it fat, and all of it around his gut.

Sherman took one look at him and said:

"You have exactly two weeks to get down to 295 pounds. From then on, for every pound you're over 295, you'll be fined $50 a day."

God, Davis had my sympathy. A man that big, and how he loved to eat! It was sheer torture to watch him. At the end of the two weeks he was down to 298, and Sherman fined him, as promised, till he got down to 295.

The problem then was that Davis was so weak he couldn't tackle your grandfather. The Giants used him as little as possible, and they let him go at the end of the season. I'll bet they hated to see all that money go, but there was nothing else they could do.

The big tragedy in the ranks of Giant draft picks was Tucker Frederickson. A great player and a great guy, who had everything. He was drafted in 1965, out of Auburn. In his senior year at Auburn, he was All-Everything. All-American according to the Associated Press, *Look* Magazine, the *Sporting News,* the Football Writers Association, Newspaper Enterprise Association. In his rookie year with the Giants he was magnificent. A total of 659 yards rushing. Rookie of the year. Then, in our tenth game in '67, against the Steelers, he was hit. The cartilage was wrenched from his knee. In '68 he gained 486 yards, in '69 136, in 1970 375 yards, and then Tucker packed it in. It's a bloody pity. It seems as if the Giants have a curse on them when it comes to draft choices.

One final guy who might have made it big was Fred Dryer.

He can still make it big, but not with the Giants. By normal standards, Fred was a nut, too, like Looney, but he was so easy, so pleasant, so carefree, that you never really could blow your stack at Fred the way you could with Looney. Fred knew he was a damned good football player, but he was never under the delusion that the whole team revolved around him.

The first time I saw Fred was the first day I reported to the Giants' training camp in 1969. I turned into the parking lot and there was a travel-dirty Volkswagen bus with California plates and a guy as big as a house sitting on the roof, wearing a T-shirt and shorts, with long blond hair down the back of his neck. In one hand he was holding a surfboard and in the other a toothbrush.

I found afterward that Fred was never far from his toothbrush. He's the only guy I ever met who had a fixation about teeth. He brushed them after meals, between meals, and sometimes because he had nothing else to do. He must have the cleanest teeth in the western hemisphere.

I learned about the surfboard, too. Fred was a first draft choice out of San Diego State as a defensive end, but his heart was still back in the country of sun and surf. His hair was as blond as it was because he was always out in the sun, and the sun had bleached it.

He was quite a piece of work, one of the best-built men I've seen, six foot six and 235 pounds, with a thirty-inch waist, and one of the quickest men I've ever seen play football. He moved like a panther on the kill, unbelievably fast, never off balance. At his size he moved like a good middleweight fighter.

But he was always himself. I remember a reception at the Essex House, a pretty high-class hotel on Central Park South.

The reception was for kids who had reached the finals in Ford's "Punt-Pass-Kick" competition in the states of New York, New Jersey, and Connecticut, and for their parents. The kids were to compete between the halves of the Giants game the next day to determine the national finalists of the competition. The Giants, to represent the team, had corraled me, Fred, and a rookie linebacker named John Douglas. Everyone was dressed to the nines—the kids, the parents, Douglas, and me—everybody except Dryer. He showed up in his T-shirt, short shorts, and sandals. And with that hair, he got quite a bit of attention just walking through the lobby before he even got to the reception.

I remember giving him a heart-to-heart talk.

"Fred, it doesn't prove you've joined the establishment if you dress up a little when you go into class places," I said. "Mr. Mara likes his players to look decent. You know, you've always got to make compromises."

Fred just laughed at me and patted me on the shoulder.

That winter Fred drove his Volkswagen bus all the way down into South America, and paddled a canoe down the Amazon River, all by himself. I don't know how far he traveled on the river, but he sent me some snapshops to prove he was there, and he also got dysentery and lost forty pounds that took him three months to get back.

The spring Alex Webster got the idea that it would be great to go around the country and see what his players were doing. What that really meant was that Webster wanted to see what shape they were in, and he took John Dziegiel, the co-trainer, around with him to check on his judgment. In Los Angeles, where Fred lived, Webster and Dziegiel tried to get Fred on the phone for a couple of days, without success. (Fred, I might add, also had not signed the contract the Giants had sent him.) Finally, at 11 A.M. one day, with Webster and Dziegiel scheduled to catch a plane for New York in a couple of hours, Fred answered the phone to Dziegiel.

"Fred, this is John Dziegiel."

"John who?" Fred asked. I don't know, he might have forgotten. Dziegiel had only been taping and rubbing him for about six months.

"Dziegiel," John answered. "Alex Webster and I are here in Los Angeles and we're heading out to the airport to catch a plane back to New York. Alex wants to talk to you. We'll meet you at the airport in half an hour. In the dining room."

"Okay," Fred said.

I'm surprised he didn't ask who Webster was.

In about half an hour John and Webster were in the dining room catching a fast bite, neatly dressed in suit and tie, when they looked up and saw Fred standing in the doorway. Puma shoes—those German warm-up shoes, black, with two slanting white stripes on each side. No socks, but plenty of powder on his ankles where he'd just taken a shower. T-shirt. Bermuda shorts. And brushing his teeth.

Fred only played two seasons for the Giants. Eventually, he went to the Rams so he could stay in Los Angeles.

Not all the Giants picks, obviously, were either hurt, screwballs, lousy, or sun-lovers. Two other guys I've been close to since I've been on the Giants were their picks. Ernie Koy was drafted right out of Texas in '65, the year before I joined the Giants. A big Texan with an innocent amicable face, six foot four and 235, a fine running back. He, Tucker Frederickson, and Steve Thurlow were the famed "Baby Bulls." Koy was also the Giants' punter.

I got to know Koy well when, in my first year with the Giants, I was sharing the apartment with Aaron Thomas at 136 East 56th Street. Koy lived maybe a hundred feet the other side of Lexington Avenue at 245 East 56th. We used to run into each other on the street all the time and the three of us generally took the subway up to the stadium together. Koy, as a big Texan, loved good food and plenty of it, and I, as a not-quite-so-big Hungarian, loved good food and plenty of it. Ernie came from a family of athletes. He had been an All-American at Texas, his brother Ted was an All-American there, and his father had been a major leaguer with the Brooklyn Dodgers. Ernie was so relaxed all the time that, on the road, they used to allow an extra fifteen minutes to get him awake enough to get up. All the time he lived in New York he never really got away from Texas. He wore cowboy boots all the time, and everyone always called him "Cowboy." He used to call me "Gogi."

"How's my little Gogi?" he'd ask.

Ernie played for the Giants for seven years and he never really made it big. I don't know why, he was a damned fine running back, but he never set the big records and he never was flashy in the way a Jimmy Brown or a Joe Namath was. But, as any football coach will tell you, he was one of the guys that *every* pro team has to have if it's going to succeed. Big, strong, a good runner, a good blocker, he wasn't the guy who'd break away for a 70-yard touchdown. He was the guy who, if you absolutely had to have four yards, would get it for you or die trying. Even if the fans didn't know what he meant to the Giants, the coaches and the other players did.

Ernie finally was cut in the summer of '71. He quit football, married a stewardess for Overseas National Airline, and retired to his cattle ranch near Bellville, Texas. I got a letter from him a while back in which he said the biggest excitement in his life now was driving thirty miles to see a movie. I remembered the times he and I and Tucker Frederickson used to go to Mr. Laff's, an athlete-and-girl type nightclub in New York run by Phil Linz, the old Yankee. The girls at Phil's place aren't the kind you'd take home to meet mother, but they have a lot going for them in other ways.

The other guy I was close to was a defensive back named Tommy Longo, now with St. Louis. Tommy was totally different from Ernie, and I think that maybe I understood Tommy better. His grandparents had come over from Italy, and they had never made it big in the land of opportunity. Tommy was damned well determined that he was going to, and the way for him was to make a name in pro football.

He used to talk to me sometimes about his childhood, sleeping in the same tiny bedroom with three of his brothers, no money, the whole family one step away from the relief rolls. Tommy came from Lyndhurst, New Jersey, where he had gone to high school, and he had gotten a scholarship to Notre Dame. At his biggest Tommy was six foot two and 200 pounds, and nobody expected him to make it big on defense at Notre Dame. Even in college, that isn't big for a defensive back. But everybody underestimated the amount of sheer guts and desire that Tommy had. Everybody else could say he couldn't make it, Tommy just didn't know it. He was going to make it if it killed him. He wasn't even All-American at Notre Dame. He was All-Midwest, and second-string Associated Press All-American.

But the pro scouts saw something that the newspapermen didn't—Tommy had come up with the Notre Dame record for most career tackles by a defensive back, and most tackles in one season. Tommy was drafted by the Philadelphia Eagles in '66, and then got hurt in the training season. The Eagles promptly cut him, and none of the other pro teams wanted an injured rookie defensive back who hadn't even made All-American. Most guys would have given up at this point, taken a job, and gone back to Lyndhurst to become an assistant football coach. Tommy wouldn't have had any trouble with the job; he already was working, offseason, for his uncle, who owned a New Jersey company called TechTorch, which made acetylene welding torches.

But not Tommy. He latched on to the Westchester Bulls, then a farm club for the Giants.

Football farm clubs in America are like going to Siberia. Most of the stadiums don't even have a locker room where the teams can dress. If it's a night game, only one side of the field is lighted; you get $100 for playing a game and bring your own arnica; there are maybe twelve hundred people in the stands and—Tommy told me—after the teams are introduced you're supposed to shake hands with as many fans as you can. Cold water in the showers.

Tommy took it. Took it *all*.

In '68, in the training season, the Giants invited Tommy up to camp for a tryout. He didn't have all the speed in the world, but he had that kind of nerve. He had married a New Jersey girl named Annette Colasurdo, and she used to drive up to Fairfield every day to watch practice, first having gone to mass and said a prayer for Tommy.

Tommy made the Giants, and played two good years for them. He was hurt in the '70 season, and he was cut after an exhibition game in the '71 season, in what Alex Webster said was one of the toughest cuts he ever had to make. Monday was always an off day for the players during the season, and none of them ever showed up at Yankee Stadium except for special reasons. It was also the day the coaches went over the films of the Sunday game, and, before the regular season started, the day on which they decided which players were going to be cut.

This Monday, Tommy was at the stadium, working out by himself. There he was out on the field, all alone, running, sprinting, trying cuts, and out came Webster. Webster is not the kind of guy to put something unpleasant off to the next day.

"The thing I hated most," Webster said, "was that he had such guts." Thank God, the Cardinals picked him up, and he played one more season for them before retiring.

I've gotten a little away from the '69 season and the shift from Sherman to Webster, but it was necessary to explain what was going on.

Alex Webster, of course, was one of the "old Giants." He was a member of the family. And a hell of a good coach, I might add. He knew everything that could happen to a football player. To be cumbersome about it, he was a player's player.

He had been through the mill.

He'd been drafted by the Redskins back in 1952 out of North Carolina State, and the Redskins had cut him in training. But he was like Longo, except he went up to Canada, where he played for the Montreal Alouettes. So Alex knows what it means to be a big star in college, get cut by the pros, and go to a minor league.

When Alex said the hardest thing he had to do was cut Tommy Longo, I believed him.

Anyway, Alex caught the Giants' interest—he'd set all kinds of rushing records in Montreal—and the Giants gave him a tryout. Obviously, he made the team, and from then on it was nothing but glory. He was a legend. All-Pro rushing back, he was one of the NFL's all-time top scorers in rushing, ahead of such big names as Bronco Nagurski and Paul Hornung. He still holds the Giants records of most rushing yardage (4805 yards) and most rushing touchdowns (39).

When Alex took over as head coach, he faced exactly the same problems that Sherman had. He didn't have the players.

We started off like a house afire. We beat the Vikings (who ended up the NFL champions that year), 24-23, in a game in which we had to come from behind. That's the kind of game that sets you up. I got the first score with a field goal, then the Vikings tied us, then they scored two touchdowns in the second quarter, so at the half, we were down 17-3. We scored a touchdown in the third quarter while they got a field goal, and it was 20-10 going into the last period with the fans feeling, well, here this one goes. But we came alive in the final quarter and scored two touchdowns.

The game really made us feel good. Even though the Lions beat us in the next game, 24-0, we still had enough momentum to get out the next week and beat the Bears, 28-24, then Pittsburgh, 10-7.

Then the roof fell in. We lost seven straight. God knows, Webster must have expected it, but it didn't make it any easier. Missed plays. Missed blocks. Fumbles. Dropped passes. He got them all. He raged the way Sherman did, except he's bigger, and his language was tougher. None of it did any good.

We not only lost the ball games where we were creamed, like St. Louis beating us 42-17 and Dallas 25-3, we lost some games that we should have won.

(Those games we "should have won." I'm beginning to sound like Webster and Sherman and every coach who ever lived.)

We had the ball on the Washington goal line three times and couldn't score. They beat us 20-14. We had Philadelphia beaten, and they punched over a touchdown with less than a minute left to win, 23-20. New Orleans hit us with a late field goal and pulled it out, 25-24.

Then, damn it, to show that we had the makings of a football team, we came back and won the last three games, rubbing it into two of the teams that had beaten us earlier. First, we beat St. Louis by a score even worse than they had handed us, 49-6. Then we beat Pittsburgh, 21-17. Then we came up against the Browns, who had already clinched the eastern title, and we beat them, 27-14.

It wasn't a season to make us think that we had it made, we were 6 and 8, and it didn't bring any bonus checks or make Webster coach of the year, but winning the last three games gave us a kind of a spark. We *could* win football games. But what was the key to becoming champions? How could we get untracked from those six-game losing streaks? How could we stop the fumbles and dropped balls? How could we lose to St. Louis 42-17, then turn around and beat them, 49-6?

I think that's where that subtle, indefinable thing called

psychology comes in. Since I can't define it, I'll try to explain it.

When I was on the Buffalo Bills, they were a damned good team, a great team, and they knew it.

If they lost a game they were sullen and depressed afterward, but their general collective attitude was:

"Aw, they're bums. Every break in the book they got. Luck, just plain horseshit luck."

And they'd go out next week and murder the opposition, just to show how good they were.

But if the Giants of the late '60s lost a game, their general attitude was:

"Christ, here we are again."

Another losing streak.

As far as I was concerned, the 1969 season was so-so. I tied with Joe Morrison as team leader in points scored—we each got 66, Joe on eleven touchdowns—but 66 points for a place kicker is nothing to go around jumping with joy about, especially since I was 11 for 21 in the field goal department, which is not a passing score. The absolute minimum passing score in the field goal department is 60 percent.

The season did convince the Giants that they didn't want me as their punter, however. During training, the Giants suddenly decided to try me out as a punter, despite the fact that I hadn't done any punting since Cornell. I didn't do too badly, either, at the start. I hit a 61-yard punt during the exhibition season, and I was averagering over 42 yards in the regular season.

Then, in the first game against the Detroit Lions, two things happened to me in the kicking department. First, if you are punting against Detroit, the idea is to keep the ball away from Lem Barney, their All-Pro corner back, and quick as a cat. I kicked a line-drive punt directly into Barney's hands so fast the Giants were barely off the line of scrimmage, and Barney danced it back for a touchdown like Fred Astaire, waving at me as he passed. It looked great on national television.

To top that performance, I missed two field goals, both of them less than 35 yards. I guess Webster decided on the spot that if he couldn't stand a punter who kicked line drives, he also couldn't put up with a place kicker who missed from under 35 yards. So I went back to full-time place kicking.

One good thing happened to me in '69, off the football field.

I met a girl. This time a special girl.

CHAPTER TEN

I Meet Kathy and the Giants Look Good

There is a type of football fan who might surprise you. He is a man anywhere between the late twenties and late forties, a successful business or professional man who somehow has been bitten by the football bug. He works for an investment firm or in the headquarters of a big corporation in New York, or for an insurance or automobile company, or an advertising agency. Some are doctors. These fans go to all the Giants games; they read a lot about football; they know a lot about football. Some of them have become good friends of mine, and I see a good deal of them socially. It was through one of them that, one weekend in June of 1969, I was invited to a cocktail party at the apartment of Dr. Frank Sirotnak on East End Avenue.

It was an ordinary, rather quiet cocktail party with maybe thirty men and women, some married and some single. Most of the men were the sort of football fan I've just described.

I hadn't been at the party very long when I noticed an extremely pretty blonde, neither tall nor short. The second thing about her that struck me was how gracefully she moved.

She moved like an athlete, easily and naturally, with a nice swing, and she had a wonderful tan. After a while she started looking around for her pocketbook, which turned out to be on a table behind me. When she came over to get it, I told her what a nice tan she had and asked her what she did.

"I'm a professional golfer," she said.

I believed her.

"What do you do?"

"I'm a professional football player," I said, and she broke into peals of laughter. She didn't believe me. It didn't really help my ego to find out, later, that she'd never even heard of me. We talked for a couple of minutes and then she drifted away and I drifted away. But I noticed that every time I looked across the room at her, she looked at me. Actually, I found out from someone at the party, she was a stewardess for Eastern Airlines, but she never told anyone that at parties. "If you tell a man at a party that you're a stewardess," she explained, "he figures that you're dumb, and easy. I always tell them either that I'm a pro golfer, or that I work in the Nedick's at Broadway and 42nd Street."

Toward the end of the party we found ourselves together again and we exchanged names, though we both already knew them. Her name was Kathy Sauer. There were two other couples standing around and one of the guys said: "Let's go over to my place and have a couple of drinks and something to eat." So we got into two cabs and went over to his place on 53rd Street. When it was getting late and time to leave, Kathy had a flight out the next morning, I offered to take her home. Another girl at the party horned in on the ride, but we took her home first. Then I took Kathy home—she lived in an apartment on East End Avenue. I got her phone number and walked her to the elevators in the lobby and slapped her on the back and said:

"I'll see you again, kid."

To a girl who was used to wrestling off dates, this was a surprise. I'm not sure her jaw didn't drop. Then I went off to Bermuda for ten days and didn't call her for almost two weeks. That was on a Wednesday, and I made a date for Friday.

I'd been going around with a lot of different girls up to then, and they all had different styles. I used to take them to the kind of places I figured suited them. There's one kind of girl you take to P. J. Clarke's, and another kind you take to the Persian Room. As a rule, they don't mix. I decided it was nothing but the best for Kathy and took her to Raffles, which is a private club in the basement of the Sherry-Netherlands Hotel. She didn't seem too much impressed—at least, not as much as her roommate. When I took Kathy home, her roommate came into the living room and asked where we had been.

"To a place called Raffles," Kathy said.

The roommate looked at me.

"Do you know someone who's a member?" she asked. I said I was a member, and she said: "Gee, I didn't know they had football players as members."

Maybe that impressed Kathy, I don't know.

Anyhow, we had dates three nights running, and even then I was pretty sure I was going to ask her to marry me. It's a strange thing. You want to get married, but it's going to be a whole new world. I was perfectly happy as I was. I *liked* being a bachelor and not exactly swinging around New York, that isn't my type, but having a great time. Getting married means a whole new kind of life, all sorts of things that are different. You're not on your own any more. You can't come and go as you please, and yet, I knew I wanted to marry Kathy.

I solved all this by going off to training camp in Fairfield. Kathy kept on flying for Eastern, and I played a whole season of football. Of course, we saw each other as much as we could, all through the fall and all through the winter. We'd even talked about marriage—the "if-we-got-married" routine, but that was as far as it got.

What precipitated my proposal was an Eastern Airlines bomb scare.

At this time Kathy was senior stewardess on those horrible night coach flights to Puerto Rico. This particular flight was to leave Kennedy Airport at midnight, and Kathy was at the airport at 11 P.M. About half of the 200 passengers had boarded the plane when the captain came back to her and said there was a report that there was a bomb on board. The passengers all had to get off. An Eastern Airlines agent came aboard and said that the stewardesses—all eight of them—should start looking for the bomb. The captain said no. He said that the entire crew would go to the crew's lounge in the airport and leave bomb-hunting to people who knew what they were doing.

After forty-five minutes, the agent came into the crew lounge and said that no bomb had been found, the flight was to get under way. So the crew went back on, and the passengers were loaded aboard. All this time, Kathy had been getting more and more worried. Forty-five minutes seemed an awfully short time to search a whole aircraft and all its luggage for anything as small as a bomb could be. She checked with the agent and found that none of the hand luggage had been searched. In addition, there was a ton-and-a-half of mail aboard, and that hadn't been checked, either.

Kathy said the hell with it, and simply led all her girls back off the plane. She went home via Carey limousine, getting there about 3 A.M. At 6 A.M. the phone rang. It was the Eastern supervisor, telling Kathy that she and all her girls were suspended until the case—refusing to obey an order to take off—could be investigated.

The next afternoon, when I called Kathy's apartment, I was greeted with a flood of words, explanations, demands for justification, and everything else.

She was thoroughly shaken up and so was I, though not as much, naturally. There's nothing for keeping your cool over a bomb scare like having been fifteen miles away. So I drove over to see her, and took her out in the car, and proposed.

She accepted. This was on St. Patrick's Day in 1970. One thing that pleased her, and I guess made her know this wasn't a spur-of-the-moment thing, was what she found when I took her to my apartment. She'd been helping me decorate it, and a few weeks earlier we had been driving around New Hope, Pennsylvania. In an antique shop she had seen a table that she told me would be "just perfect" for my place. Later, I had driven down there, bought it, and brought it back. So, when she came to my place, there was the table as an engagement present.

Telling her father wasn't the easiest thing in the world, I don't know why. He's a hospital administrator, and a very nice guy. But I didn't know exactly how to do it, and I kept putting it off. Finally one evening, Kathy insisted. So, after dinner we drove over to Plainfield, New Jersey, where her parents lived, and didn't get there until about eleven o'clock. Her parents had already gone up to bed, but her father came down in his pajamas, slippers, and bathrobe, half asleep.

I had gotten my courage all screwed up to just the right pitch, and I started off right away:

"Mr. Sauer, I have something to tell you."

He paid absolutely no attention.

Yawning, he moved straight into the kitchen.

"Let's get something to eat," he said.

Not exactly the reception a tense man wants.

Kathy and I followed him out. He started puttering around in the refrigerator, yawning and talking about what was new with Kathy and the stewardess business, asking me how the Giants were going to do that year, and I kept muttering, Mr. Sauer, I have something to tell you. He paid no attention whatsoever.

Finally I took him by the shoulder.

"Mr. Sauer," I said. "How would you like a football player for a son-in-law?"

"Oh, my God," he said. At least I had gotten him awake. He shook my hand, and turned back to the refrigerator. "This calls for beer," he said. "No, by God, champagne!"

Kathy and I were married on May 30th in the Crescent Avenue Presbyterian Church in Plainfield. Because she's a Protestant, the officiating minister was the church pastor, Dr. Charles Mead, and because I'm a Catholic, also officiating was Father Benedict Dudley, the chaplain for the Giants.

Two things I remember about the ceremony.

Dr. Mead had been explaining all the details in advance, including the fact that in this ceremony, instead of saying

"I do," I was supposed to say "I will." I told Kathy I wasn't too fond of that. She said:

"We can change it if you want. But what's wrong with 'I will'?"

"Because I'm Hungarian," I said. "When I say it, it comes out 'I vill.' "

And afterward she told me:

"All my life I swore that when I got married and got rid of the name of Sauer, I was going to have a nice, simple, Anglo-Saxon name like Brewster or something. And what do I trade Sauer for? Gogolak!"

After the ceremony, we took a limousine back to New York, to the Plaza. The next day we went to Hawaii for our honeymoon.

That's one thing about marrying an airline stewardess, men. The tickets were $3 per person each way. We spent all the rest of our honeymoon money treating ourselves in Hawaii.

We started the 1970 season with a players' strike. The NFLPA (National Football League Players Association) had been negotiating with the owners for some time, basically for better pensions and better pay for pre-season games. (Medical and dental benefits were also involved.) The thing that had been griping the older players was that baseball players had worked out a much better pension deal, and the thing that had been griping the younger players was the exhibition pay scale. For exhibition games then there was a sliding scale based on years of experience, starting with $70 a game for a first-year man, and going up in steps of $70 until you reached a maximum of $350 for a five-year man.

I wasn't actively involved with the Players Association. None of the Giant veterans really were, because Mr. Mara was always pretty good to us and we had no argument with the Giants. But since we were all members of the NFLPA, we decided that we'd go along with the association and not show up at training camp. There wasn't any meeting about this, since we all were at our homes hundreds and maybe thousands of miles away when we got the letters telling us about the strike, but everybody seemed to adopt the same general attitude:

"Everybody else is going to be out, how can I show up?"

When the Giant training camp opened, only a handful of guys showed, draft choices and free agents. This situation continued for two weeks, with the Giant veterans at home getting more and more restive. More and more they began to feel, hell, I'm a football player, let's play football. More and more, I began to feel so edgy that I don't know how Kathy put up with me.

Finally, the strike was settled—the players didn't get all they wanted, but they vastly improved the pension deal—and we all showed up for training.

The strike proved one theory of mine. If you keep yourself in shape, you don't need five weeks in a training camp to get ready for the season. I know the coaches need it to look at the rookies and free agents, but for even a second-year veteran, in shape, you don't really need more than three weeks. Players today are a lot more conscious of their bodies than they were even in the days when I first started playing. Football players still like to eat—I'm one of the leaders in this field—but nowadays, in the off season, they get on the scales every three or four days and if they find themselves ballooning, they just force themselves onto a diet. The player who shows up thirty pounds overweight today knows that the only laughs he's going to get will come from the reporters, who have nothing to do with paying his salary.

When we finally started training, we found out—it took us a week or two to realize this—that the Giants, during the off-season, had made themselves one hell of a trade.

To the general surprise of the reporters and the fans, the Giants had traded Homer Jones to Cleveland. Homer had seemed a Giant fixture, nobody like him. Homer's problem, as far as his quarterback was concerned, was his talent for improvisation. The Giants have as many pass patterns as the next team but suddenly, as Homer lined up waiting for the ball to be snapped, he'd decide that none of these pass patterns suited his mood and he was going to do something different. No one, including Homer, knew what this "something different" was going to be.

Tarkenton told me that in moments of stress he'd simply shut his eyes, throw the ball as hard as he could to where Homer might conceivably be aiming for, and yell:

"Heeeyyy, Homer!"

"You know," Tarkenton said, "it's amazing how often he was there."

Homer had been around a lot before he came up to the Giants in 1964, but all the time I was on the team, the program listed Homer's age as twenty-nine. Never a year older.

Maybe he wasn't getting older on the program, but he wasn't fooling his legs. Sometimes Tarkenton would yell Hey, Homer, and Homer would be a half stride away from the ball. That's enough.

At any rate, Homer went to Cleveland and in return the

Giants got two players who turned out to be real nuggets. (The Giants also got a linebacker named Wayne Meylan, who wasn't.) The first was Jim Kanicki, a six foot four, 270 pound defensive tackle who had been the Browns' No. 2 draft choice out of Michigan State. The other was Ron Johnson, the Browns' No. 1 draft choice from the University of Michigan in '69.

All I have to say about Johnson is that in his first year with the Giants, he became the first back in the history of the team to gain over 1,000 yards.

I don't think even the Giant front office knows how they ended up with Johnson.

One story I heard is that the Giants really wanted Kanicki, to shore up the defense, and they were willing to give up Homer just for him, but they wanted more for Homer—standard operating procedure in trading. The Browns said Meylan, and the Giants said *that* wasn't enough.

So, according to the story, the Browns' guy said:

"What about Johnson?"

Now, the Browns had three or four guys named Johnson on the roster, and the Giants' guy didn't even ask which one. He had gotten another player in the deal, which was what he wanted, and that was enough for him. So he said, okay.

So, the Giants got Ron Johnson.

As far as I was concerned personally, there were three other changes at the start of the '70 season, none of them as important as the Kanicki-Johnson trade.

The first was that I had changed my style of training. I was sick and tired of my performance in the '69 season, and I decided to do something drastic. I was getting into my late twenties, and I just felt that I didn't have the "pop" in my leg that I used to have. "Pop" means you don't just kick a football, you kick it with such power that the minute you hit it, it goes "pop" exactly where you want it to. It's a great feeling. It comes from power, and my formula is that strength and speed, in equal proportions, equal power. I don't think I had lost any strength in my leg—at least, it felt as strong as it always had—but the "pop" was gone.

Since there's no way to play soccer in the off-season in the United States, which I would have loved to do, what I did mostly was run. I was not one for much weightlifting because trainers had told me that, while weightlifting develops your muscles and your strength, it takes away from your flexibility. A good part of place kicking depends on the "feel" of the ball, just as in soccer, or punting. If you get your leg so musclebound that you don't have the "feel" of the ball, you won't be able to kick it right. You'd have to kick the ball just as hard as you could every time to make sure that you had enough power. This might be all right for a conventional kicker, but in soccer-style kicking, where you're swinging your foot in an arc—like the head of a golf club—the ball can hook or slice on you, just as a golf ball can. So, in soccer-style kicking, if you're in close, say kicking from the 22-yard line, and you hit the ball as hard as you can, it may slice right off into the stands. Weight-lifting, I felt, could be perfect for a lineman, or even a fullback, where you need every ounce of power you can get in your legs, but not for me.

I decided to stick basically with running, somewhat spurred on by a letter I got from Webster in the off-season (all the players got them, I wasn't singled out for this honor) saying that on the first day in training camp, Webster and the coaches were going to put the players on the running track to see how far each one could run in twelve minutes.

That was fine with me. In March, I started going up to the Yankee Stadium to use the running track, where seven laps around the track is one and three-quarters miles. I had moved into my apartment at 84th Street and Second Avenue by this time (though I wasn't married to Kathy yet) and it was pretty convenient.

Except for the fact that the Yankees were still playing baseball. Sometimes I practically had to fight my way into the dressing room if their game had gone into extra innings. I got to know the Yankee schedule as well as their players did. The Giants have a year-round training office at the Stadium, manned by John Dziegiel, though nothing like the year-round training complex that Kansas City and some of the other teams maintain. They tell us that when the Giants move to Jersey, they'll have real year-round facilities for us to train at, which will be great for guys like me who live around the metropolitan area.

That year the Giants had bought a thing called "The Universal Gym," which contained every known device for building up your strength. Weights, bars, pulleys, you name it, it was there. I decided to try that out, and for the first time, I tried a little weightlifting. Not much, but some. I'm something of a nut on physical conditioning, not the way Joe Don Looney was, but something, and I'd heard that doing nothing but running develops runner's muscles the way a swimmer develops a swimmer's muscles—long and graceful. Not built for instant power.

After four months of running two miles a day and doing some weightlifting, I felt absolutely great. My leg felt as strong as it ever had. I hadn't been able to do much kicking, but I knew inside myself that the "pop" would be there. It was, too.

I started by saying that there were three things different in the '70 season. The first was my training; the second was that we were established in training on the campus of C. W. Post College in Brookville, Long Island, much easier to get to from Manhattan than Fairfield was. The third was that Webster decided to give up having the team, on the night before a home game, stay at the Summit Hotel at Lexington Avenue and 51st Street. The Summit was where Sherman put us. We always had a light Saturday afternoon practice at the Stadium, then we got into the bus for Manhattan. The Summit was big and brassy, with plenty of noise, and right in the middle of things. Webster thought it had "too many distractions." He changed us to the Doral, a tiny, quiet, French-staffed hotel at Park Avenue and 39th Street. We stayed there every home game, but the little Frenchman at the desk never seemed to be able to get used to the sight of forty football players coming into his lobby.

"Messieurs, messieurs," he kept clucking at us.

Another thing Webster changed: When Sherman had us stay at the Summit, we all had to have dinner together in the big commercial-type dining room. The dining room at the Doral probably could have handled us, but what high-class hotel wants forty football players taking up half the space, all of them wanting nothing more than a thick steak or two with potatoes, vegetables, salad, and milk? Webster gave us meal money—ten bucks. Eat anywhere, provided you were back in your room at 11 P.M. Ernie Koy, Tommy Longo, and I always went to the Pen & Pencil because I had become good friends with John Bruno, the owner. If you have to keep in shape, a problem with being the friend of a restaurant owner is that you keep having more food put in front of you. Koy and Longo and I would finally tell them to stop, and we'd get back to the hotel. Rosy Brown and Jim Katcavage were the checking coaches then. They had the master key from the desk and a little after eleven you could count on the door being opened, without so much as a rap, and there would be one of those monsters peeking at you. If you'd managed to hide what they called an "unauthorized person" in the room, it was no time for her to giggle.

In the morning Father Dudley would have an 8 o'clock low mass in one of the hotel conference rooms. You didn't have to be a Catholic to go to the mass, but I guess a lot of the non-Catholics were self-conscious about it. "If the team won the week before," Father Dudley said once, "I have about ten players at the service. If it lost, I have twenty. It's miraculous what losing a football game does for religion."

Of course, Wellington Mara was always at the service with Mrs. Mara, and some of their children, a few of the coaches and trainers, and maybe a couple of newspapermen.

Then, at 9 A.M., we had breakfast. At this hour the Doral would get it up—juice, fruit, cereal, eggs, steak. Some guys eat breakfast as if they hadn't eaten for a week; some have maybe a glass of juice and a cup of coffee. In all the time I knew Fran Tarkenton on the team, I never saw him eat breakfast on the day of a game.

About Sunday at breakfast the tension starts building up. Dinner Saturday night it was all jokes and laughter. Now, suddenly, almost quiet. The bus always left the hotel promptly at 11—the game started at 1 P.M.—and I mean *left*.

If you weren't on the bus, you got yourself a taxi out to the Stadium plus a lot of conversation later about what had happened. Some of the guys would have the trainers start taping them up before we left the hotel so there wouldn't be so much to do when they got to the field.

Eleven o'clock on a Sunday morning on Park Avenue has to be one of the quietest times of the week. Very few cars, only the occasional toot of a horn. Very few people except perhaps an elderly couple going to church or coming back, and a doorman or two walking a dog. Nothing else. The only excitement we ever had getting on the bus was once in '70 when a great big defensive end of ours named John Baker, who had come down from Canada, came out of the hotel carrying a very high-class looking attache case. All you ever needed for overnight at the hotel was a pair of clean socks, clean underwear, a clean shirt, and a shaving kit. Most guys just jammed all this into one of those little airline kit bags, but here was John with his attache case, and just as he started to get on the bus, he tripped, the case fell, and it flew open. Besides his underclothes, John had about five different kinds of deodorant: spray, rub-on, stick; he had two bottles of cologne, and two bottles of whisky. Half-pints, I grant you, but two bottles of whisky and all that deodorant on a bus to the Stadium?

At any rate, to get back to the '70 season, we started off by losing the first three games as I've already explained. Sounds like the same old story as '69? It wasn't, though. Somehow, this year, we had that *feeling* that we were going to win. The spirit I was talking about.

We felt that we had everything going for us. Besides the bright spots of Ron Johnson and Jim Kanicki, our No. 1

draft choice, Jim Files out of Oklahoma, won the middle linebacking spot, and Bob Tucker, a free agent who had been cut by both the Boston Patriots (in 1968) and the Philadelphia Eagles (in '69) suddenly emerged as the damndest pass-catching tight end you ever saw. He was the third best receiver on the Giants that year, with forty catches for nearly 600 yards and five touchdowns. In addition to that, Tucker Frederickson was having one of his healthy years, and wouldn't miss a single game. Our defense wasn't the toughest in the League, but it was better than it had been for a long, long time.

We lost our first game against Chicago, 24-16, though we might have won it with a little luck. We were leading, 13-10 at half time, but the Bears scored a touchdown in the third quarter and again in the fourth. As for myself, I felt pretty good. I kicked three field goals, one of them for 45 yards. The "pop" was back in my leg.

Then we lost the Dallas game, 28-10, and there was no way we could have won that one. Again, we were leading 10-0 at the half, but in the second half Dallas just ran us off the field. They scored 14 points in the third quarter and 14 more in the fourth. We were just simply outplayed.

The third game we should have won, and the game films proved it. Everyone who saw that game live on television or on film afterward knows it.

New Orleans was leading us, 14-10, late in the fourth quarter, when Tarkenton threw a perfect pass to Aaron Thomas in the end zone for a touchdown. What the New Orleans management had done that year, however, was to paint a bright green strip, much brighter than the grass. One yard wide, *inside* the sidelines in both end zones, between the goal line and the end zone marker. When Thomas caught the ball, he came down on this green strip. There wasn't a New Orleans player within yards of him, so Aaron slammed down the ball, and there was our touchdown, we thought.

What we forgot was that no official alive is going to call a play in New Orleans that will mean the home team will lose if he can help it. The New Orleans stadium is one of the worst in the country to play in. In the first place, especially this early in the season, it's so damned hot you think you'll never get through the game. A temperature of 100 degrees on the playing field is nothing down there. In the second place the stands at the end zones are so close to the playing field that the fans can practically spit on you.

So, when Thomas caught Tarkenton's pass and scored, the official simply ruled that he was out of bounds. There was one official who wasn't going to be running for his life.

When we had the regular Tuesday meeting, I've never seen so many frustrated men. Even Webster seemed bewildered. He gave us his "little talk," and he was pretty damned raunchy, but he also talked as if he were a little baffled.

We ran and re-ran the game films over and over and they always showed the same thing: there was Aaron Thomas with the ball on the green stripe the New Orleans types had put down, a good yard inside the sideline, and there was the linesman, a solid twenty yards back up the field, running down and signaling that Thomas was out of bounds.

I'll admit it wasn't a perfect game on our part. We should have been two touchdowns ahead of them and then there would have been no question. But we had won the game, there was no question about that.

And that was what led to our feeling of frustration at the

meeting. We *were* playing good ball. Everybody was putting out, we had no real injuries, and still we were losing.

Well, we went through the week with the knowledge that *something* had to change. We were just playing too good ball not to start winning.

We did. We beat Philadelphia the next Sunday, 30-23. Ron Johnson had two great runs, one for 34 yards and one for 68 yards, both for touchdowns, and Bobby Duhon ran back a punt 45 yards for another. I had a couple of respectable field goals, one of 40 yards and one of 45, so I contributed a total of nine points. (With the three PATs.)

I'll tell you one thing about playing Philadelphia, and Pittsburgh, too. They're the two roughest teams in the league; physically rough. You can win from them, but you come out of the game feeling like you've been through a meat grinder. Dallas or the Vikings will out-cute you and out-fox you and out-finesse you, but with the Eagles and the Steelers it's just one long afternoon of assault and battery. Guys come out of those games—not me, thank God—bleeding and bruised and aching in every muscle. The trainers' room looks like a hospital ward. I think it was that first Philadelphia game that Scott Eaton was hurt, and we lost him for three or four games in the defensive backfield.

After we beat the Eagles, we won five more games in a row, and we were right up there in contention for the Eastern title in the National Conference. We were in it up to the final game, as a matter of fact.

After the Philadelphia win, we beat the Boston Patriots with little trouble, 16-0. I had three short field goals (the longest was 22 yards) and, of course, a PAT for a total of 10 points.

I was on my way to my best season with the Giants—one of my best seasons ever. I ended up as the Giants' leading scorer with 107 points, and set a Giant record for the most points scored by any player in a single season. (It also brought me up to third in all-time points scoring for the Giants, with a career total of 374. I was 25 for 41 in field goal completions that year, and 32 for 32 in the PAT department.

We beat St. Louis 35-17 with Tucker taking two touchdown passes from Tarkenton. All I had was five PATs.

We beat the Jets, 22-10, then we played Dallas, for the second time, at the Stadium.

This is the game I described in Chapter One, so I won't go back over it again except to say that in this game the defense was really clicking again. The Dallas backfield combination of Calvin Hill and Duane Thomas was one of the most formidable groundgaining outfits in all of pro ball, but our defense held Hill to 26 yards and Thomas to 23. On top of that, the defense dropped Craig Morton four times for losses totaling 30 yards.

By the time the game was over, we were all on Cloud 9.

The next game was against Washington, and we won a squeaker, doing away with the talk about the Giants being a first-half team. We had to come from behind to win that one. We were trailing 33-14 at the end of the third quarter, but Tarkenton went to work. He got one touchdown on a 71-yard drive, then in the very next series he hit Frederickson with a 57-yard bomb, and the score was 33-28. Then Tarkenton went 73 yards in eleven plays, and we had this game, too.

The dream of finishing with an eleven-three record, or at the very least ten-four, began to look a little shaky in our next game. We lost to Philadelphia, 23-20. We could have won it and we should have won it, but we got a series of those breaks that, if you let them, will drive you straight up the wall.

After the really first-rate, championship-caliber ball we'd been playing for weeks, listen to this for a record in the Philadelphia game: We fumbled four times, with the Eagles recovering three of them. We let Billy Walik run back two kickoffs (I know, I know, who gets half the blame for that?) for 45 and 57 yards. One of the runbacks set up a touchdown and the other a field goal. And then, to put the icing on the cake, we got a bad pass from center over the head of Bill Johnson, who was back to punt, and the Eagles recovered on our 1-yard line. Maybe I shouldn't have said we "should" have won that game. We could have won, yes, but with mistakes like that, you couldn't beat Harvard.

I'll pass over what Webster had to say after that game. It seems only fair to all concerned.

We got back on the winning side in the next game against Washington, just barely. We were leading by 24-10 at the end of the third quarter, but ol' Sonny Jurgensen came back with two touchdown drives, and brought the Redskins to a 24-24 tie. Then Willie Williams made an interception for us, and gave us the ball on our own 49-yard line. Tarkenton gave the ball to Bobby Duhon, and he went 38 yards off tackle. That got us within field goal range, and I made it. We came out of that winners, 27-24.

We won our next game against my old team, the Bills, without any trouble. As I've said, the Bills had begun to go downhill steadily after the '65 season. The first half was something of a struggle. The only scoring was on field goals, one by me and two by the Buffalo kicker, Grant Guthrie. But in the second half we came awake again. Fran Tarkenton again staged two of his drives for 77 yards and 74, and Ron Johnson had another of his 100-yard days. The defense had a good day, so good that Spider Lockhart was named the NFL defensive player of the week. Four times, on the safety blitz, he dumped the Buffalo quarterback.

The game was our eighth win, and no matter what happened from then on, we would have a winning season, our first since '63. And we still had a crack at the title. God, how we started thinking back. If the New Orleans game hadn't been stolen from us, and if we hadn't blown the Philadelphia game, we now would have won ten, and we would have been unbeatable for the division title.

The game against the Cardinals the next week put us back on Cloud 9. St. Louis was the division leader, and we knocked them off in what baseball players call a "laughter." Unlike the Eagles game, we couldn't do anything wrong. At one point in the second quarter, we led 21-0. The Cardinals hit a place kick in the second quarter to make the half time score 21-3. In the second half I hit two field goals, one in the third quarter for 27 yards and one in the fourth for 46, and Tarkenton threw a touchdown pass to Ron Johnson. The final score: Good guys, 34, the bad guys, 17. This was the game in which I was officially credited with my first tackle in professional football.

From Lou Saban on, through Sherman and Webster, the rule had been for me never to go downfield after a kickoff, just drift back and be safety. I've already explained, there are just enough guys in football looking for the cheap shot so that the kicker's proper place is away from the action.

So, I had kicked off against the Cardinals and was drifting back, positive I had kicked the ball far enough so it wouldn't be run back. Suddenly I realized that MacArthur Lane had not only taken the ball but, worse than that, he was bringing it out.

MacArthur Lane was not only the most ferocious running back on the Cardinals, he was one of the most ferocious in all football. Six feet four, 240 pounds, and fast. He'd gotten by our whole team and he was on his way. The only man between him and the goal line was me. I realized this because I looked behind me for help, and there was none. I was the only Giant there. The crowd was suddenly silent. I had to make the tackle—me, the only guy on the field in a clean uniform, with no hip, thigh, or shoulder pads. I decided, what the hell, hit him low, make him stumble, maybe help will come. Under no circumstances was I about to try to tackle him head on.

MacArthur was about eight yards away from me and decided he would make a quick cut around me. That should have been no problem, I ran the hundred in 13 seconds, and I'm not quick. He started to plant one foot for his cut, and the foot came right down on my kicking tee. The foot twisted, he tripped and slammed into me, already falling to the ground, and I fell down on top of him. Everybody in the stadium, including the coaches, thought I had made the tackle. Nobody knew the truth except me and MacArthur Lane.

The plane trip home from that game was one of the things that makes life worth living. You know, you fly home from a game like the New Orleans one, and the plane is a flying morgue. Everybody's sour, nobody wants to talk to anybody, the slightest comment and you get your head snapped off.

All you want to do is to be left alone, to look out the window and wait for the trip to be over.

After you win—especially when you knock off the division leaders—the plane trip home is a short hop to Heaven. Jokes, gags, everybody roaming around, slapping each other on the back, going back over the game play by play—"Man, you remember that time it was third and four . . ."—happy as you can be. On our charter flights home the beer is always free, and after a game like that it disappears by the case. And the poor stewardesses, they should get combat pay.

It's funny what winning does for a pro team. I think we'd had the spirit since the first St. Louis game. We were winners. Just the way when you're losing, nothing goes right, everybody's on edge looking for somebody else to blame until the whole team is nothing but a bunch of scapegoats. When you're winning, everyone's a hero. You drop a pass, or fumble, or miss a field goal on a losing team, and you're the world's biggest slob. And everybody lets you know it. "If you hadn't . . ." You do the same thing on a winning team, and it's nothing. A little slip anybody could make. "Don't let it get you down, kid. What the hell, I remember once . . ."

It was that way with the winning Giants. We began to have informal parties, something we'd never had up to that time while I'd been on the team. The offensive linemen used to get together once a week, just to sit around and drink beer. Guys on the team used to call you up. "The wife and I are having a couple of people in tomorrow night, and we wondered . . ." A warm feeling. A good feeling.

I guess the last game of the season was inevitable. As I said, if we had the New Orleans game or the Philadelphia game on our side, the last game wouldn't have made any difference.

We played the Rams at New York, and we'd seldom been colder. The Rams had seldom been hotter. I scored the first points in the game, a 42-yard field goal in the first five minutes, but from then on, we might as well have been in Chillicothe. Roman Gabriel passed us dizzy; Pat Studstill, Les Josephson and Willie Ellison had a field day running. We ended up on the short end of 31-3, out of the division title race. There was no dancing with the stewardesses in the aisles this time.

When we'd licked our wounds, we began to feel a little better. The season hadn't been all that bad—in fact, in retrospect, it had been a hell of a good season. We'd won nine games, which was more than we'd won since the championship days of Allie Sherman, giving us a nine-five record. We ranked fourth offensively in the National Football Conference, second in pass defense—and fifth in rushing defense. Johnson gained a total of 1514 yards (he caught 48 passes for 487 yards to go with his 1,027 yards rushing), and Fran Tarkenton had the best season ever in his ten-year career, with 219 passes completed out of 389 attempted, for a 56.3 percent average and 2,777 yards. He ranked third in the conference. Tucker Frederickson was our No. 2 rusher, with 375 yards, and he got 408 more yards catching passes. Oh, it was great. We had a damned good team, and we all said, wait till next year.

CHAPTER ELEVEN

Year of Disaster

The next year, in 1971, we were five wins and nine losses.
What happened to us?

Everything.

The first thing was the hassle between Tarkenton and
Mara. I don't know all the ins and outs of that, but I do know
that we flew out to Houston to play our first exhibition game
of the season in the Astrodome, and the night before the
game, Fran checked out of the motel we were staying in and
flew back to Atlanta without a word to anyone.

All of us on the team knew that Fran, besides being one of
the finest quarterbacks in football—he was the fifth-ranking
all time pro quarterback at this time—was also a hard-work-
ing business man. He had a lot of real estate interests in and
around Atlanta, Georgia, where he lived; he had a fast-food
chain called "Scrambler's Delight" which, unlike Joe Namath's ill-fated venture with the "Broadway Joe's" hamburger chain, was actually making money; he was in a business
that sold electronic teaching aids to school systems, and he
headed a foundation that taught skills to the underprivileged.

227

This foundation had received a $2-million grant from the Federal government, so I assume it was a pretty big operation.

At any rate Fran had decided that, instead of keeping after the Giants for a raise in salary every year, he wanted a loan from them. The newspaper reporters speculated that it was as high as $500,000, but half that was a more realistic figure. Fran had precedent on his side. Two or three other pro football team managements had made big loans to top-rank quarterbacks.

It was simple business. If your salary is $100,000 a year—which Fran's was in 1970—you're hell and gone up in the upper salary bracket tax squeeze. On the other hand, if you get a $100,000 loan, you pay $6,000 a year interest, at 6 percent, which you can deduct at a rate of 70 percent on your income tax, so you are only spending $1,800 a year of your own money for the loan. In the meanwhile, of course, you have the money.

None of us on the team realized that Fran had come up with this proposal to Wellington Mara, and that after the practice at C. W. Post on the previous Friday, Mara told Fran that he'd been all through all the business about the loan with the lawyers for the Giants and because of the team's corporate structure, the loan was impossible.

Apparently Fran brooded about this all the way to Houston—naturally without telling anyone on the team—because the next thing that happened, according to what we heard afterward, was that after Sunday practice in Houston, Fran again broached the subject to Mara and told him that he thought the loan was essential. Mara said no again. Then Fran said he thought he'd better go back to Atlanta.

"Do you need me to play against the Oilers?" he asked.

Mara said no.

I guess Mara's feeling was that it would be better to get this straightened out, once and for all.

At any rate Fran left without a word, and the official announcement was given to us at the dinner we were eating in the motel at 4 P.M., only a few hours before the game.

Most of us felt as if the bottom had dropped out of the club. Fran had done a great deal to make the season the year before. Certainly he couldn't have done it by himself, he had to have the playing he got, but without him we wouldn't have had the record we did, and we knew it.

The second major thing that ruined us in the '71 season was injuries.

Even in practice, and before, the injuries had started to hit us.

Our great '70 runner, Ron Johnson—a dedicated ball player, the kind I like best—had hurt his leg so bad playing basketball during the off-season that he had to have an operation. (I got a letter from the Giants early in 1972—all the players did—saying that the team wanted to do everything it could do discourage its players from getting involved with basketball, and that it would no longer regard off-season basketball injuries as coming under its medical plan.)

Junior Coffey was hurt. He was a top running back. He had been a Most Valuable Player for the Atlanta Falcons before the Giants got him in a trade in 1969 and he'd gained 722 in each of two successive seasons. But he'd cracked his Achilles tendon in spring training for the Giants in '70, and had sat out the entire season. Now he was hurt again.

Don Hermann, our wide receiver who'd had such a great

season in '70 had broken his shoulder in training. Tucker Frederickson was hurt.

Oh, the start of a beautiful season! I never realized that the human body could get racked up so many ways, especially the human knee. I think the Giants had eleven knee operations that season. The human knee is not adapted to play pro football, and the orthopedic specialist who invents a device that will allow the knee to move back and forth with complete flexibility but will prevent it from cracking when it's hit sideways has a fortune waiting for him. Not a device that guarantees against a popped knee, just one that will give you a fifty-fifty chance of walking off the field after you've been hit, instead of being carried.

So, we'd gone out to the Houston game without Johnson, Frederickson, Coffey, Hermann, and, to put the icing on the cake, without Les Shy, who was Hermann's replacement and who had then gotten himself hurt in practice.

And now we didn't have Tarkenton.

We were a great team as we took the field. This was the first time we'd ever played Houston and the first time we'd ever played in the Astrodome. It should have been a big deal, one of the top teams from the old NFL come West, playing in the Astrodome and all that. It wasn't. I think subconsciously we expected to lose, and we did.

Houston beat us, 35-6, and the fact that our points were made on our two field goals didn't make me feel once ounce better. We played horribly. The defense was worse than the year before, and the offense couldn't get untracked. Tarkenton's replacements were Dick Shiner, and a kid named Ed Baker from LaFayette who had been picked up in 1970 as free agent, and who had spent the '70 season on the taxi squad.

Shiner probably had the worst play of the day only because it was so obvious. He was trying to pass; the defense got through and a Houston linebacker named George Webster took the ball right out of his hands and ran it in for a touchdown. (It went into the game record as an intercepted pass.)

But there's no sense in picking on Shiner; we were all terrible. The trip home was like the flying morgue I mentioned. The worst part of it was still Tarkenton. We still didn't know whether he would come back or not, though he was under contract to the Giants.

I also foresaw problems for myself during the year: Fran was slated to do the holding for me. I belong one thousand percent to the school of thought that a playing quarterback should not do the holding for a place kicker—certainly not for a soccer-style kicker like myself.

One half of my reason, as I've explained, is that I don't see how the playing quarterback can utterly, totally, and completely switch his mind from quarterbacking to holding. The second half of the reason is that the playing quarterback can't practice enough. It's only reasonable. You can't expect a first-string quarterback, in practice, to take the time off from his primary job to practice holding for a place kicker. But again, especially with a soccer-style kicker, the timing for the holder is of the utmost importance. If it isn't honed down to the last hundredth of a second, the kicker is in trouble.

My holder turned out to be the least of our troubles in '71, however. Or of mine, either.

The Tarkenton-Mara hassle was fixed up on Thursday of that week, at least on the surface. Fran flew into New York to tape a couple of television shows, and he came out to C. W. Post College—he left his luggage in his hotel in New York, that's how uncertain he was—for a two-and-a-half hour talk with Mara.

Fran came out first and then Mara, and both said that Fran had signed for the season. The newspaper figure was $125,000, which is probably right.

The hassle wasn't really fixed up, though, under the surface. I somehow have the feeling still that Mara—who, among other things, is a stubborn, hard-nosed Irishman—felt deep down that he shouldn't have taken Tarkenton back. Sink or swim without him, would be my guess on Mara's instinct.

And I can't help but feel that it affected Tarkenton's attitude, too. Not that he didn't put out a hundred percent. But he was an established star with ten years of topnotch playing behind him. He didn't have to prove anything. If he had quit football his name would still be up there in the record books and everybody would know who Fran Tarkenton was. And he had publicly lost a fight with the management, one that had gotten headlines from coast to coast. Fran was tougher and edgier that season than I'd ever seen him in my life.

And the damned injuries continued to murder us. We drafted a guy as a back-up for Tucker Frederickson who later turned out to be a great football player—Charlie Evans, a six foot one, 215-pound running back (and blocker) out of USC. In training nobody even expected him to make the team (he was a 14th draft choice), but he did, and he was doing a top job. Boom. Hit hard from the side, out for the season.

We drafted a guy named Coleman Zeno, a six foot four, 210-pound wide receiver from Grambling, 17th-round choice, nobody ever expected him to make the team. He'll be another great one. Runs the 40 in 4.5 seconds, caught two touchdown passes in our first game. Following Tuesday. Practice. Hit. Broken arm. Boom. Our for the season.

I could go on, but I won't.

Our exhibition game after the Houston fiasco was another fiasco. Against the New England Patriots, as they now were officially named, in their brand new stadium at Foxboro, Massachusetts, a thriving metropolis of some three thousand souls located halfway between Boston and Providence. The stadium was one of those things that developers think up. As far as I could see, all they'd forgotten was to put in any access roads. It was the opening game for the new stadium, and at half time the announcer said that the jam of cars outside still trying to get in should be cleared up in time for everybody to be able to start home after the game was over.

Maybe the reason I've dwelt on the traffic so much is that, no matter how bad it was, it wasn't any worse than the game we played. We were on the short end of a 20-14 score, the first win the Patriots had ever had against a former NFL team. At the end of the first half, the score was 13-7 for the Patriots, and the only score we had was when Rocky Thompson—another of the Giants great draft choices, a wide receiver from West Texas State—ran a kickoff back 90 yards. (Thompson, who was born in Bermuda, won the British Empire 100-meter title in 10.1 seconds, and has done the 100-yards in 9.2.)

Mike Taliaferro was the Patriots' quarterback through the first three quarters, and by then it was so obvious we couldn't catch them that they brought in their prize draft pick, Jim Plunkett of Stanford. Even though Plunkett was intercepted four times, and we had Tarkenton in for the whole second half, we were only able to score one more touchdown.

Our next game, against the Jets in New Haven, showed us that '71 was going to be a long, hard season. The thoughts of improving on the '70 season began to look more and more nebulous. We lost, 27-14, and Namath wasn't even playing. (He had hurt his knee badly making a tackle.) Al Woodall was at quarterback; Emerson Boozer ran for 110 yards and John Riggins, their first draft choice, got 73 yards. For our part, at half time we had a rushing yardage of minus one; Tarkenton was tackled five times for losses; Tom Blanchard got off a punt of 21 yards at a time when it hurt, and Frederickson, normally old reliable, fell down on a simple pass pattern.

Giant people were beginning to lose their cool. Webster gave us a chewing out the likes of which I had seldom heard, and even Tarkenton, who never talks when he doesn't have to—he was zero for eight in the first half—told reporters: "I just don't know what's happening out there." It's a hell of a thing when your quarterback doesn't know. Tarkenton talked more after our next defeat, which was in our next game, 26 to 14 to the Eagles. Nobody was supposed to lose to the Eagles that year, especially the way we did. The Eagles ran for 202 yards against us, and gained another 142 passing, and Tarkenton was nailed three times behind the line of scrimmage.

"Damn it," Tarkenton said after the game, "I've never seen playing like this. I don't have to take this kind of crap."

Well, he was to see worse. We lost the next two exhibition games, to the Browns, 30-7 (a game in which the Browns scored the first four times they had the ball, and I missed a

46-yard field goal) and then to the Steelers, 20-3. In this game even Tarkenton didn't look sharp. He was intercepted three times.

So, the exhibition season was over, and none too soon. We had lost six, won none, and this time we didn't have the feeling that it was just the breaks that were murdering us.

The regular season didn't start off as badly as it might have, everything considered. By "everything considered" I mean that the Giants were not the sort of team the Packers used to be and that Dallas was, with a sprinkling of super-stars, two or three good men deep at every position. The Giants had some good football players, but no superstars; it wasn't two or three men deep at any position—some positions it wasn't even one man deep. It had more rookies than any coach likes to have starting, and some of the best players— Johnson, Frederickson, Hermann, to mention only three— were hurting badly. It was the kind of team where, to win, every man would have to play above his head in every game, and we would have to get the breaks in the bargain.

The first game we beat the Packers. Or more precisely, we lucked it out. We got two touchdowns on fumbles, one of a fumbled kickoff. This is the way the gods were on our side all through the game: The Packers got the ball on their 46-yard line with just over two minutes left. With one minute and 32 seconds left, they had the ball on our 36, third down and 5. They were in field goal range, two downs to go, and trailing by only two points. For reasons unknown to me, Scott Hunter, their quarterback, decided to throw a pass. If he'd been four points behind, I could have understood it. But two points? At any rate, Jim Files dropped back, intercepted, and ran the ball back to the Packer 43. We ran out the clock and had the game.

But the way we had played worried Webster and the other coaches. They knew, better than anyone, that we'd lucked it.

What bothered me was that I missed three field goal tries— and not impossible ones, either. One from the 47, one from the 45, and one from the 37. In addition, Green Bay had scored on the runback of a kickoff, which is another big black mark. I couldn't blame it on anybody else, either. It was me.

There is absolutely nothing you can say to a field goal kicker to buck up his spirits after he's missed three in a game. It gets you so far down that you feel you'll never climb back.

The only other game in which I remember missing three was the New Orleans game in '70, when I went out onto the field with us trailing 7-0, the ball on the left hash mark at the 28-yard line. I missed it, off to the left. I went back to the bench, feeling like a fool, sat down all by myself at one end, trying to figure out what had happened.

I knew I was making a mistake, thinking, because in kicking you have to concentrate only on what you're doing at the time, you have to go out there and kick easily and naturally. The minute you start thinking "I should do this" or "I should do that" in the middle of a game, you're spoiling your concentration. Even knowing that, with us trailing by a touchdown, with all the pressure on, I found myself thinking: "It went off to the left, so compensate for it, if you're kicking from the left side of the field, play the ball more to the right."

To prove I was right, a little later in the first half, I was called out on the field, and the ball was in almost identically the same spot, on the left hash mark, except this time it was the 31-yard line instead of the 28. I kicked, and it went off to the right.

I could hardly walk back to the bench. I could hear the roar of the crowd, but all I could do was think to myself: "What's going on here? What's happening? How could you possibly miss two easy field goals, ones that are so easy you don't even practice that close in?"

And I didn't have an answer. I went and sat on the bench and kept working myself into a worse and worse stew. All sorts of things went through my head that had nothing to do with my job, like "My God, what must people be thinking?" and even "This game is being televised back to New York, what must they be saying there?"

Finally I got so I couldn't even sit on the bench and I got up and started pacing back and forth behind it, something I practically never do. A couple of the guys said: "Don't let it bother you, Pete," but I just shook my head. I asked one of the trainers to get me a different pair of shoes and I changed into them there on the field. Jim Garrett came over and said: "Okay, Pete, just concentrate on the next one. Take it easy. Just concentrate on the next one."

I tried to. The next one was only 11 yards and I made it—just barely. It may have been the worst ball I ever hit in a game. It was sheer luck it went over. It just shows you what the pressure will do.

Just before the end of the first half I missed my third one, but oddly enough I didn't feel as badly about it as I had about the second one. I had shaken off my fit of desperation thinking and I had gotten my concentration back. It was a 46-yard attempt and I hit it right, and hard; I had the distance, the ball just slid off about four inches to the right. Of course, it doesn't matter whether you miss by four inches or four feet or four yards, you missed. But it was a miss I could live with.

The second-worse part about missing is going home on the plane after the team has lost. I just went off by myself as far away from everybody as I could and stared out the window. A couple of the guys came along and patted me on the back and said: "Forget it, Pete, even if you'd made them we still would have lost." It didn't make me feel any better.

We get paid every other week, right after the game, and on this flight the Giants guy came down the aisle handing everybody his check in an envelope and I kind of looked at mine as he held it out to me, as if I didn't really deserve to get it.

But I took it.

What bothered me about my misses in the Green Bay game was, I felt, more serious. The "pop" was gone from my leg.

Now, I think, the mistake I made was in my own personal, off-season training. I just ran too much.

I had decided that if running had given me such a good year in 1970, the way to have a better year in '71 was to run more. I had started a business of my own by that time, Peter Gogolak Sports, Inc., which was mostly a speaking bureau for things like father-and-son banquets, business luncheons, product promotions and so on, a certain amount of public relations. No matter how late I left my office, I'd go home, change into sweat clothes, drive up to Central Park and run twice around the reservoir, 1.52 miles per lap. Running around that reservoir tends to build up your speed. If it's before dusk, there are some very odd-looking characters who titter at you;

if it's after dusk, there are some equally odd-looking characters who drift off behind the bushes as you go by. Fairies or muggers, they keep up your speed. Running at least three miles five days a week, and sometimes five miles, when I got to training camp, I *felt* great. But I had run too much. I didn't have the "pop." I was down to 190 pounds, and I should have been a minimum of 205.

So, for the missed field goals in the Packer game, I have no one but myself to blame, myself and my training.

The next game was against the Redskins, and while we lost it, we could sort of talk ourselves out of the loss. The Redskins that year were George Allen's "old geezers," as he called them. George had come to Washington from the Los Angeles Rams, and he had brought along what seemed like half of the Rams team from the year before. They were no patsies.

The holes in our defense really showed up in that one. Bill Kilmer was quarterbacking the Redskins that day—Sonny Jurgensen had been injured—and it seemed to me that every time I looked, Kilmer was completing a pass. I thought, our pass defense isn't *that* bad, but Kilmer was 23 for 32, and every time I looked at Tarkenton, he was buried under a pass rush. To top it all off, we had suddenly developed a bad case of "drop it." Frederickson, McNeil, Houston, all dropped what looked like sure completions.

It is the psychology thing again which, to repeat, I can't explain. If a team is going good, clicking, guys you'd never expect to catch passes, catch ones that never under God's sky should they have caught. If a team is going lousy, a quarterback can hit his best receiver square in the chest with no defender within ten yards, and the guy will drop it.

But, as I said, we could talk ourselves out of the Redskin defeat. We got a little boost from the St. Louis game, where we won 21-20, due to Webster, Tarkenton, and Rocky Thompson. Webster decided to stop using the balanced offense, and put in a little razzle-dazzle. Double handoffs, run-pass options, all the rest. It paid off. Rocky Thompson took a kickoff back for 93 yards, and Tarkenton, who has the guts of ten burglars, with a minute to go and third and 3, threw a pass to Clifton McNeil.

So, we won.

My contribution was to miss two field goals from 42 yards, and I felt like hell. God knows how Kathy put up with me. I didn't want to see anyone, and I didn't want to talk to anyone. I still didn't have the pop, and even with the season barely started, I didn't know any way to get it back in time to help the team. You can't build up a leg for kicking just in a week or two.

It's a horrible feeling. To train all that time, and then find that what you absolutely have to have isn't there. It's like a boxer training the best way he knows for months, getting into the ring feeling absolutely great, on top of the world, and then, when the fight starts, suddenly find that he has no punch at all. Sure, he can use all the technical skills he has so that he doesn't look like a living disaster, but he knows that the one thing he *must* have, he doesn't.

I didn't either.

Next week, we went to Dallas to play the Cowboys. Since, as it turned out, the Cowboys were on their way to a Super Bowl win, we were expected to lose by up to three touchdowns according to the odds-makers.

The funny thing was, with a little bit of luck we might

have won. Dallas was almost as bad as we were, but not quite. They won 20-13, and frankly, neither team deserved to win. There was a total of twelve fumbles, the Cowboys and we each lost possession five times. How can anybody win a game like that? If we'd only fumbled once. Or twice. Because we didn't play that badly.

But fumbling is a catching disease. Thank God I'm not a runner. It's enough to give you the idea that on our first running play, we fumbled, and on our last play of the game, we fumbled.

At this point, our season record was 2-2, and for anybody who didn't know football, it might not have looked too bad. After all, in '70, we'd lost our first three games and at that point in that season we were 1-3.

In the next game, however, the fumbling really began to catch up with us. As one newspaperman wrote: "The Giants now not only fumble on the offense, they've also taught the defense how to fumble."

The game was in the Stadium against Baltimore, and it was a great day for the newspapermen because it was the first time that Johnny Unitas had played in Yankee Stadium since 1958, when he had passed for 359 yards to beat the old Giants 23-17 in a sudden-death championship game in the old NFL.

Old 19 didn't trot onto the field until the fourth quarter, and by that time Earl Morrall had the game sewed up for him. Morrall may not have matched Unitas' old record, but he had completed 8 of 17 passes for 128 yards and three touchdowns, and that monster running back of theirs, Norm Bulaich, had gotten 108 yards, most of them after breaking Giant tackles. Tarkenton was intercepted three times. The Colts had scored two of their touchdowns after the interceptions and one on a Giant fumble on the 2-yard line.

Oh, the hell with it. The final score was Baltimore 31, New York 7.

It would only hurt me to go through the next games torture by torture. We lost to the Eagles, 23-7, the first game the Eagles had won all season. They did it by running. Their quarterback, Pete Liske, couldn't find a receiver so they turned to the running game with two second-string runners, Al Davis and Ronnie Bull. And they won by two touchdowns.

The next three games we at least looked like a football team.

We lost to the Vikings, the division leaders, but for a change people weren't laughing at us.

Maybe we had gotten tired of people laughing at us, maybe it was that we had gotten some of the walking wounded back. Jim Kanicki, whom we had needed all the time, was in; Ron Johnson was in the backfield for the first time that season; Frederickson was back at work; Don Hermann was back; Bob Tucker and Willie Williams were in great form. The Vikings only won in the last minute, on a touchdown pass from Norm Snead to Bob Grim, and the only reason that Snead was in was that Kanicki had racked up Gary Cuozzo on a pass rush about halfway through the fourth quarter.

But, finally, we looked like a professional football team, and we proved it the next week when we beat the Chargers 35-17. We got 412 yards on the offense, with Charlie Evans scoring three touchdowns. Coleman Zeno caught four passes for 90 yards, Spider Lockhart had two interceptions and Willie Williams had one.

But the important thing for us, I thought, was that late in

the third quarter, the score was only 21-17, with us ahead, and that was when we really began to go to work. That is the point in a game where you either win it or blow it. That is where your defense has to hold. Ours did. And that is where, next time, your offense has to score. We did.

Then we faced the Falcons, which gave the newspaper reporters an even bigger field day than they had had with Johnny Unitas in the Stadium.

The elements in the Falcons game were just too big to be overlooked. First, the Falcons were coached by Norm van Brocklin, with whom Tarkenton had had a highly publicized fight when van Brocklin was coaching the Vikings and Fran was quarterback. Second, Dick Skiner, my old place-kick holder on the Giants, was the starting quarterback for the Falcons. Third, Atlanta was where Tarkenton lived and worked off-season.

The Falcons game looked as good for us as the Chargers game. We were down 17-7 at one point. Tarkenton then engineered an eight-and-a-half-minute drive for a touchdown, so we were only down 17-14. In the closing minutes, Tarkenton got us down to the 2-yard line, fourth down, 31 seconds to play. A field goal would have tied it, but Tarkenton and Webster decided to go for the touchdown. In the huddle Tarkenton called what we call a "Dive 33," which was simply a hand-off to Frederickson to let him dive through. When Fran got the ball, however, he suddenly saw this beautiful hole open right up in front of him, and he charged through himself. I don't think Fran was trying to grandstand in front of the hometown crowd. I think he just reacted like an old footballer. He saw the hole, and he went through.

From then on, the season was a disaster. We lost to the

Steelers 17-13, even though we played what, on statistics, was our best game of the season. Our yardage was 419 compared to 175 for the Steelers; we ran off 73 plays to their 45; Tarkenton completed 27 passes for 302 yards to their twelve completions for 75 yards. And we lost.

It was a miserable, bitter, windy day with flurries of snow. I missed a 36-yarder in the midst of a gust of snow, and when I was trying a 51-yarder, Fran bobbled the snap. I'd already started my move, so when I kicked there was nothing there; Fran was chasing the ball. He got it and threw it downfield, hoping that it might go as an incomplete pass or, even if it were intercepted, the Steelers would be back on about their 20-yard line. No such luck; the ball was intercepted all right, and the Steelers ran it back for a touchdown.

At the end of the game, Fran said:

"It just looks like we're not supposed to win."

How right he was. It was proven in the last four games, which saw us in the cellar with a five-nine record, the worst we'd had since the horrendous one-twelve-one year.

Headline after headline carried the same old story: "Giants Give Game Away."

The Dallas game was a disaster. It was not only that we lost, 42-14, it was that at the end we looked like an infantry company that had just come out of the Battle of the Bulge. We had ten players injured, five of them seriously. Three had to have operations: Spider Lockhart for a separated shoulder, Houston for a fractured cheekbone, and Duhon for a major cartilage operation on his left knee. Hermann, Scott Eaton, Junior Coffey, they were all hurt, Frederickson, Don Johnson, Charlie Evans, Jerry Shay, Willie Williams, Coleman Zeno. What a mess!

The final game of the season, against the Eagles at the Stadium, was an anti-climax. We lost, 41-28. The "coup de grace," one writer put it, and it was true. Fran Tarkenton didn't even play, the first game in his major league career that he didn't even have a minute of time on the field. The only pleasant note of the whole game was that Bob Tucker became the first tight end in the history of the National Football League to win the receiving title, 29 season receptions for a total of 793 yards.

I can't begin to describe how badly I felt at the end of the season. I think that being the loner I am made it worse. Being a place kicker forces you into loneliness, as I've said. You're not in the physical battle with everyone else, you don't even build up the sort of personal relationship that even a quarterback, who is also supposed to stay out of the blood-and-guts conflict, has with other players. The place kicker is paid for one thing: Go in for one play and put points on the scoreboard. No planning, no strategy, no game plan. And, above all, no second chance. One play. That's it. People sometimes ask me what really goes on in a football huddle. How the hell would I know? I'm never in a huddle in practice, I'm off at the end of the field, kicking a soccer ball in the air. And in a game I'm in a huddle at most maybe six times. I can tell you what happens there. The quarterback says: "Field goal. Play starts when the kicker is ready." He never even says, "when Gogolak is ready." And what *really* happens between the halves? How would I know? I'm sitting off by myself, sucking oranges.

At the end of a bad season, being a loner brings you close to desperation. All you can think of is the field goals you missed, and you can't blame anybody else for them. A quarterback can have a bad year, but he can rationalize it. Maybe he didn't get the blocking, maybe his receivers fell down. A running back can have a bad year, maybe his pulling guards had slowed down a step. A place kicker? No excuses. Oh, maybe there were some bad snaps during the season, maybe the blocking broke down a few times—but three missed field goals in one game? How do you rationalize that? It all comes back to you, you and the "pop" in your leg. Have you really lost it?

And there's no one you can go to for advice. I was the first of the soccer-style kickers in American football and as I said when I was back at the Ogdensburg Free Academy, there were no books on the subject. If a golf professional finds he's going sour he can go to another pro and say: "Watch my swing and tell me what I'm doing wrong."

But who could I go to? I talked to Charlie, of course, but he couldn't help me. He looked at the game films, and he couldn't see anything wrong.

So there I was, back on my own.

What I did during the winter and spring, after worrying myself silly, was to completely change my way of training. I wanted to get the power back in my leg, strength plus speed. Instead of running three miles a day, I ran only one, and in a new way: jog fifty steps, then sprint fifty. Jog and sprint. Jog and sprint. And I stepped up on weightlifting, especially weightlifting with the leg.

I simply had to find that "pop" again. After the '71 season, I knew the Giants would have tryout kickers in training camp. If I didn't find the "pop" I'd find myself a free agent.

We Come Back

I don't know why I described the 1971 season at such length except that it's like the old story about the man who kept hitting himself over the head because it felt so good when he stopped. And most football books tell nothing except what great seasons the player had. There's another side to football.

The '71 Giants were lousy. And I was terrible.

Within myself, lived with worry. There was always the nagging doubt, had I lost it?

It didn't help this doubt at all when I read in the sports stories that "it's an open secret" that the Giants were looking for another place kicker. I had already figured that out for myself.

It was hell.

What made it worse was that this feeling had been building up all through the season. If a kicker is playing for a winning team and he misses one, he thinks: "What the hell, I made the last four and I'll make the next one." It's a good attitude. You *know* you'll make the next kick. If you're on a losing team and you miss one, even if it's almost impossible, in a driving rain and fifty yards out, you think: "Oh, Jesus! I've missed three in a row and the next one will be from fifty-two yards!" You know you'll miss the next one. Missing one big kick makes you feel bad enough. Like committing suicide. Missing two or three in a game makes you feel—you can't describe it. I've already tried. You want to resign from the human race. But when it goes on game after game—that's how I felt at the end of the '71 season.

I reported for training on July 11 at Monmouth College in West Long Branch, New Jersey. Monmouth has a beautiful campus made up of several estates of wealthy people who used to live on the Jersey shore. There were a number of reasons for switching from C. W. Post. Post was not the easiest place in the world to get to because of the summer traffic on Long Island, and it had a full schedule of summer classes, which meant there were always a lot of students around. In addition, if we were going to become the Jersey Giants in the near future, it seemed sensible to begin to build up ties with New Jersey by training there. And besides, as far as I personally was concerned, the Post football field had only one set of goal posts, which meant that I had to wait until the team got through practicing before I could start my own real work.

Obviously, I didn't report to Monmouth in the best of all possible frames of mind. First, we were coming off a season in which I had given the worst performance of my entire professional career—six field goals out of seventeen attempts. Second, there were a lot of new faces. Fran Tarkenton and Fred Dryer had been traded; Norm Snead had arrived (Bob

Grim, the wide receiver we got in the same trade, was in a fight over the terms of his contract and hadn't showed up); Jim Garrett had switched from offensive backfield coach to be head defensive coach; Ray Wietecha, an All-Pro center who had played for the Giants from 1953 to 1962 had come from the Green Bay Packers to be offensive line coach. How would this new team do? I looked at the roster of players and realized that, of the forty players who had been on the team in 1966 when I joined the Giants, only four were on this squad: myself, Greg Larson, Joe Morrison, starting his four-teenth year with the Giants, and Spider Lockhart. It was a startling thought. I was an old-timer.

And, again obviously, the three new men I was most in-terested in were the three who were trying to get my job as kicker. I remembered how I felt when I first went up to the Buffalo Bills and watched the veterans looking at the new players, measuring them, wondering and worrying whether the new boys were good enough to take their jobs. This is a tough side of pro ball, tougher even than the physical side. Standing there and thinking to yourself: "I'm thirty years old and I may be standing here watching my job and my whole career go right down the drain." I guess it's that brutal and naked in all professional sports, but you never fully real-ize the hard, basic, ruthlessness of it until it's happening to you.

The first guy I watched was Skip Butler—William F. But-ler—a No. 4 draft choice of the Packers in 1970 who had been cut and had gone to New Orleans. He'd been picked up by the Giants toward the end of the '71 season. The second guy was Paul Rogers, a strong boy from Nebraska who had set all kinds of college kicking records. (In the 1969 Sun Bowl he had been voted the most valuable player for kicking four field goals.) The third kicker was Jack Simcsak, another Hungarian, who had played his college ball at Virginia Polytechnic Institute, where he had kicked a record 55-yard field goal, and who had played one pro season at Denver.

What began to make me feel better after the first few days of practice were two things. The first was my own performance; the second was a growing, indefinable feeling about the quality of the team.

I had gone into the practice season knowing that the thing I had to do, from the very first day, was to impress the coaching staff. *I* felt in the best shape of my life, but an athlete can never make an objective judgment about that. He can feel he's really in the best shape—and not psyching himself up, *really* feeling it, better than he was five years ago, stronger and all the rest of it—and yet the coach off on the sidelines will say: "You know, Gogolak looks pretty good, but I don't think he's got the fire he had five years ago."

So I knew I had to impress the coaches, and on our first endurance run, for the whole squad, I finished fifth in a squad of eighty-five. The thing that made me look so good was that it was an endurance run. As I've said before, speed is not my thing. What it showed the coaching staff was that I was in shape.

Also, in practice, I was consistently hitting the ball from over 50 yards out. This was a kind of negative plus. The coaches know, as well as the kickers do, that what you can do in practice isn't the final judgment on what you can do in a game. But if you can't kick from 50 yards out in practice, you might as well forget it. Within me, I felt obvious. My training had paid off. The "pop" was back!

Still, I can't describe the feeling of relief I had when, after the first two weeks of training camp, the three try-out kickers were released. The cuts came so fast—I'd never seen cuts in the first two weeks before, except for guys who were obviously incompetent from the very start—that even I had some qualms. All these guys were good ball players, they all were hard workers, they were all good kickers. I think the factor that swung the Giant decision for me was my experience. I had kicked as well, or better, than any of the three during practice, and I had been kicking for the Giants for six years. If you went back to the 1970 season, I had scored 107 points for them.

Even so, I went to these guys and told them I was sorry to see them go. I was, too. If one of them had gotten my job I would have hated his guts, but now—it's too complicated to explain. I was sorry to see them go. I told them that this early in the practice season they could get picked up by another team, and Butler was picked up by Houston. Rogers and Simcsak—all I can say is that I'm glad I'm not trying to break into pro ball today. It's tough, tough, tough.

After the load of my own job was off my back, I began to look around more at the rest of the team and I suddenly began to realize, you know, we've got some guys here who can really play football. It was totally unlike my first season with the Giants, when I came up and thought, the Buffalo Bills could beat this team any game in the season.

There was a new atmosphere in the Monmouth training camp. Off our record in '71, there had to be. Alex Webster was a hell of a lot tougher. There was a lot more hitting, starting early and going late. When we were training at C. W.

Post, the team was supposed to practice an hour and twenty minutes every morning and every afternoon, but sometimes when it was really hot, the afternoon sessions were dropped. Not at Monmouth. There the practice sessions were an hour and forty minutes, every morning and every afternoon. On July afternoons on the Jersey shore the sun glaring down can make you pant like a dog; but we practiced. I've seen offensive linemen looking as if they belonged in an oxygen tent. And if you want to see a man suffer, watch a 240-pound offensive guard practicing pulling plays under a hot July sun.

We had schedules that I hadn't seen before. You had to be in a certain place at a certain time, and if you weren't there, you were in trouble.

As far as the team was concerned, even in training camp, things seemed to be jelling. The trades, the drafts, the coaching changes, all seemed to be coming together.

Jim Garrett, for example. Garrett is one of those coaches who eats, drinks, sleeps, and thinks nothing but football. You tell someone Garrett has eight kids and the standard answer is: "How did he get the time?" In training camp, you get up at 5:30 in the morning to go to the john, and when you pass Garrett's room you hear the little whirr of the projector as he sits there rerunning defensive plays. Like Sherman, Garrett is unbelievable. Once last year he and I got to talking about the 1964 Buffalo team, the year I went up, and Garrett told me the name of every one of the twenty-two players on the starting line-up for that season, height and weight, where he'd gone to college, how he'd played, and everything that had happened to him since, including where he was then living, what he was doing and how many kids he had. As I say, unbelievable. I think he can do the same thing about every living man who has played pro ball, and most of those who are dead. He's the only coach I know in pro ball who gives his players *written* tests and grades them on the answers.

Besides the famed "rover" defense he installed in the '72 season with Jack Gregory, he installed eight different basic formations for defensive backs against the opposition offense, and his written questions for his defensive backs would go:

"You are six minutes into the fourth quarter and we are ahead, 10-7, the opposition has the ball on our 26-yard line, they have a second and four situation, and you see that the offensive end opposite you has now lined up 20 yards from the line of scrimmage. What is your primary responsibility?"

As you see, playing football for the New York Giants is not like playing for Cornell.

Garrett should also get credit for bringing Jack Gregory to the Giants. Gregory was a big defensive end with Cleveland—by big I mean six foot five and 250 pounds—before he played out his option, and at least four teams were after him. Garrett, however, went down to Gregory's hometown in Okolona, Mississippi, and got him for the Giants.

But beyond Gregory, almost all the Giants trades and drafts worked in '72. In earlier years the Giant training camp was like a revolving door. Twenty or thirty guys would go through camp in a couple of weeks. You'd see a guy for a week, and—zap—he'd be gone. If a guy was cut from another team, the first phone call he'd make would be to the Giants. This year, our trades and our draft picks stuck. Besides Gregory, who was a standout, our first two draft picks were Larry Jacobson of Nebraska, a six foot six, 260-pound defensive end who made the starting team as a rookie, and Eldridge Small from Texas A & I, a six foot one, 190-pound wide receiver who turned out to be a top player as a defensive back. Bob Grim, after reporting late, never did get the chance to play much. Our four-year veteran wide receivers, Don Hermann and Rich Houston, had such a good year that nobody could have bumped them from their jobs.

A couple of other guys who stood out were John Mendenhall and Vince Clements. John was a defensive tackle from Grambling who went at six foot one and 255. That's a little short for that position in the pros, but Eddie Robinson, the famous coach of Grambling, said John "couldn't miss" in the pros. Considering the number of his players who made it in the pros, Robinson should have known, and he was right. What Mendenhall didn't have in height, he made up for with quickness, and on top of that, he's one of the strongest and toughest football players I've ever seen.

What Clements had going for him was that complete and utter determination to play football that I described in Tommy Longo. Vince was a kind of throw-in with Grim and Snead in the Fran Tarkenton deal. I got to know Clements because he's a Connecticut boy (he lives in Southington) and I had rented a house for a year in Darien, Connecticut. A lot of times during the season I'd give him a ride into the Stadium, and on those rides he told me again and again how glad he was to be playing for the Giants.

"It's giving me a chance to prove myself," he kept saying.

Vince had played his college ball for the University of Connecticut, where he had been named to the Coaches' All-American, but he had sat out the '71 season with the Vikings because of knee surgery. Vince was a running back, six feet four inches and 205 pounds, one of those deceptive runners who's always moving faster than you think he is.

He proved himself, too. He got Alex Webster's old number, 29, and he had two games in which he gained more than 100 yards.

The defense looked pretty good in practice, but practice isn't a game. Garrett had installed his new "rover" system with a lot of new twists, and we had three new men starting in the defensive line—Jacobson, Mendenhall, and Dick Enderle, a six foot two, 250-pound guard whom the Giants had gotten from the Atlanta Falcons during the off-season. Enderle played so well for us that I still can't figure out how the Falcons let him go, though I guess it was because, like a lot of other players, he couldn't get along with Norm van Brocklin. Even with these guys beefing up our defense, nobody really knew how the defense would stand up in real games. Any half-decent player can look good in practice. If the defense gave up points in games, the question became, how many points could the offense score? The newspapers were already saying that if the Giants could manage to win six games it would be a good season, and if we won seven it would be a miracle.

On offense, we had Charlie Evans back after his '71 injury, and Ron Johnson back after knee surgery. Ron had had a thigh operation during the '71 training season, and the postseason knee operation was for torn cartilage, absolutely the worst kind for a running back. But Johnson is another of those unbelievables. He knew the number of running backs who *never* came back from a cartilage operation. So, after the operation, he told me, all through the off-season he worked his butt off to get that leg back in shape. And it paid off. He doesn't think he's quite as good as he was before the operation, but he was good enough for us in '72 to gain 1183 yards, second only to Larry Brown of the Redskins. And for all the publicity Brown got as the big running back on a team that went to the Super Bowl, I think that Johnson is a better carrier than Brown. For one thing, he's quicker.

So, in training, our running game looked set. The big question mark, of course, was at quarterback, the key to the offense. Randy Johnson had had a fine game against Philadelphia to end the 1971 season—30 of 47 passes complete with three touchdowns—but he'd played behind Tarkenton all year and practically all of his season record was achieved in that Philadelphia game. For the season, he'd only been in long enough to complete 41 out of 74, and all his touchdown passes were in the Eagles game. And Snead—pro ball players knew that Snead was a first-rate quarterback, but he was thirty-three, he'd played his first three pro years with Washington in the early sixties, when they were hardly a powerhouse. Then he'd been quarterback for the Eagles for seven years. They were not years of glory. With the Vikings in the '71 season, Snead had thrown only 75 times for 37 completions. Behind Gary Cuozzo, Snead hadn't seen too much action.

Most of the guys on the Giants thought of Snead as back-up insurance for Johnson, and a lot of them thought he was over the hill.

In fact, Snead and his wife, Susie, had a little of that feeling. I was talking to Snead once about what had happened in Minnesota and what he said was:

"I won both of the exhibition games I played in, but Grant wanted to go with Cuozzo."

And Susie said:

"Yes, when Norm didn't make it in Minnesota we both

wondered if he was over the hill. When he was traded to New York, we both knew that this was the last stop."

I found out afterward that the Giants front office hadn't felt that way. They'd had their eye on Snead for a long time. They'd gone after Snead while he was still playing for the Eagles, before they'd gotten Tarkenton. The Giants have never been a team to build up a young quarterback. Pittsburgh builds up a Terry Bradshaw, Cleveland a Mike Phipps, the Dolphins a Bob Griese, but when the Giants want a quarterback they go after a veteran—Y. A. Tittle, Earl Morrall, Fran Tarkenton. Johnson. Snead.

Snead himself is not the flashy, Joe Namath type of quarterback. He's the steady, old-pro type who never loses control. Snead has his ups and downs, like any quarterback, but I've never seen him have a really bad game (except maybe once) or throw a really bad pass.

I noticed that when he came to the Giants, he rented a house in the Candlewood Lake section of Connecticut. Several Giants players live in that area including, most important of all for a quarterback, Greg Larson, the center.

The relationship between the center and the quarterback has to be one of the most psychic in pro ball. They have to get to know each other's minds so well, each other's way of thinking, that in a game they each know almost intuitively what the other is going to do.

That was our quarterback situation.

I don't know why I should be talking so much about the team when I should be talking about myself.

Psychologically, I was a thousand percent better after the Giants had let the three tryout kickers go, but as far as *my* kicking was concerned, I still had an old, familiar problem.

I had a new holder.

This season, with Tarkenton gone, my holder was Tom Blanchard, the punter. The familiar problem was the coordination between Larson, Blanchard, and me. We worked it out by the end of the season, but in training camp, we were still having our problems.

All things considered, except for my own performance in the Jets game at New Haven, we had a good exhibition season. Our first game was the Hall of Fame game in Canton, Ohio, against the Kansas City Chiefs—a big, tough team that had won its division title in '71. I remember thinking on the way out to the game:

"My God, they're a powerhouse. We're going to get creamed."

The surprising thing is, we weren't. They beat us, 23-17, but we looked pretty good. Our defense was better than in '71, and the offense got us some points. On the way back from the game, we felt almost as good as if we'd won. We'd been expecting to lose by two or three touchdowns.

The next game was the Steelers game and they creamed us, 28-10. It wasn't just the score, it was that we looked so lousy. Even though I had a 45-yard field goal on the last play of the first half, I felt lousy. The feeling that we had after the Chiefs game, that maybe we had a real football team, went straight out the window.

On the bus back from the Three River Stadium to the airport, I sat beside Doug Van Horn, a good, big guard, and about the only thing he said on the whole ride was:

"The same old bullshit. The same goddamned 1971 season all over again."

I felt the same way. The last half of the game I'd felt the way I'd so often felt in 1971. Won't this game ever be over?

I felt even worse after our next game, the Jets game. It was a wild and woolly game, a high scoring game with the lead changing back and forth. Our defense looked pretty good— Namath was intercepted five times, for one thing—and the offense was clicking. In the closing seconds the score was tied 31-31, and I went in for a 38-yard field goal. A pipe.

I missed.

That's all. I missed. I know that Tom Blanchard and I were still not working together perfectly and that I was tense and overconcentrating, not comfortable and automatic the way I should have been, but that's no excuse, and Lord knows it wasn't Blanchard's fault. I missed off to the right.

I went into the locker room and took a two-and-a-half hour shower. I don't think I'd ever felt so plain frustrated. I had visions of doing even worse than I had in '71, and no excuses. While I was getting dressed a friend tracked me down and said:

"Pete, there are three tough-looking characters outside waiting for you and they say they're going to wait all night. They blew a bundle on this game."

So I went out the back door and sneaked to my car, where Kathy was waiting with two couples we had invited to the game. I got in and, as we started off, my pal brought out a bottle. I had the longest drink I've ever had in my life.

Gradually, over the rest of the exhibition season, I began to forget the Jets game. Blanchard and I were working together better all the time, and the Giants won the last three games to give us our first winning exhibition season in thirteen years—three won, two lost and one tied.

Randy Johnson was injured on the last play of the Jets game, so Snead was quarterback in the following game—against the Patriots in Foxboro, Massachusetts—and in the final two, a charity game at Princeton, New Jersey, against the Eagles, sponsored by the New Jersey Chamber of Commerce, and against Cleveland in the Stadium.

Snead looked good in the Patriots game, which we won 31-10, and I had a less than great day. I kicked an 11-yard field goal. We played a sloppy game against the Eagles, but they were sloppier and we won that, 27-12. I had two field goals, nothing to brag about—both under 25 yards—but at least I was making them. In the Cleveland game, which we won 28-21, Webster said we played "super" ball, and we had our winning exhibition season. Charlie Evans and Ron Johnson couldn't have played better and Snead definitely had the quarterback job locked up.

But when we began playing football for keeps, in the regular season, we started off even worse than we had in '71. Then, at least, we had split our first two games. In '72, we lost them both.

Our first game was against Detroit in Detroit, and we lost 30-16. The defense looked tired and the offense couldn't get going. The only bright spot of the whole game was a 92-yard kickoff return by Rocky Thompson. I had the kind of day that made me begin to wonder what the hell I was doing. I made a 42-yard field goal, and I missed a PAT. Sure, I have an explanation for it. The field in Detroit is natural grass and it had been all chewed up by the cleats. As I kicked, the side of the sole of my shoe hit the dirt and instead of hitting the ball with my instep, I hit it with the side of my foot.

But explanations don't impress coaches, and they don't impress me. I should have made it. It was the first PAT I'd missed in three years. I could just see another tryout kicker in camp.

The next game—thank God it was a turning point.

The next game was terrible. Terrible for the Giants, and terrible for me. It was against Dallas and we lost, 23-14. "Mistakes costly," the papers pointed out, and went on to point out that it was our seventh straight NFC defeat. I missed a 45-yarder that didn't make me feel too good, but then later, I missed a 24-yarder. I had kicked that field goal from 19 yards, but one of our guys had lined up wrong and we were penalized five yards, so that I had to kick again. This time, I was off. Webster was really teed off at me, and I don't blame him.

When I got myself partly pulled together the day after the game, I tried to analyze what had gone wrong with me. As I said, I never had felt better in my life, and I was kicking from over 50 yards out in practice. I finally decided I wasn't getting enough practice under game conditions. The way the practice schedule was set up, I only kicked once a week under a rush. And I decided that the very first thing I was going to do was to talk to Webster. If I had to go through another season like '71, I was going to quit.

My decision to talk to Webster may have been the smartest thing I'd ever done. The people I knew who know football were all talking about how lousy the Giants were doing—the papers were even saying we might have a *worse* season than '71—and about how bad I was. There were rumors that the Giants were going to try to get my brother Charlie from the Patriots to replace me. Not that I think the Giants would have, and I'm sure Charlie wouldn't have come, but that was the talk. Webster was so worried about my kicking that he actually did bring up that tryout guy I was worried about, a guy who had kicked for Philadelphia, Mark Moseley, but on Tuesday I had gone to Alex and said:

"Alex, I don't want to be a kicker if I miss from 24 yards. I've been worrying about it and I think it's because I really only kick about five minutes a week against the rush. In practice. I can kick all day with a center and a holder, but I need the rush so I can get the feel of it. Give me three times a week against the rush."

Webster agreed. I would get eight kicks against a rush three times a week, before regular practice started. The next day, Moseley was gone. I don't know, maybe Webster brought him up to scare me. He needn't have.

But the Dallas game was a turning point. We beat the Eagles in our next game, a Monday night game at Philadelphia, by 27 to 12. I missed a PAT again, but this was because Tom Blanchard dropped the snap from center, so I wasn't too worried. In that game, Snead moved into eighth on the all-time passing list, completing over 67 percent of his passes to give him a total of 25,047 yards. And, in the next game, we beat New Orleans, 45-21, at the Stadium.

It was in our fifth game, against San Francisco, that we really came into our own.

San Francisco was a top contender. They'd finished first in their division in '71, and were favored to repeat. We went into the game a solid underdog, and we beat them. I don't mean that we just won the game, sometimes a poor team beats a better one just on luck. We beat them.

Four things stick in my mind about that game, beyond the fact that Charlie Evans had a great game. First, Snead had a sensational day, bringing his passing-completion percentage to 67.9, which is almost unbelievable. Second, that rover defense began to come into its own. Gregory nailed Brodie far behind the line on a third-down play that put the 49ers deep in a hole when they had a chance to even the score. Third, I got three field goals, none of them sensational, but they gave us 9 of our 23 points. (San Francisco had two touchdowns and a field goal for 17 points.)

And fourth, I made the first real tackle I ever made in pro ball. You remember that MacArthur Lane one was a fluke, but my tackle of Vic Washington was for real.

The game was played in Candlestick Park, which I don't like for a variety of reasons, two of which are those winds that swirl around and another that it has Astroturf, which gets horribly slippery when it's wet. It was a wet, rainy day and the ball was both slippery and heavy—soggy. I kicked off and Washington, who had stationed himself just behind the goal line, timed it to catch the ball on the dead run at about the 10-yard line. If a return man is going full speed on wet ground when he gets the ball, the chances are the first two or three kick coverers will run or skid by him, and this is what happened to us. Two or three of our guys missed him, and Washington started up the middle. (In a play-off game against Dallas in '71, Washington had a 98-yard runback for a touchdown.) Washington put on a burst of speed and by the time he'd gotten to the 30-yard line, he was past all of our guys except the outside coverers, and they had no chance of getting him.

So here I was, sort of standing around on the 50-yard line with Washington on his way. The only thought I had was:

"Hit him low, if you hit him high he'll run through you."

And I guess Washington had roughly the same idea.

He was probably thinking, here's the guy in the clean uniform, the field's too wet to cut around him, run over him.

So I hit Washington, as low and as hard as I could, and I not only stopped him, I knocked the ball out of his hands. Willie Williams had caught up to us by that time, and he picked up the ball and ran it back for a touchdown. But it didn't count. The referee ruled that he had blown his whistle, the ball belonged to us, but Willie couldn't advance it.

On the next series of plays we scored anyway, but I never got as many congratulations from the team as I did for that tackle. When you get congratulated by about forty football players, it means you can't sit down for an hour. There has to be a different way of congratulating a guy. And it's a fine thing when a professional ball player gets a headline in a newspaper because he made a tackle.

The 49ers game gave us back the feeling we had first gotten in the Kansas City exhibition game. Now, we *knew* we could play ball against a top team.

We proved it in the next game, against the Cards, when we came from behind after the half—we were trailing, 7-to-21—to win, 27-21.

I began to hit the ball in that game. Obviously, the defenses did one hell of a job, since the Cards didn't score a point in the second half, and our offense came to life in the third quarter with two touchdowns, so at the start of the last period we were tied, 21-21. Then I hit two field goals, one only 19 yards, but one for 43.

I had that old feeling, and the whole team had it, that now we were really with it. We could beat anybody.

Actually, we should have won the next game, against the Washington Redskins. I know that every player always says that, and also that it was calls by the referee that beat them, but look at the facts. And remember that I'm the kind of player who figures if a call goes against you, what the hell. There's no use yelling. That Washington game was one of the few where I really wanted to join in a posse to lynch the referee.

The first disputed call was when Snead completed a pass to Don Hermann for a touchdown. The referee ruled that Rich Houston had interfered with a defensive player—about 30 yards from where the action was taking place. Okay, the call on that went against us.

The next call, I don't understand to this day. We were playing good, tough, ball. (I had three field goals in that game, one from 43 yards.) The score was 14-13 at this point, Washington ahead, but we were really moving. It was third down for us, and Snead gave the ball to Ron Johnson on a running play. Johnson had the first down and more when he was stopped by two Washington tackles. One had him high, one low, and he was just stopped, dead in his tracks, standing up. The play was over. Our whole bench, watching, just sort of turned away from the play, thinking, okay, first down, *now* let's go!

Everybody thought the play was over except the referee.

While Johnson was still being held there, at a dead stop, the Washington linebacker, Chris Hanburger, grabbed the ball out of his arms and started to run. He was flattened instantly, but the referee ruled he hadn't blown his whistle, the ball was still in play, it was the Redskins' ball on our 40-yard line. I don't know what they ought to do about football refereeing, but God knows they should do something. I know it's not the easiest job in the world, but what was Johnson supposed to do after he was stopped cold?

Well, we lost the game, 23-16, and I still say we should have won it.

I have to admit that when we played the Redskins two weeks later (in the interim game we beat the Denver Broncos, 29-17, but it was a tragic game for us because Charlie Evans broke his leg again and was out for the rest of the season), Washington really beat us.

For fifty-eight minutes we played as well as the Redskins. Both teams were able to score, but neither team was able to put together two consecutive scores that might have broken the game open. Eldridge Small took the opening kickoff of the second half back to the Washington 13-yard line—and we couldn't get a touchdown. The score at that time was 7-6 in our favor, but we had to settle for a field goal, which meant the score was 10-6 instead of 14-6. We went into the last two minutes of play with the score 13-13. Then Larry Brown went in to score for the Redskins.

That was bad enough, but there was worse to come. With 25 seconds to go, we were intercepted, and the Redskins had the ball on our 10-yard line. Obviously, we had lost the ball game. Most coaches would run out the clock. Not George Allen. Before the game, Jim Garrett had told reporters that he would guarantee that the Giants defense would hold Brown to under 100 yards. Up till that last 25 seconds, Brown had gained 96 yards. So Allen started calling time outs, and when the ball was put in play, it went to Brown. Two straight plays, Brown scored another touchdown, he gained 106 yards, and the score was 27-13.

The next time the Giants and the Redskins play, it's going to be for blood.

Right after the game, some assistant coach on the Redskins started yelling at Garrett and Garrett went charging over, and they were in a real, honest-to-God fist fight in the middle of the field that had to be broken up by some of the players. And Webster went over to shake Allen's hand and congratulate him, but Allen had already left the field. Alex's face turned the color of a Hawaii sunset. The veins in his neck were pumping. All I know is, I wouldn't want Mr. Webster that mad at me. Webster doesn't take kindly to that sort of performance.

I think the difference between the old Giants, before '72, and the new Giants, in '72, showed up best in our next game, on November 19 against the Cardinals. We were sloppy, we played badly, and we won, 13-7. The '71 Giants would have lost by four touchdowns. We were giving up ground as if we didn't want it, but only between the 30-yard lines. Donny Anderson was getting six and seven yards at a whack, till they got inside our 30-yard line. Then they were stopped.

About the next game, there isn't much I can say that everybody doesn't know. Giants 62, Philadelphia 10, and Garrett boiling mad because the defense gave up a touchdown on the last series of plays.

We weren't trying to rub it in, either. Webster isn't that kind of guy. The club set a scoring record, and I got a record eight PATs, but it was just that the Eagles were so bad. I don't know what's the matter with that team. They aren't that bad. They have good players, and they've had good players in the past. Maybe it's a matter of morale. I don't know what it is. They'll run two or three good sets of plays against you and look like world beaters, and suddenly they go to pieces.

Be that as it may, after the Eagles game our record was 7-4 —better than anyone had expected, including us—and to get into the playoffs we had to win two of our last three. None of them would be easy: the Bengals, the Dolphins, and the Cowboys.

We figured that we simply had to win the game against the Bengals, but against them we played one of our worst games of the season, and Cincinnati beat us, 13-10.

The biggest thing the Giants lacked in '72 was depth, and it showed in that game. Spider Lockhart was out, injured, and we didn't have a back-up to really fill his shoes. The defense looked terrible, and Snead was going so badly that Webster put Johnson in. Johnson threw a touchdown pass, but he also threw two interceptions.

There went any hopes of making the playoffs. In '72.

In the next game, against Miami, we played even worse. We had four fumbles, two interceptions, and I missed a PAT. Counting that Miami game, we only had ten fumbles and twelve interceptions altogether, so you can see what a nightmare the game was. The score doesn't even reflect the way we played. And my missed PAT gave me a total of four for the season, the most I've ever had in a season in my entire career. It was the same old story, I hit the ball with the side of my foot instead of my instep, but that's only an explanation, not an excuse. Yepremian wasn't missing, and the turf was as bumpy for him as it was for me.

By explaining how bad we were, I don't want to take anything away from the Dolphins. Don Shula has done a magnificent job of molding that collection of "unknown" guys into an unbeatable football team. Of course, in Paul Warfield he has, in my opinion, the best receiver in pro ball. I know it's a big claim, but once in the Miami game we had Spider Lockhart and Willie Williams both on Warfield and he went up and caught the ball. If you can get a ball in between those two guys, you have to be the best. And every team in the league is always laying for the Dolphins. I know we were. The first team to knock off the Dolphins has got to look impressive. But Miami went through the whole season, and the play-offs *and* the Super Bowl undefeated. You can't be any better than that.

In the last game of the season, against Dallas, we really looked like a great team ourselves. I don't know what happened to Dallas in '72. On paper they look unbeatable; the Lord knows, they have the players, and they have a good coaching staff. Maybe they have *too* many good players. They don't have the spark that, say, the old Packers had. The old Packers just didn't know when they were beaten. The Cowboys play top-flight precision football, but they never seem to catch fire.

It was the first time we had played in the Cowboys' new stadium at Irving, Texas, and, man, that's the place to play ball. It's more like a theater than a football stadium. It's all enclosed except for an opening in the top. It's ringed, above the stadium seats, with private boxes that those rich oil men paid $50,000 apiece for. That's just the price of the box; everything else, including the tickets, is extra. When we went onto the field for practice, we could look up and see all those people—lovely women, dressed to the nines—eating their steak dinners.

There's never any wind, and the footing is Tartan turf, the best of the artificial covers I've played on. I could kick in that stadium for the next ten years.

In this game Vince Clements gained over 100 yards again, Ron Johnson brought his year's yardage up to 1,183 and scored his fourteenth touchdown, an NFC record, and Snead completed 16 of 18 passes to give him a year's percentage of 60.31. That broke Y. A. Tittle's old 1963 record of 60.22 percent.

I had three field goals, from 49, 22, and 26 yards. I had one blocked, but it was a guy coming right through the center, so it didn't bother me too much. If a place kicker is blocked by a guy coming in from the side, it is his fault—he was too slow getting the ball away. If he's blocked from the front, it means that the blocking broke down.

And, thank God, I didn't have a PAT blocked. I made a crack earlier about Bob Timberlake bringing the excitement back to PATs—you never knew whether he was going to make it or not. I was beginning to think maybe that wasn't quite so funny. Every one of my missed PATs hit Larson right in the rear end and after that happened once, I heard one of the guys on the team say to Larson:

"Christ, Greg, you're blocking more kicks for us than all the opposition put together."

Not funny.

That aside—and I *know* I'm going to have to work on it—'72 was a comeback year for me.

I made 21 field goals in 31 attempts for a percentage of .677. As I've written, any kicker doing better than 60 percent is doing his job. I made 34 PATs, which means the Giants got a total of 97 points from me—more than any other player —and made me the Giants' all-time leading scorer, with 519 points. (Frank Gifford was the old leader, with 484.)

The flight back from Texas was one long celebration. We were on Cloud 9, and all I could hear was: "Wait till next year!" But it wasn't a cry of desperation, the way it had been in '71. We *had* come back, and with a little bit of luck, we could have been in the playoffs. In '73, with a little more depth, we *will* be in the playoffs.

Over the Christmas holidays, Kathy and I were to take our young son David Gogolak (born September 8, 1971) to visit our parents—first mine, because Hungarians celebrate Christmas on what is Christmas Eve in the States, then hers, in Jersey. Never, never, never have I gone through so much good food, first a Hungarian Christmas, then an American one.

We drove up to my parents, in upstate New York, the Thursday before Christmas, Kathy, David, me and our part-Labrador puppy, Duna. (Hungarian for Danube.) It hadn't snowed all winter where we lived, but as we drove north we saw more and more snow on the ground. The hospital where my father works is set high in the wooded hills near Lake George, and the road that winds up to it is very narrow. Cars sometime have to stop and sort of work their way past each other, instead of passing.

By the time we arrived it was dark, and as I drove the car slowly up and up that black narrow road through the black, snow-patched woods, all I could remember was how we had made our way through the black woods coming out of Hungary.

When we got to the house, it was all lighted. In the window I could see my mother and the two grandmothers, ninety-one and eighty-seven, watching and waiting for us.

God, it was good to be home!

We left all the presents in the car and went inside for our reunion. The smells of Christmas already permeated the house, from the Christmas tree set up in the study, to the cooking and baking. Being at my mother's at Christmas time is like four days in a Hungarian bakery. She always makes exactly seven different kinds of cakes and cookies for Christmas and whenever the supply starts to run low, she's off to the kitchen to make some more.

The table was all set and through everything I could smell my favorite dinner, chicken paprika.

First we had to talk, all the greetings, little David being admired, the victory of the Dallas game. The grandmothers, who don't speak a word of English but who watch every football game on television, knew as much about the Dallas game as I did. Johnny, now a freshman in high school, was there, but Charlie hadn't been able to get away from Denver.

I remembered when, long ago, I had been the center of attraction at Christmas. But that *was* long ago. With Hungarians, children always come first, perhaps that's why the children have so much love and respect for their parents. And the younger the child, the more attention he gets. This Christmas, young David was stage center.

For the four days Kathy and I were there, we hardly did more than eat, drink, and sleep. I don't mean eating just at meals—I mean starting first thing in the morning, and finishing with a midnight snack. My mother thinks that if you're not eating, you must be sick. I ended up twelve pounds overweight.

Early on the morning of Christmas Eve, we all carried our presents into the study and stacked them along the wall. Then my father ordered us out of the room and locked the door behind us. He was to play the role of the little Christ child and the Christmas angels. He was going to trim the tree and arrange the presents. As far as he was concerned, the only flaw was that he couldn't use real candles as he would have in Hungary, and had to settle for electric ones. He spent half the day in the study. Then, just before 7 o'clock that evening, he slipped back in and promptly at 7, my mother rang the Christmas bell. My father opened the study doors.

There was the Christmas room, all in darkness except for the blazing lights of the tree, the presents ranged around it. We all knelt down to say the Christmas prayer and then we went in to start opening the presents.

At about 9 o'clock we sat down to the special fish dinner that Hungarians always have for Christmas, paprika hal. The way my mother makes that, she fries slices of bacon (five per person) moderately well done, then sautés onions in the hot bacon fat. She uses haddock (you can also use cod), bought fresh and whole, boned and salted at home. Into a casserole she puts alternate layers of haddock, bacon, and onions, covering each layer with a sauce made of tomato paste, sour cream, and various seasonings. The seasonings *have* to include equal parts of two Hungarian paprikas, the sweet and the hot. Then the whole thing is stewed for about half an hour. It's absolutely delicious. It's served with rice and salad, and I don't know of anything better. Except maybe chicken paprika.

Early on Christmas Day, Kathy and I and young David and Duna started the drive to Kathy's parents, down the same twisting road through those cold and barren hills.

Kathy and I talked about the Christmas, and about my parents.

They had achieved the greatest event of my life, the escape from Hungary.

They had made it possible for Charlie and me and Johnny to come to a free country, for me to go to Cornell and become a football player and for Charlie to go to Princeton and become a football player and a lawyer. And for Johnny to do whatever he wants to and can.

All I hope is that young David can be as proud of Kathy and me as I am of my parents.